In the Company of Rivers

12/12/07

Ezra,

Wishing you a Happy Birthday and some good fishing in the year ahead!

All the best,
Margie

In the Company of Rivers

◆

An Angler's Stories & Recollections

Ed Quigley

iUniverse, Inc.
New York Lincoln Shanghai

In the Company of Rivers
An Angler's Stories & Recollections

Copyright © 2007 by Edward J. Quigley

All rights reserved. No part of this book may be used or reproduced by any means, graphic, electronic, or mechanical, including photocopying, recording, taping or by any information storage retrieval system without the written permission of the publisher except in the case of brief quotations embodied in critical articles and reviews.

iUniverse books may be ordered through booksellers or by contacting:

iUniverse
2021 Pine Lake Road, Suite 100
Lincoln, NE 68512
www.iuniverse.com
1-800-Authors (1-800-288-4677)

Because of the dynamic nature of the Internet, any Web addresses or links contained in this book may have changed since publication and may no longer be valid.

The views expressed in this work are solely those of the author and do not necessarily reflect the views of the publisher, and the publisher hereby disclaims any responsibility for them.

ISBN: 978-0-595-44682-7 (pbk)
ISBN: 978-0-595-69580-5 (cloth)
ISBN: 978-0-595-89005-7 (ebk)

Printed in the United States of America

"The Legend of Savannah Sound" originally appeared in *Yale Anglers' Journal,* Volume VII, Number 1.

"Muskrat at the Bar" originally appeared in *Art of Angling Journal,* Volume 2, Issue 1.

"Anglers' Apothecary" originally appeared in *Fly Fisherman* magazine, Volume 7, Number 3.

This book is dedicated to the memory of Judy's mother, Betty Lee.

Contents

CHAPTER 1   IF YOU LOVE RIVERS 1
"... you find reasons to be near them."

CHAPTER 2   NYPD GOLD 4
A badge, a brogue and blarney are used to master a gentle art.

CHAPTER 3   THE LEGEND OF SAVANNAH SOUND 16
Wishful thinking spawns a bonefishing legend.

CHAPTER 4   THE TOOLBOX 42
A snicker at one man's obsession with steelhead fishing.

CHAPTER 5   FIRST TROUT 48
A boy catches his first trout in the West Virginia mountains.

CHAPTER 6   HULK HOGAN 59
Battle with a mighty Alaskan rainbow.

CHAPTER 7   THE BUTTERFLY TATTOO 68
A bar, a bear and a bird in the wilds of central Quebec.

CHAPTER 8   THE THIRTY YEAR DEER 73
Musings about first blood after thirty years of trying.

CHAPTER 9   MUSKRAT AT THE BAR 82
Encounter at the Antrim Lodge on New York's legendary Beaverkill.

CHAPTER 10   THE ANGLERS' APOTHECARY 87
A visit to the Anglers' Roost on 42nd Street.

CHAPTER 11   BAD DOG 91
A visit to a Pepsi shack on the Catawba River in the Carolinas.

x   In the Company of Rivers

Chapter 12   ANGLING ATTIRE 97
If clothes make the man, they also fashion one's expectations of the man.

Chapter 13   PAINTED LADIES 105
The discovery of a fly-fishing theory at The Waldorf.

Chapter 14   DIVINE PROVIDENCE 111
Acts of generosity on Ireland's Culdaff River.

Chapter 15   WITH PENELOPE ON THE MINIPI 125
A poem in praise of a girl guide in Canada's Labrador.

Chapter 16   THE TRUTH ABOUT FALSE ALBACORE 128
Extreme fly-fishing off North Carolina's Outer Banks.

Chapter 17   GETTING THERE 138
Schlepping through Britain; seeking salmon in Scotland.

Chapter 18   GOD'S COUNTRY 163
Old-time religion in Pennsylvania's fabled Potter County.

Chapter 19   THE LAST PLACE ON EARTH 172
Keeping regular and regularly catching giant Brook trout.

Chapter 20   THE KEYS TO THE KINGDOM 178
Fly fishing for the great Silver King in the Florida Keys.

Chapter 21   ON THE UPPER DELAWARE 186
Nothing's happening on a float trip down the West Branch.

Chapter 22   CATCH & RELEASE 199
A comment on this subject plus one on "hookless" fly fishing.

Chapter 23   MINIPI MEMORIES 206
Fly fishing adventures in the Labradorean wilds.

Chapter 24   WALKER'S CAY 228
Ship's Log: Ten days aboard "The Getaway".

Chapter 25   AN IRISH COTTAGE 251
A poem that shows there's more to home than a hearth.

Acknowledgements

Here's to …
Ann McNulty, the olive in my Martini.
Rosey Rosone, a friend and pseudo-son.
Ken Raichle, who replaced the brother I lost track of.
Jim Van Loan, the closest friend for the longest years.
Barney Leonard, the valued friend who followed me to Minipi.
John Kowalski, encourager-in-chief, a true-believer all these years.
Doug Johnson, the pole-vaulter who put my electronic files together.
Wayne Earp, who handed me the keys to his vacation home at the shore.
Dick Nixon, who drives me up to the Pohopoco in his new pink-lavender limo.
Jack, Lorraine, and their son, Robin, who made my Minipi Memories possible.
Steve Alexander of the good ship Getaway, who made Walker's Cay possible.
Deb McBride, once a colleague, always a friend, now my editor, who is not to be blamed for boo-boos.

And especially to Judith Q. Kirkland, my treasured daughter, who followed in her father's footsteps and made me an incredibly proud Dad.

1

IF YOU LOVE RIVERS

♦

"... you find reasons to be near them."

"When I die, if heaven isn't like the Rogue River, I won't go."
Willie Illingworth, 1942-2007

"A river is the most human and companionable of all inanimate things."
Henry Van Dyke, Little Rivers.

Jerry Dennis wrote that first quote in his book, *A Place on the Water*. The second is from a sign that hung in Willie's office. Dennis is right. Willie right on. Henry Van Dyke wrong. Well, half wrong.

Contrary to what Van Dyke says, rivers are by any measure certainly not "inanimate things." They are living, breathing, tumbling, running, roaring, rollicking animate things. Some of the most animate things, I'd say, on God's green earth. But Van Dyke gets the other half right: rivers are supremely "companionable." Sometimes I think more companionable than human beings. And, like most human beings, they have personalities. And possibilities.

Thus, when I look down the long corridor of my life, I see the names of a multitude of rivers. The Green, the Grass, the Bighorn, the Salmon, the Perkiomen, the Willowemoc, the Beaverkill, the Elk, the Umpqua. I see the names of people, too.

That's what this book is about: water, the sweet and the salt; and memories of people, the sweet and the salt.

I have always been a stream-seeker. The kind of person who slows down when crossing bridges, even on the Interstate, to get a glimpse of the waters running beneath them. Wondering what their names are, wondering what kinds of fish swim in them.

Like the people I have known, the rivers I have known exhibit different moods. Some are, at times, forlorn and sorrowful. Downright funereal. At other times happy and playful.

Once in late October, I remember standing alone in a cold rain under a gray-blue, crushed-velvet sky on the banks of the Salmon River in upstate New York near the town of Pulaski. There in the shallows, along the river's edge, among the charcoal-colored rocks asleep beneath coverlets of frost, fringed with emerald moss, lay the black sarcophagi of giant salmon. Through the shallows, through the thin curtains of mist and rain, fishermen slogged slowly and silently past them, looking down as they passed like reverent guests at a viewing.

I remember another time standing beside a river in late March in the northeast after a long winter of heavy snow. The ferocious waters, the color of frothy cappuccino, were filled with drowning debris. The river had boiled, like a forgotten pot, over its banks. It surged past me like wild dogs pursuing deer. It gnawed and tore at the roots and trunks of trees, which, in July and August, had stood calmly back from the river, dry and unafraid.

But, by late spring, in another week or two, the wild dogs will be gone and most of the debris will have disappeared. A fallen tree will have created a new fishing hole with tempting possibilities. The river will now be as calm and as clear as moonshine. The banks will have reappeared. Where once there was all rush and roar, there will now be only the buzz of insects and the chirp of birds.

In the fall, this same river, will be low and slow and well within its banks. It will be strewn with yellow leaves collecting like Post-It™ notes in stacks one upon the other in front of trailing limbs and in helter-skelter piles in eddies behind the rocks. More leaves will slowly pinwheel down settling on the surface like gentle rain. The kind of rain e. e. cummings said had "such small hands." The kind of leaves that make you flinch when one flutters into your cheek and ruins your cast, and reminds you that another summer on the water has come to an end.

Yet, for all their seasons, and all their and moods—malevolent, or merry, mild, or wild—no, because of them—I have seldom met a river I couldn't somehow love … or, because of pollution, pity. My affection for them extends to their little relatives, the narrow creeks and tree-shaded brooks, the tiny mountain springs, the slender salamander sluice that trickles through the swampy bottom of a low, wet meadow. I love these little fellows, too.

What *is* it about rivers?

Well, a truly learned friend of mine, Ted Zeigler, once said, speaking, I think, about life in general, "You are always drilling over oil-bearing strata." And so it is with rivers … and with fishing in particular. You are always exploring possibilities, always tempting the potential that a fish will rise and strike your fly. Do everything right, and, if the time of day, the season, the hatch, the moon … if your mood and the mood of the river is right, you may, indeed, persuade a fish to rise and take your fly. It is this flirtation with possibilities—drilling over oil bearing strata—that give rivers and the act of fishing such a potentially rich and compelling allure.

That's why I so often fish the dry fly. Because it lets you see the moment when possibility becomes reality. Nothing is hidden. That's why I especially love to cast my floating flies on the calm, smooth summer glides and glassy pools because nothing here seems quick but the fish.

Cast a floating fly and you can see it touch the water leaving behind a tiny telltale wink of light and around it a migration of tiny ringlets. Then, best of all, you may see the flash of the trout coming to your fly. See his take and turn. His splash and swirl. Feel his frantic tug.

If you share my love of flowing water, and the solitude of the woods, the excitement of the salt—standing ankle-deep in the sapphire and sand of the flats—then follow me. We will visit the rivers of my memory, and I will introduce you to the people I have met along their banks and share a laugh or two and flirt with endless possibilities. Perhaps, although we are not looking for them, together we might find some parables right here in the company of rivers.

2

NYPD GOLD

Random House Unabridged defines "fishing" as *"the act of catching fish."* And "angling" as *"the act and art of catching fish with a hook and line."* Both definitions should immediately be corrected to read *"the act of* trying *to catch fish."* That's because, unlike linguistics professors, all fishermen know that if fishing *always* resulted in catching fish, it would be called *"catching,"* not *"fishing."*

This dictionary also fails to reveal that the words "fishing" and "angling" for that matter have other meanings as well. For example, "he was *fishing* for compliments." Or, "he was *angling* for a raise."

In other words, "fishing" and "angling" have other meanings that go beyond the act of trying to catch fish, meanings that have to do with attempting to acquire things other than *fish* by "fishing" around for them.

This linguistic song and dance brings me to the story of my dear old fishing buddy, Sergeant William Cotter, a most engaging man who had a most unusual way of fishing for his fishing gear.

His success depended, in large part, upon something that he always carried in his wallet, not money but gold: his NYPD badge.

As I said my friend's name was Bill Cotter. William Daniel Patrick Cotter. I use his real name because, try as I have, no fictitious name will suit my recollections of him. There never was and never will be another Cotter.

The good Lord already knows him, has forgiven his few venial sins and is right now, as I speak, enjoying his company. Those of us left here on earth will, I know, be equally quick to overlook any faults that might be revealed here.

Remember, Bill was a New York cop and they enjoy a pocketful of dispensations denied to all ordinary men and women.

Bill was tall and handsome with a bearing not unlike Gary Cooper's. If you don't remember Gary Cooper, then think of George Clooney. He was that sort of a guy. Never touched a drop (unlike Mr. Clooney) and I never heard him curse or raise his voice.

Speaking of his voice. His vocal chords were strung as tight as the strings on Willie Nelson's Martin guitar. Cotter unplugged. This lent that familiar Yankee, New Yorker twang to his speech. Listen, I bet you can hear it when he says, "Ya gotta see dis t'ing here, Eddie, babe." He could turn good grammar on and off like a spigot. Of course, he had no such control over his Yankee accent.

I first met Cotter on the banks of the Croton River just below the big stone dam. He was wearing a black and white plaid flannel shirt, a crushed and faded NY Yankees baseball cap with his dark curly hair poking out the hole in the back. His Red Ball hippers were turned down to his knees like a pirate's boots. The rubberized canvas was crackled like the varnish on an antique dresser. He had a just-lit Chesterfield between his lips. He was, I'd guess, forty-three. Maybe older. And, for all of his being so loosely put together, he had a smoothly subtle elegance about him, a kind of untutored gentility twinkling through. You could see it in the way he talked, in the fluid way he walked.

Once he told me matter-of-factly that he made it a practice of reading every book on the *New York Times* bestseller list. After you got caught up, he said, it was easy. What's more, he said that he read every word in the Sunday *Times*, too. Even the Shipping News. Every Sunday. That kind of stuff, he said, came in handy, especially when dealing with those uptown perps.

His first words to me that day were, "Doin' any mischief, lad?"

Now Cotter sidled up to everything like a crab. Ideas, people, angling, everything. Talked that way too. Sideways. You know, from the corner of his mouth (or as he called it, "mout"). His already mentioned New York twang was overlaid with a deeply melodic Gaelic lilt. The sound, if not the very manner, that the Irish poet Seamus Heaney said he remembered hearing as a boy. It was the way, Heaney said, the "scullions" talked. And it was the way Sgt. Cotter talked, giving his every sentence the sound and rhythm of a pronouncement. Something said *ex cathedra* as if he were Father Flanagan lecturing to his boys.

He lived in a little white Victorian cottage with an encircling, generously spindled porch down by the mouth of the Croton River in the town of Croton in the county of Westchester. The town, like the river, is named Croton. Croton-on-the-Hudson, New York, to be precise.

This town was, once, like many of the little towns strung from New York City north along the banks of the Hudson, a popular summer-home site for well-heeled city folks. And a permanent residence for those with thinner heels—the Italian stone masons, for example, who came to Croton to build the Croton dam to form the Croton reservoir. And Cotter's cottage, indeed, once a summer cottage, long ago winterized (in a fashion), perched above the lower part of the Croton River just upstream from where it enters the wide and mighty Hudson. On Mulberry Lane.

He had a wife ("da bride" he used to call her), a son, Michael and a daughter, Colleen. And a blue Chevy station wagon, I'd say five years old. He was a daily-mass-going Roman Catholic. And, of course, a cop. A New York City police officer. NYPD blue. He rode the train to work on duty days rubbing shoulders with all the other commuters in their Brooks Brothers suits. Me included.

"Was always in the tick 'o t'ings, ya gotta know, Eddie. Never shirked my duty. Oh, Lord, I seen a lotta t'ings I wished I'd never seen. T'ings that swim around in a man's mind for years. Carried dis .38 Special for years, I did. Near twenty years now. No, more. Smith & Wesson. Never once pulled the trigger. Must, by now, the barrel, you know, must be all plugged up with lint as t'ick as you'd find in da belly button of a Bowery bum. Green mildew on the barrel, Kelly green, you know, from the dampness in the leather holster. Wadda ya say, Eddie, babe? Pretty colorful stuff, I'd say."

The day we met I had broken my front tooth trying to bite a fly off the end of my tippet. Bit down on the eye of the hook instead of the knot. I couldn't keep my tongue away from the jagged edge. Never knew where that hunk of tooth went. Damn near half the tooth! Swallowed it, maybe. Spit it into the river, maybe. Who knows? But, anyway, I was glad to run across someone who could assess the damage for me.

"Yeah, doing mischief," I replied, "like I just broke my tooth. Broke the damn thing in half it feels like. Can you see it?" I lisped.

"See it? Looks ta me like the entrance to Lincoln Tunnel. Like the black hole of Calcutta. Now, if asked, and I *was*, I'd say it looks like it's gonna need some fixin', lad. Some serious fixin'."

"That bad, huh?"

"Let's just say, not good. But here's the real question: Does it hurt?"

"No, I don't feel a thing."

"OK then let's get back to fishin'. The fixin' can come later. Old Sidney Rosenfeld, friend of mine and fellow fisher, he can fix it. Got his office right up there on the hill, on the way home. You live up there in the village don't ya? Tell him I sent ya. Made me these choppers. Wadda ya t'ink?" he smiled like a model in a Pepsodent ™ ad, "Name's Cotter. What's yours?"

Now Cotter may have sidled up to things but once he got there, he'd get hold of them real tight. By the throat. In those days he had just sidled up to the art of fly fishing. And he was always spilling over with questions about it.

"Hey, Eddie," he'd say, "if you was gonna have the best rod, know what I mean, old pal, the best rod, the very best, what would it be?"

Or, "Hey, Eddie, what kinda reel do the heavy hitters use? You know, what's a guy like Nelson Bryant or Joe Brooks use? The real McCoy."

And one day he asked, "Hey, Eddie, if you could buy any waders, any waders in the world, the best, what would they be, my boy?"

I'd always patiently answer his questions, like, for example, the one about waders.

"Well, Mr. Cotter, old buddy, it would be Hodgman waders. Hands down. They're the best. The very best. And I'd get chest-highs. Not hippers. With matching suspenders. And a belt around the middle. I'd put felt soles on 'em.

You know, thick enough so I could walk up the side of Croton dam in an ice storm."

"Hodgman, huh. Hodgman waders? Chest highs. Spell it for me, Eddie."

"H-O-D-G-M-A-N. Hodgman. They're imported. Come from England."

"Ah, all the way from Merry Old England. Musta lost the 'e' on da way over, huh? Whoda guessed?"

It was a few weeks later (Sidney Rosenfeld, D.D.S., who turned out to be a wise old fly fisherman himself, had fixed my tooth) when Cotter called me on the telephone.

"Eddie," he said, "got me some fine and fancy new fishing gear. Some real hummers. Let's us, you and I, sashay down to the banks of the ole Croton River this very minute, if not sooner, and test these t'ings. Wadda ya say, Eddie, me boy?"

So, I went. And, there he was, lean and lank, resplendent in a sparkling pair of right-out-of-the-box British tan chest-high Hodgmans. Matching suspenders, belt and all.

"How do I look?" he said, removing his baseball cap and sweeping it in a half circle as he bowed.

"Well, Mr. Cotter, damned if you don't look like Mr. Nelson Bryant himself. An autograph would be in order."

"Yes, Nellie—that's what I'd imagine his downtown buddies at da *Times* call Mr. Bryant—he never looked so good. And, you might ask, Eddie, babe, not for an ortergraph but for the amazin' story of how I did become so prepossessing by possessing such a fine pair of British waders." He finished the sentence with another theatrical pirouette and tucked his thumbs into the web belt cinched around his middle.

"OK, Mr. Cotter, tell me the amazing story of where you got your waders?"

"Well, since you asked, Eddie, babe, and nice it was of you to ask, I'll tell ya the story.

"Starts out while I was eatin' my lunch and mindin' my business—ham and cheese on Wonder Bread—and drinkin' a brewsky down by the wharf. Ya know where I mean, Eddie? Down the waterfront. Downtown. It's important ya know I was down where all the big ships come in to New York harbor. Ah, yes, the BIG ships, Eddie, from across the great pond. And wadda ya know, there's this here boat from Merry Old England. And there's this here little Puerto Rican lad scurrying about, hither and thither, fetching sandmidges and sodas and brewskies for the longshoremen, and I calls him over and I says to him, 'Hey, my little lad,' what's up with that boat? That ta one, says I pointing like this. What's the guys unloadin? And he says, 'Dunno, stuff from England, man. Hey, want me to getcha anudder beer?' And I says, naw, already gotta a beer. What I need is a pair of waders. Watcha call fishin' boots. Think there's boots watcha call waders in dem boxes dere?' 'Boots?' he says, 'How ta hell would I know?' "Well, you *ask*, little feller. That's what you do, says I. You go right over dere and you ask them guys, de ones right dere.

"Well, he goes over. And glory be to God, there is a shipment of boots on that boat. And I says to that there little Spanish fellow, I says, why, you know, lad, I'm wondering if they're the kinda boots we high-class fishing fellows call 'waders,' more precisely 'chest waders.' "How th' hell would I know!' says he. "OK, OK," says I, "I'll go over dere myself and ask.

"Now I don't really need to ask 'cause I know what's on that ship. No surprise ta me, laddy. I checked the shipping news in the *Times* and confirmed it with O'Brien who's down there on the wharf beat. So, I'm what you might say, fishin' in well-stocked waters. And now I says to the little Spanish lad, do them boxes every fall offa that forklift thingamajig?' 'Sure they do, well, sometimes they do,' he says.

"Well, if that happened and if a box broke open and spilled out a pair of watcha call, listen careful, *chest-high waders*—say that, *chest waders*. And he says, 'Aw come on man.' And I says, just remember this, lad, that's a real tall boot, that's what it is, lad, comes near up to your armpits. You getting' my drift? 'Cause if you ain't what I'm saying to ya is dis—if an accident was ta happen and if dem boxes was ta spill out onto the wharf and if in da box dere happened to be a pair of waders my very size—that's nine wide, nine wide, my lad, *nine wide and chest high,* if dat was ta happen, well, know what I'd do? I'd give you—and the thingamajig driver—a fiver, that's a fiver each, just to pick 'em up and fetch 'em here fur me to see."

'Man, you gotta be kidding. I can't do shit like that,' says he. 'Those guys ud smack me up th' side-da m'head if I grabbed holt a box a boots.' Not likely, my lad, ya just go over dere, tell the forklift driver that you work for Sgt. Cotter, tell him about the fiver, point over ta me and I'll wave back."

"Eddie, are ya listenin'?

Well, that little lad, he goes over dere and God Almighty in Heaven be my witness to da trut, it weren't more'n a minute when a whole load of boxes topples helter-skelter offa that fork lift thingamajig, and, ya musta guessed it by now, them boxes, Eddie, the trut, I swear, had the very words 'Hodgman Ltd, U.K.' stamped on 'em. And that little lad, he runs over there yellin' back ta me, 'Hey, man what's your size? What's your size? I forgot.' "Nine wide," yells I, *chest highs, nine wide.*" And like a Labrador 'triever, he squirts in among all them boxes that spilt offa the lift t'ing, while me, I'm sitting there waving, and he comes back with nine-wide-chest-highs. Job well-done, says I slipping him a fiver and I walks myself over to the driver and says, "You OK dere, pal?" and slips him a fiver and waves to the other longshoremen and off I walks with these here sweet and supple honey-colored British boots draped over me arm. Nine wide. Chest highs. The very same that now grace my nimble body."

Cotter pirouettes yet again hooking his thumbs under the matching suspenders that hold up his gleamingly new Hodgmans and pull them tight up under his armpits.

"Now, Mr. Cotter," says I, "can we please go fishing?"

"Why don't mind if I do. Like they say, Eddie, deer's a million stories in dat city. Maybe more. And, you just heard only one of 'em."

Yes, and it's only one of the stories of how my pal Cotter went about the task of fishing for his fishing gear—"da finest t'ings dat money (or in this case an NYPD badge) can buy."

There was, for example, the gorgeous Orvis Battenkill bamboo seven-footer with its perfectly balanced Orvis CFO reel and slippery-smooth ivory-colored fly line that he discovered in the back of his Chevy when he returned to Mulberry Lane after graduating with honors from the Orvis Fly-fishing School up there in Manchester, Vermont.

"Dis rod, Eddie, it was my faithful companion during my wholt time up dere. And we formed dis bond, one wid de udder. And after we's all t'ru fishin' we'd stack all de rods in a barrel dere like umbrellas. And, dis here rod, obviously overcome with deep and abiding affection for me, musta leaped into the back of ole blue Sally and come home wid me. Now, Eddie, Eddie, tell me, how could I turn my back on such devotion? 'Sides, Orvis ain't gonna miss one itty-bitty rod and reel. Dey got trillions."

And then there was his fly-fishing vest:

"So Jimmy Gallagher says ta me, Sgt. Cotter, I knows how much you like ta fish and dere's not a fancier sporting goods store than the one on my beat, right on Madison Avenue. Abercrombie & Fitch. So, if you walks my Madison beat next week, I'll walk yours.

"So we trades beats for a week. And in I walks the Madison Avenue beat on Monday and goes inta Abercrombie and starts right off chewin' th' fat wid th' manager, a fine gentleman named Mr. Frederick Atkinson, and he tells me that all the world's best-known anglers, they all buys their stuff here, comes here ta be 'outfitted,' he says, and so I says, Freddie, 'What's a guy like that, say, a guy like Mr. Nelson Bryant or Joe Brooks or Lee Wulff wear when he's a-stream?" And he shows me a khaki vest wid a zillion pockets for fly boxes, zippers more you cudda count, says it was designed by none other than Lee Wulff hisself and I says, dats beautiful, beeootiful, but, Freddie, pal, way, way otta my reach pricewise. And waddya know, Eddie, this I know will stretch your credulity, but when I goes up to say goodbye to Freddie on Friday, he hands me dis box all wrapped up in dark green paper, little gold elastic bands on da corners and de words 'Abercrombie & Fitch' in gold 'crost it and he says 'tight lines, Sergeant, hope to see you someday on the Amawalk.'

"Well, my face turned red with joy and gratitude, my eyes filled with salty tears and I says, "Freddie you are a true gentleman and a scholar and in your debt I shall remain et cetera, et cetera.

"And, thus, I got me dis here gen-u-wine khaki Lee Wulff fly fishing vest. Oh, look here at the label, embroidered, look, it says 'Abercrombie & Fitch.' See da label? Now, tell me, what daya t'ink, Eddie, is dis de cat's meow, or what?"

Now that I've mentioned, or rather now that Mr. Frederick Atkinson mentioned the Amawalk; I have to tell you another Cotter story.

The Amawalk is a well-known little stream—at least among the cognoscenti of downstate New York anglers. It is filled with trout. At least it was then and I pray it still is. It is a fly fishing only, artificial lure only, catch-and-release tailwater that percolates from under the Amawalk Reservoir dam in Westchester County. Yes, the water is as clear as polished window glass and cool all year round. The air above the stream is filled with the buzz of plentiful and predictable hatches.

So close to New York City is this stream that it gets visited day in and day out by well-equipped anglers of the very highest sophistication and skill. As a consequence, the brown trout in its waters are equally skilled and sophisticated, a breed of the most fastidious and discriminating gourmet brown trout to be found anywhere, I suspect, on the planet.

They never rush up to snatch a dry fly off the surface. Even during prolific hatches. Instead, they tilt their bodies to elevate their nose casually and drift back underneath a fly, natural or otherwise, sometimes even moving up slowly to actually nudge it with their nose, sniffing as if they were wine tasters. Then and only then, if the fly meets their list of criteria, will they sip it in with the grace and elegant good manners of a lady of a certain age sipping afternoon tea at the St. Regis on Park Avenue.

Now, obviously, their chief criterion is that the fly appears NOT to be tied onto anything. It has to drift freely with the current. This means that the line, the very end of the line, which in fly fishing circles is called the "tippet," has to be of the smallest diameter possible. That means having at least 32 inches of an 8x tippet, which is finer than a spider web, tied with a surgeon's knot onto the end of a 12-foot long 7x leader.

Such gossamer tippets were at the time all imported from France. To tie a fly onto such a fine French tippet, besides the patience of a saint and the vision of an eagle, you had to use a size 28 fly ... or, if truth be told, smaller.

Fact is, speaking of surgeons, I once met a heart surgeon from Einstein Hospital on the Amawalk who was using and claimed that he regularly used size 32 flies. I have heard of none smaller. They were, he claimed, Royal Coachmen. But I had to take his word for that. You see, a fly that small is about the size of a mustard seed.

What's more, the trout have also become so acclimated to the constant parade of anglers that they do not abandon their feeding stations as we marched by on the path above the stream. What did they care? Their razor-sharp discrimination and their infallible good taste would save them from the prick of a hook. And, if, by chance, one did get hooked, he would not fight with much gusto. After all, he knew that he was fortunate enough to live in a catch-and-release stream and although being caught was embarrassing, he knew he would immediately be released by the gentle touch of a patrician hand. Therefore, few anglers, except the Amawalk regulars, and they only after long practice, much refinement of gear and many frustrating hours, could even get an Amawalk trout to rise to their fly.

It was to this stream that I took Cotter one sunny day in June and showed him a big brown trout (18 inches at least) holding languidly at the top of the infamous curve pool. After one full hour of incessantly casting to this fish, he gave into frustration, turned and plucked a Japanese beetle from a stream-side laurel leaf, tore the feathers off his fly with tweezers and impaled the struggling beetle on his now bare number 12 hook and cast it with a plunk four inches above the nose of that implacable fish.

The fish surfaced with the characteristic nonchalance of its kind, examined the struggling beetle for a moment, tipped his nose up, nudged it, drifted back in the current underneath it and sipped it in like a Geisha at tea ceremony.

Out of pure spite, Cotter wanted to kill that fish on the spot; but at my urging he released it and rebaited his hook with another freshly captured beetle.

He had just impaled the second beetle on his hook when a New York State fish and game officer strolled up. In a mannerly yet authoritarian fashion, the officer said, "Good afternoon, gentlemen," and asked to see our licenses and to inspect the flies on the ends of our lines.

After commenting on the beauty of the day, Cotter launched into litany of inquiries, asking about the health and well-being of the officer and his wife, the names, age and gender of his children and while doing so Cotter produced his fishing license from the bowels of his bulging wallet. In so doing, he casually displayed the gleaming gold of his NYPD badge pinned inside.

By this time the officer had Cotter's hook and beetle in his hand.

"Sir, you have a live beetle on your hook," he said calmly. "Do you know, sir, that using live bait—anything but an artificial fly—on this stream, you do know you are on the Amawalk, is against the law?"

"Not possible," said Cotter, using his best grammar. "That's an artificial Japanese beetle. I tied it myself with the finest peacock herl and a copper-painted piece of cork. Sir, for you to think it is real is an unexpected, yet welcome tribute—yes, compliment—to the skill and artistry of my fly tying."

"This beetle, sir," replied the officer, "is not only real. It is alive."

"No, sir, I assure you. Not possible, sir," said Cotter shaking his head with innocent conviction. He then raised the bill on his cap, bent over and peered down at the beetle wiggling in the palm of the officer's hand, "Well, glory be to God," he said with mock astonishment, "so it is, real, real by God, alive and wiggling. How's that possible? By what divine intervention ... well, I must have snared that Jap fellow from the bush on my back cast. Plucked the little foreign devil right out of the laurels. Must have impaled the poor unfortunate creature on my back cast. Shows you, there's an explanation for everything."

"And what, sir," replied the officer, "did he do with your peacock herl and copper-painted cork imitation?"

"Well, he must have thought it was the very real thing and attacked it on my back cast in a mating frenzy. Tried to mate with the artfully crafted imitation on my hook and the frenzy of copulation pulled it clear off my hook and got himself speared in the very act. This has got to be one of the wonders of nature. An article for *Fly Fisherman* magazine or *Annals of Etymology*. Can you believe this?"

"No, I can't," replied the officer.

"Would I lie to a fellow officer?" inquired Cotter.

"Sir, in spite of whatever divine intervention occurred here, the fact is that you are fishing with live bait on the Amawalk. And that is a serious offense."

"But an accident, it was. No, a miracle of nature. An accident of nature. Surely that mitigates the severity of my alleged transgression?" said Cotter.

"Sir, I am holding in my hand the live beetle you are fishing with, and accident or not, that is against the law."

"Then, sir," replied Cotter, "as a fellow officer, husband, father and member of the Mother Church, I have no alternative but to pray for your mercy. I can only hope that in making your decision regarding the sanction for this alleged offense, you will weigh the part this foreign beetle himself may have, could have played in my entrapment."

So it was that instead of a costly and embarrassing encounter with the law, Sergeant Cotter got no more than a warning. He was, you might say, like the brown trout of the Amawalk, caught and released by a touch of mercy and the gentle hand of what men of the law call professional courtesy.

I know that Mr. Cotter, my good ole fishing buddy, enjoyed a long retirement from the NYPD. I know he replaced old blue Sally with a big SUV stuffed with the finest fly fishing gear you could find anywhere in the world, the very best that charm and guile and the glitter of NYPD gold could bring his way. Although I know better, I like to think that he is still casting about for trout and the impedimenta to catch them with and that every now and then he looks over his shoulder, and says, with his melodic Gaelic lilt, "Hey, Eddie, babe, waddaya t'ink a dat?"

And I reply, "Hey, Bill, wait up. I'm on my way.

3

THE LEGEND OF SAVANNAH SOUND

I have trouble falling asleep. So, what I do is this. I crawl under the covers, punch a head-hole in my goose down pillow, close my eyes and go fishing in the waters of my imagination.

I put myself where ever I want to be ... wading or in a boat ... in Chile, Labrador, New Zealand, Belize or the Florida Keys. Anywhere.

I make the weather warm, the winds gentle, the waters smooth ... and, depending on my mood, I either fill the water with hungry fish or with just one fish, a giant one, a particularly elusive one of the species of choice. Often trout. Sometimes tarpon. Last night bonefish.

I call it dream fishing. Actually dream catching because in my wakeful imaginings, I never, unless I want to, fail to stalk, hook and, after an epic battle, capture the fish.

Real fishing is different. It always puts hope and the lessons of experience to the test. Pits imagination and expectation against reality.

That's why, in the arena of fishing, as, for example, in politics, Truth is often a no-show. That's why, when it comes to the arena of fishing, there are always plenty of seats available for the more rowdy fans, like Exaggeration and Wishful Thinking.

◆ ◆ ◆

On Monday, a storm spread its vast cumulous wings, soared across the Gulf of Mexico, banked northeastward, casting a shadow of torrential rain and brutal winds below.

On Tuesday, both the Miami and Fort Lauderdale airports were closed. Marathon, Florida, was evacuated; it's streets awash in a powerful nor'easter.

The fisherman beat the storm to the Bahamas, arriving Monday afternoon. But late that night at Heron Hill, on Eleuthera, east of Nassau, he was awakened by the Venetian blinds chattering like sea birds over a shoal of baitfish. The wind blew the bedroom door open and slammed it shut. He closed the windows, cranked the jalousies down in the bathroom, used a towel to mop the windowsills and lay back to listen to the wind, the surf and the rain.

◆ ◆ ◆

That same night, five miles south, in the waters of the Caribbean just off Savannah Sound, a fish sank slowly beneath the breakers into its sanctuary in the shadow of a coral ledge. There she would ride out the storm. In the textbooks, she is known as *Abula vulpes*. To fly fishermen, she is the exalted bonefish capable of sustained runs of 24.7 mph. By comparison, the rainbow trout chugs along at 4.7.

Her feeding grounds are the shallow, translucent flats dappled with green sea grass and mangrove clumps surrounding the islands. Her prey, the myriad snapping shrimp, small crabs and clams that inhabit them.

On Tuesday at dawn, she moves her pectoral fins imperceptibly and rises above the reef to ride the incoming tide toward the entrance to Savannah Sound, a narrow passageway of deep water flowing between Eleuthera and the northern tip of Windermere Island.

She is not alone. For through this narrows hundreds of her kind will pass as they enter and leave the feeding grounds, coming and going on the ebb and flow of the tides, moving as one, just inches below the surface in teeming pods.

And once they enter the flats, you can see them, say the guides, if you look carefully for "nervous water," patches that resemble what sailors call cat's paws—patches that look like tiny rain squalls moving across the surface of the water.

Not all of the bonefish will enter the sound itself. Some will remain in the deep channel that flows from the Caribbean side of the island to the Atlantic along the western shore of Windermere. If you stand on the little bridge connecting Windermere to the mainland, if you are lucky, you may actually see them darting through the mangrove-lined channel on their way to the flats on the Atlantic side.

They come to the flats hungry, quick and wary like wild dogs to a garbage dump. Once on the flats they disperse to forage on their own. This day she remains among those who leave the deep channel and fan out across Savannah Sound, maneuvering through the clumps of sea grass that lie like green stains on white cloths. She stalks through the narrow, shadowy pathways between the sea grass, avoiding, at first, the wide, creamy pink patches of sunlit coral sand.

Sometimes larger bonefish and larger fish only, do not leave the flats with the outgoing tide; instead, they find safe havens either among the mangrove roots or in pockets of deeper water along the edges of the grass. This is what she does today, holding in a shallow depression, shouldering against the grass, lying as still as a barracuda, her only movement caused by the undulations of the wind-stirred water.

She is twenty-six inches long. A gleaming, living broadsword. At that length, according to the formula in Dick Brown's book, she weighs nine pounds, eleven ounces. A giant for this place and this season. A trophy. She is in her eighth year. A clear adipose covering, like a scuba diver's goggles, protects her black, yellow-rimmed, unblinking eyes that are the size of doubloons. Her polished silver scales mirror her surroundings, making her virtually invisible. She is, in fact, revealed only by the shadow she casts beneath her as she slides above the white sand. Or by her large, pointed, deeply forked tail when it breaks the surface and flickers in the sun as she tips her head down to dig in the sand in the ankle-deep water of the flats.

◆　◆　◆

By Tuesday morning, the rain stops. The clouds break apart. But the wind still blows out of the northeast, chasing the remaining shards of clouds across the sky so fast that it looks like time-lapse photography. It is chilly. The fisherman puts on a sweatshirt. No one else on Heron Hill is awake yet.

The storm has littered Heron Hill's long curving gravel drive with palm fronds and coconuts. Andrew Bethel, the caretaker, has already filled the bed of his small brown truck, the color of stale chocolate, with a load of the storm's debris. He'll give ten or twelve of the green coconuts to the baker at Palmetto Point. The rest will go to the dump.

The fisherman has rented a chalky white, two-door 1987 Olds Cutlass Supreme and now he drives it between the black waters of the turtle bog and Margaret Hill Cemetery, past the gigantic, ancient cotton-silk tree into North Palmetto Point. There he turns north on the macadam road and drives five miles farther to Governor's Harbour. There's a red rubber band on his left index finger to remind him to drive on the left-hand side of the road.

His destination is Pammie's. That's where he's been told he will find Gladstone Petty, "Bonefish, Reef & Deep Sea Fishing Guide."

Pammie's, windowless, squats on pink cinderblock haunches at the very edge of the road across from Governor Harbour's liquor store. Inside are three white, chrome-edged Formica tables. Clustered around each are four tubular aluminum chairs with red plastic seats. A white and gold ceiling fan slowly stirs the air, which smells like the downwind side of an egg roll stand on Sansom Street at noon.

Behind the bar—white Formica—are bottles or dark rum, whiskey, scotch, gin, vodka, and some bottles of beer—a gold bottle of Kalik, a green bottle of Beck.

Pammie's is empty and silent except for the buzzing of flies.

The door to the kitchen is a yellow cloth curtain. The waitress (or is she the cook?) pushes it aside and steps out. Two small black faces are attached to her thighs. She is wearing a pink bandanna, metallic gold lipstick and metallic chartreuse eye shadow. Her nails are long and painted to match her eye shadow. Her blouse is red. It's first two or three buttons are open revealing a dark valley between two mountainous breasts. She wipes her hands on her red-and-white-checkered apron. She is expressionless. Says nothing. Only looks at him blankly. Something sizzles behind her on the stove.

"Is Gladstone here? It's about fishing," he says.

"No. He is not here. Not now. He will be back soon. You can wait."

She and the small faces disappear behind the curtain. He goes outside to blow the smell of twice-or-thrice-cooked grease from his nostrils.

Across the street, at the liquor store, the fisherman buys a case and a single cold bottle of Kalik, the Bahamian beer, named for the sound that the island's cow bells used to make—ca-lick, ca-lick—before the insidious black spiders drove all the cattle off the island. The single bottle is wrapped in a brown paper bag. He uses the opener mounted on the doorjamb. The cap clicks off and falls into the pile of caps beneath the opener.

The clouds are back now. The rain has begun again. The wind is blowing. He drinks the beer, sitting in his car. And waits. And waits. There is no sign of Gladstone.

Leaning against Pammie's is a narrow figure in a yellow rain slicker. A figure that turns now and then to look up and down the road as if watching and waiting for someone. The figure now walks over to his car, walks, even in the windy rain and under the stiffness of the slicker, with an unusually erect, yet casual, slow, smooth motion, like a person marching in a procession.

The fisherman rolls down the window.

"Are you going up the road?"
"Do you want a ride?"
"I am going to J.C."
"Where's J.C.?"
"Up the road, that way." The figure raises its arm and points a finger north.

"How far is it?"

"Not far."

"Ah, OK I guess." He has nothing better to do.

The figure in the rain slicker opens the passenger-side door and slides in.

"My name is Georgiana." There is a tender seductive music in her voice.

"Georgiana!" Yikes, a girl, a child! Sixteen, hell, maybe, thirteen, he thinks. God, I've probably just broken some law.

She unsnaps the slicker and he sees that she is as thin and supple and the color of as a # 3 bamboo fly rod.

"Ah, why aren't you in school?"

"The schools are closed today."

"Closed? Why? Is it a holiday?"

"No. Closed because of the rain. Because of the storm."

"The rain? Funny, we only close our schools because of snow."

"Snow? We have no snow here. Only rain. Where are you from?"

"Philadelphia."

"Why did you come here?"

"To fish. To fish for bonefish."

"The fishing is very good here in the summer."

"You mean it's no good now?" He swung the Cutlass around and drove north.

"Oh, well, not so good now, better in the summer when the water is warmer."

"Do you know where the bonefishing is good; I mean where people go on the flats to fish?"

"Oh, everywhere. They go everywhere. Right there," she points out across Governor's Harbour itself.

The water in the harbor is whipped into froth by the winds. Contained by the seawalls, it looks like the top of a giant Key Lime pie. In fact, driving out of Governor's Harbour along the breakwater is like driving through a car wash. He rolls the windows up.

"All along here, too, right here, too, they fish right here," again she waves her hand toward the choppy flats along the side of the road.

"You mean I could stop and fish right along here? Anywhere along here?"

"Of course you can. But you must be very careful here. You must lock the car. They might take the car. They take the car and repaint it, change the numbers and no one knows the difference."

"Ah, but this is Dwight Pindar's car. They would have to deal with him."

As they passed the airport, she pointed again.

"Back there, too. See back there. Behind the airport. Lots of people go there. There's a big flat there just inside the reefs. Lots of fish are caught there. Mostly in the summer."

Eleuthera (they say it means "freedom," but in what language?) wallows like a giant antediluvian crocodile with its dark green back exposed above the turquoise waters near the edge of the Caribbean Sea at Latitude 25 N., Longitude 76W,

There is only one macadam road on the island. It runs north/south along the narrow central ridge from Southeast Point through a litany of tiny settlements of pastel-colored cinder-block houses for 110 miles, up through The Bogues, to the Harbour Island ferry moorings.

The fisherman and the schoolgirl have run out of conversation as they approach J.C., one of these tiny settlements named James' Cistern, presumable for a man named James who built a cistern there. It is, like all the others, a cluster of dwellings situated five miles north of the airport. And when he lets Georgiana out there, she walks up a narrow, ragged path, up a hill between white, yellow, pink, green, pale orange and sky blue houses. A small golden-brown brindled dog runs out to sniff at her heels. She doesn't notice it. She does not look back and never breaks that smooth, processional stride of hers.

As the fisherman turns the car around, he sees two boys beside the road. They are hitchhiking. One is tall like the girl. The other is short. He stops the car.

"Where are you going?" he asks them.

"To Governor's Harbour. Will you take us there?"

"Maybe, maybe not. First, let me ask you: Do you know anything about fishing?"

"Fishing? Everybody knows something about fishing," says the tall one.

"Then hop in." They both slide into the back seat.

"My name is Kareem. This is Luke. He is my brother,"

"Kareem?"

"Yes, like Kareem Abdul Jabbar," says the tall one.

"Do you guys know anything about this place behind the airport?"

"Everybody knows that place."

"Everybody?"

"Yes, everybody but the tourists. They know, too, but they never go there. Almost never."

"Will you take me there?"

"Sure, mon, we will take you there." They both slide forward and cross their arms on the back of the front seat.

The rain has stopped. The sky is blue. The sun is bright.

"Here, here, right here," Kareem points to a narrow unmarked, unpaved road. It winds behind and then alongside the airport runway, and then turns left through the bush toward the ocean. It runs a long way, or so it seems, especially since it is a sand road with potholes and great cement-gray puddles.

The fisherman turns in at Kareem's command and stops in front of one of the more formidable puddles. "Kareem, will you get out and tell me how deep that puddle is?"

Without hesitation, Kareem leaps out of the car and wades cautiously into the puddle.

"OK, no problem, c'mon. OK, c'mon, c'mon," he motions with his one hand and points ahead with the other. The gray water laps up to his knees. It is as thick as house paint and colors his legs gray. There is a manly expression on his face.

After creeping from puddle to puddle with the brush scraping the sides of Mr. Pindar's car, they suddenly break into a clearing. And there it is. On either side of them. The Dump. Two great undulating mounds of trash—rusting cars, refrigerators, stoves, crumpled cardboard boxes and cans and bottles of every description—and above them, wheeling, hovering and darting like pieces of blown paper are sea birds, although such birds are not plentiful on the island until summer.

Kareem tests the final puddle, the largest of them all. The water is up to his calves. He wades slowly through hiking up his short pants, and steps aside. Then, with his legs painted Cape Cod gray, he motions the fisherman forward. When the fisherman stops the car on the other side, Luke bolts out of the back seat and together, he and Kareem scamper up and over the rocks and across the dunes and down toward the water, like escapees from Devil's Island, never looking back.

They have guided him through the dump to the edge of a beautiful sapphire bay, a vast flat dappled with mangroves and turtle grass. The boys are galloping now along its rim, their short baggy pants and over-sized T-shirts flapping like flags in a high wind. This is The Place … the place Georgiana spoke of … but on this day the trailing edge of the nor'easter makes it unfishable.

The two boys have blown down the beach like stringless kites and he yells at them.
"Kareem, Luke, c'mon. C'mon back you guys!"

With the boys recaptured, he turns the car around and heads back through that formidable puddle. Both Luke and Kareem are now guiding him. Both walking in front of the car, both with painted legs.

Suddenly, as they navigate the channel between the mountains of trash and garbage, a pack of dogs, all clones of one another—all exactly like the one that sniffed Georgiana's heels, all terrier-sized, brindled golden-brown, short haired with erect, pencil-pointed ears, tiger-yellow eyes—twelve, maybe fourteen of them—they pop up seemingly from everywhere, yet nowhere, and run hell-bent up, out of and across the trash mountains and disappear into the bush without a bark.

"See! See!" yells Kareem jumping up and down and waving his arms, "Tourists, they don't like that much, not very much. None at all."

Kareem and Luke look into the bush. The explosion of dogs has happened so quickly that the fisherman has no time to like it or not like it. It's almost as if it never happened or happened in a dream that's now impossible to remember.

Once back at Governor's Harbour, the fisherman gives a five-dollar bill to Kareem, who's up in the front seat now, having assumed the position of Senior Navigator. And then the fisherman turns, reaches back and gives Luke a one-dollar bill.

"Thanks, Kareem. You, too, Luke, you're good guides.'

"You know," says Kareem in a low, thoughtful voice, "I could take you fishing on Saturday."

"We'll see. I know where to find you. In J.C. right? You boys enjoy your day off"

The fisherman stops again in front of Pammie's. The elusive Gladstone has still not returned. So, he resumes his vigil in the car. Then grows impatient, enters Pammie's, goes behind the bar and picks up a card with Gladstone's phone number on it and then crosses the street, buys another cold Kalik and lights a Te-Amo Robusto. He'll call Gladstone when he gets back to Heron Hill.

As he pulls into the drive, Andrew is squatting beneath a palm tree, one of many on Heron Hill's sloping lawn. He is using his machete to manicure a little flowerbed beneath the tree. The fisherman stops and gets out to talk.

"What do you think, Andrew?

"Well, the sky is clear now but the wind is still bad," says Andrew looking up at the sky." Usually it takes only one day for a storm to blow out but this one will take two." He removes his hat and rubs his head, scratching at his gray temple. "Two days for sure, maybe more."

They lean together against the little chocolate-colored truck. "You should try some fresh bait. Do you have bait? You know there's plenty around here. All over. I'll show you."

Andrew puts his machete down and walks to the edge of the lawn, crouches and steps a few feet into the bush. He's barefooted, wearing shorts and a T-shirt. He stoops to rummage with his bare hands through a tangled pile of discarded palm fronds and rotting coconuts.

There are snakes on the island. Not poisonous ones mind you, just shy, benign creatures, so they say, that, on a diet of baby chickens and mice, reportedly grow up to six feet long. Members of the boa family. This thought makes the hair tingle on the back of the fisherman's neck as he watches Andrew rummage around moving deeper and deeper into the bush until he disappears.

When Andrew reappears from the darkness of the deep bush, he has five small crabs squirming in the palm of his hand. They have what looks like a snail's shell centered behind their small claws. He pulls off one of the shells to reveal a glistening, succulent pink nub of flesh perfectly designed for a fishhook. He drops the little crabs, plunk! plunk! and the naked nub of crab meat into a black plastic bucket.

"We make sand balls with these. Want to see? I'll take you fishing this afternoon. Down below. Over there, behind the other house. I know the people. We can use their steps. It is a good place. Very good. You go have lunch. I'll get more bait. You come back and fetch me and we'll go."

Heron Hill perches on a bluff above the eastern shore of Eleuthera overlooking the Atlantic. Another private home sits several hundred yards to the right screened from Heron Hill by a thick grove of palms and dense brush. Andrew pointed in that direction.

After lunch the fisherman returns to the yard and fetches Andrew, who by now has filled the black bucket with a swarming mass of crabs. They walk together down to the road then up the driveway to the neighboring house; go behind it and down the wooden steps clinging to the face of the fifty-foot cliff to the ocean behind the house. The tide is in and they must walk single file on a narrow wet band of beach between the face of the cliffs and the breakers.

The fisherman carries his small gear bag and a spinning rod and reel. The rod is a Browning "noodle rod," a whippy affair nine feet long. Andrew carries the bait bucket.

He follows Andrew up the beach for about fifty yards. Then, Andrew stops and looks at the breakers.

"This is the place."

Andrew picks a crab out of the black bucket, pulls off its shell and puts the naked nub of flesh on the fisherman's # 6 stainless steel hook. Then he bends over and pulls the shells off six crabs, places them all on a flat rock and, with the butt of his knife, pounds their flesh into small, ragged pieces. Then he scoops up two handfuls of wet sand and fashions a two-fist-sized ball of compacted sand and crab flesh,

"Ready? he says, holding the sand ball in his hand and looking back at the fisherman,

"Ready."

Andrew lobs the ball into the arc of a cresting wave. When it hits the water it explodes into a cloud of sand and crab bits. As a new wave crests, the fisherman sees what Andrew calls hound fish (narrow, knife blades of fish like small sterling silver barracuda about fourteen inches long) darting through the crab chum. First one and then another and another. They are clearly visible as the sun flashes off their sides in the cresting waves.

The waves are high, four feet, and frequent. The water is chilly. The fisherman is standing in it up to his thighs. Shivering.

"OK, now," says Andrew.

Following Andrew's instructions, he casts the baited hook up over and beyond the breakers and lets it drift on a taut line with the current.

"There are bonefish even here jacks, too," says Andrew matter-of-factly. "We fish with hand lines. Throw the sand balls, then the baited hook. I catch lots of fish right here. In the summer."

Now they have run out of bait. So the fisherman returns to the wet sand strip and clips off the hook (he'd had only one bite, a bump and a tug, for his dozen casts and drifts). He reaches into his bag. There he finds and ties on a Hopkins lure, a piece of oblong tapered chrome dimpled like the surface of a golf ball. It is three inches long and trails a treble hook. He is soaked and shivering. Again, he wades out into the surf up to his belt.

"Watch out now," cautions Andrew as a big wave rises up to menace the fisherman.

He raises the rod over his head and turns his back to the wave, struggling to keep his balance as the cold water crashes over him.

Andrew runs down the beach to retrieve the fisherman's hat.

Now he regains his balance and his hat and casts again. With the noodle rod and the quarter ounce weight of the Hopkins, all it takes is a flick of his wrist to send the lure sailing out beyond the breakers.

"Mon, oh, mon that sure go far. Never seen the likes of it," marvels Andrew.

Just then, as the lure flashes through the curl of an incoming wave, a yard-long fish appears, like a silver scimitar, and slashes at it, bumps it, but misses.

"Oh, mon, that's a bone, big bone for sure. Look at that! See that? Look at that, a bone for sure," says Andrew.

The fisherman reels in, wades to the beach and offers the rod to Andrew.

"Here, try it."

"Oh, I don't know. Never done this. Never use a rod."
But he's a natural and flicks the rod with his wrist. "Mon, that thing goes far. Mon. this be good for jacks, mackerel too."

Andrew has thrown the Hopkins in a high arc beyond the breakers. "Never been in the water like this in the winter, you know. Cold, what it is."

A couple of hours have passed. They have had no luck. So they quit and retrace their steps along the narrow beach, climb up the wooden steps and walk back down the road to Heron Hill.

"Come on, get the car, mon, I show you more spots," says Andrew.

With the fisherman driving and Andrew guiding, they go south to a place called Ten Bay. The wind there is intense and the water on the flat is all white caps and gray with clouds of sand.

"Not good here today. But when the water is calm this is a big flat. Smooth, easy to wade. Lots of fish. Sometimes hundreds. Remember this place."

Next they go to Savannah Sound.

"It can be good here," says Andrew.

The fisherman sees that the sound is sheltered. The wind is not as strong here. The flats are relatively calm. He sees two conch fishermen coming in across the shallow flat, pushing their wooden rowboat ahead of them in ankle deep water. They load their catch into a wheelbarrow, push it up the shore and disappear. The shore near the path is littered with conch shells and piles of enormous empty lobster shells, once belonging to what in the Keys they call Florida lobsters, actually giant crayfish.

"It's good here on this small flat, even in the wind."

That evening the search for Gladstone continues with a phone call to Pammie' s. He's still not there. If the fishing is so bad, where the hell is he? But at 8:30 that evening, Gladstone's son, Paul, returns the call.

"Bad weather, mon. The wind is wrong. The water, it is rough. And cold. Still too rough. The fish can't see de bait and we can't see dem. Tell you what. I go out tomorrow early and look at the sky. Call you back. Early tomorrow. 7:30 in the morning. OK? We see then."

Paul Petty does call back on Wednesday. Exactly at 7:30. But with the same story. Rough water and high winds. A cold front seems to be sitting off the island. Going nowhere.

"Too bad. We try again tomorrow. I call you. Same time, OK?"

"OK"

Thursday is the same. The fisherman bides his time, reads Dick Brown's book on bonefishing, fiddles with his gear, sorts his flies, lines them up all his Crazy Charlies in his boxes like little toy soldiers, and dreams of big, hungry bonefish fish swimming in shallow tranquil water.

Friday, early, around 8:30 AM, he drives to Savannah Sound, alone. A goat is grazing beneath the palm trees on green grass apron of the sound. The flat itself is as calm as it was when he and Andrew were there on Tuesday. The conch fishermen's boat is moored out there in ankle-deep water close to a clump of mangroves. There is no sign of them. Or their wheelbarrow.

He rigs his rod, an 8-weight, 7-and-a-half-foot Orvis Madison. It's bamboo, but unlike today's brassy blonde Orvis bamboos, this stick is a classy mahogany brunette of a certain age, not unlike the 2 and a half ounce 7-and-a-half-foot Bakelite that Lee Wulff used in the fifties to fish the waters of Newfoundland. The fisherman's venerable Madison has been one of his favorite fishing companions for thirty years now. Yet, having been refurbished by Orvis several years ago, it looks like it just came out of the box.

He fits a same-vintage, but much the worse for wear, Hardy Princess reel into the German silver handle, snugs up the locking ring, and threads an 8-weight, weight-forward floating line through the guides. The line is ninety feet long, Mint green. The reel has 175 yards of white woven Dacron backing on it.

He threads a loop-ended twelve-pound test mono leader through the braided loop in the end of the fly line and uses a Duncan loop (sometimes called a circle knot) to tie a #8 Crazy Charlie to the tippet. It is a big-eyed fly as pink as Pammie's walls, touched with tinsel, trailing two strands of Flashabou. The circle knot allows it to wiggle freely when it's in the water, like a living, free-swimming shrimp,

Gusts of wind squeeze through the narrow channel formed on one side by a crooked tip of Eleuthera's mainland and on the other by the northern end of Windermere Island. He pulls on the brim of his cap to snug it down to his ears. His small cherry red canvas chest pack dangles from a black strap around his neck as he shuffled across the thin water—it is up to his calves now.

He is heading to where he sees two large clusters of turtle grass lying in dark green tangles among bright, barren patches of sand. The dark green grass, the aqua and emerald of the deep-water channel that lies ahead, the turquoise and sapphire and gold of the shallows, the creamy white and pink of the sand lie before him like a luminous, living quilt of neon light.

As he slides his feet forward, the strategy recommended to prevent one from stepping on a stingray sleeping under the carpet of coral sand, he notices softball-sized indentations scattered all over the surface of the submerged sand. Among them are numerous dime-sized holes with folded collars of sand encircling them. These Lilliputian volcanoes are breathing holes made by crustaceans buried in the sand. The miniature craters reveal where bonefish have rooted out their unlucky brethren. This is all good sign.

For an hour and a half, he methodically works the edges of the turtle grass and the open water between them, blind casting. Every so often he stops and watches intently, looking with his Polaroid glasses into the water for the telltale shadow of a bonefish moving across the flat, or scanning the surface of the water for the flash of tailing fish. Looking for nervous water. But he sees nothing.

Then, at around nine forty-five, he senses someone approaching behind him. Another angler is coming across the flat. He turns and sees, parked beside his Cutlass, a matte black van. There's a black man beside it in black pants, white shirt and red tie. And now in the water beside him is a young man. He's in his thirties wearing fashionable granny glasses with clip-on Polaroid's, a stone-green baseball cap with its frayed brim teased into a perfect arch, a Khaki twill shirt with epaulets and a mint-green bandanna tied around the collar. He's got his gear in a purple Jansen daypack.

"Any luck?" he says.

"No. Nothing. Really"

"What's the drill here? Seen anything moving?"

"No. I've just been working the edge of the grass. Blind casting. See right along there?" The fisherman points, thinking of all the tips and tricks he's garnered from reading Dick Brown's book.

"Yeah. That where they are?"

"Sometimes they'll hold along there and wait out the ebb tide. In little pockets along the edge. Shouldering up to the patches of grass. This is a good place because you can cast to the open water, too, if and when you see fish coming across, but in the meantime you can pattern your casts along the edge there." He's trying to sound like a wise old hand, sage and savvy, like the old timers he'd met as a young man.

The newcomer has a Sage 8-footer for 8-weight line and a brand new large arbor Bauer reel.

"What's a good fly? What are you using?"

"Crazy Charlie. Pink"

The newcomer secures his rod under his right arm and reaches into his shirt pocket, extracts an aluminum box. Inside are neat rainbow rows of rather complex, life-like imitations of crabs. Epoxy crabs, wools crabs.

"Crazy Charlie?"

"Like this, "the fisherman holds up his fly. "Pink."

"Humm, looks like I don't have one."

The fisherman reaches into his chest pack, pulls out his fly box, opens it and plucks out a number 8 pink Crazy Charlie and says, "Now you do."

"Great! Thanks."

"Ah, do you strip it?"

"Yup."

"Short or long strips? Fast or slow?"

"Both ways, really. Like this."

The fisherman throws a back cast smartly into the air behind him, pauses for that liquid bamboo flex, then pulls the line down sharply with his left hand, and drives his right forearm forward executing a double haul. He ends the maneuver with the Madison parallel to the waters and waist high as the line he held in his left hand shoots out through the guides. The fly lands right along the edge of the grass sixty-five feet away. He grabs the line hanging beneath the butt of the rod with his left hand and begins to strip the fly back with smooth yard-long rhythmic pulls. Strip, pause, strip, pause.

"I try to get it right along the edge like that and move it through the open water so if a fish is lying there the fly will not come at him. That spooks them. You want them so see the fly when you present it, like out to their right, or to the left. Let it hit the water, pause to let it sink, only a second, then move it away fast like a shrimp caught out in the open trying to escape. Never move it toward them, always away."

"Damn, you're using a wooden rod. Gees. Like in the olden days. Ah, how lung's your leader?"

"Nine feet. Twelve-pound test. That's plenty. Say, look, why don't you fish here? I'll move on up the flat."

The flat is about two hundred yards long and as wide. Plenty of room for two of fishermen. But there is a protocol among fly fishermen that says you relinquish your spot—if you've been there for a reasonable amount of time—to a newcomer. The offer is not altogether an altruistic act. You have, after all, fished the water in the spot and exhausted its possibilities. Now the new angler gives you an excuse to move on to virgin water. Certainly you do not want this new boy to fish the virgin water to your left or right. Better to start him here, on the water you've whipped for hours. Of course, the flip side of this protocol of place requires him to accept the barren bounty of your seemingly unselfish generosity. It would violate the protocol to say, "Oh, you go ahead. I'll fish up there." Unless, of course, the new boy knows better, which is usually not the case.

And knowing no better the newcomer says, "Thanks."

The fisherman moves up the flat and positions himself about twenty five yards to the left of the young man, opposite a place he's been lusting after since he began to fish the flat. He was saving it for later and now as he fishes it he sinks back into concentration.

Meanwhile, the newcomer casts his pink Crazy Charlie, splashing it into the water behind him on his back cast, to the spot the fisherman had pointed out to him. He's not an accomplished caster but the wind is light, his rod is good and well balanced and the fly goes almost exactly where he wants it to go—close to the edge of the grass.

On his forth or fifth cast he sees something there that does not appear to be part of the patch of grass. A shadow. A long shadow lying four or five inches out from the edge of the grass. It was not there before.

◆ ◆ ◆

She could feel the tide coming in now, lifting her as it spilled and spread across Savannah Sound. She grew more alert, sharpening her focus on a 180-degree slice of the bright sand bottom in front of her. Visibility is perfect.

It is perfect for the newcomer, too. Through his Polarized clip-ones he can see now that that shadow is a fish. A big one. And remembering the fisherman's instructions, he false casts several times to measure out the line and sight in on a spot a few feet to the right of where the fish lies. When he has the distance measured and the spot targeted, he releases the cast. Nothing fancy. The line rolls out in an ungainly loop and the fly careens onto the surface of the water and dives to the bottom.

When he makes the first strip, the fly kicks up a tiny puff of sand, the tinsel and the trailing Flashabou on the Crazy Charlie sparkles in the sun as the fly darts forward.

She sees the puff of sand. And the Flashabou sparkles. Reflexively, instantaneously, she lunges like a thrown dagger, covering the four feet between her and the fly in half syllable of time,

The newcomer had his eye on the sparkle of his fly and he saw the bright silver instant of her lunge. Reflexively, he raised the rod tip. And struck.

Since she eats mostly hard-shelled crustaceans, there was, at first, no reason for her to be alarmed by the hardness of the morsel in her mouth. But as she clamps down on it, it leaps forward, piercing the corner of her mouth and jerking her head around violently.

Now in surprise, frustration and anger, she wheels around and surges toward the narrows, toward the deep water, toward her sanctuary beneath the reef. She will, in this first powerful surge, in 11.7 seconds, cover 125 yards of water. When she stops, the newcomer has only fifty yards of backing left on his new Bauer reel.

As her surge begins, he grabs the rod with his left hand just below the ferrule and pulls it back toward his chest while pushing the rod handle forward and up with his right hand. When he has the rod back as far as he can get it, he dips the rod tip, releases his right-hand grip on the butt and reaches for the reel handle.

She feels this change in direction; she feels the pressure ease. At first she thought she was free of this thing and now she is bewildered. She shakes her head from side to side. What is this strong, savage thing in the corner of her mouth? And for a moment she gives in to its relentless pull and allows herself to lead like a dog on a leash back from the very threshold of her sanctuary.

The newcomer, sensing her momentary capitulation, again grasps the rod just below the ferrule with his left hand and pulls hard, raising the rod and bending it into a taut arc.

Feeling the pressure increase, she swirls, turns away from the narrows and dashes seventy-five yards along the edge of the deep-water channel.

He shifts both hands down to the rod's cork handle and raises it high over his head again.

The fisherman is aware of none of this until he hears Nelson Mingo, the black man who had been leaning on the black van smoking a cigarette, yell, "Hey, Mon, you got a fish?"

The fisherman looks to his right and sees the newcomer's bent rod. "Oh, God, he's caught in the grass," he thought.

The newcomer says nothing. He's concentrating on playing the fish. Nelson Mingo takes off his black wingtips, rolls up his black pants and trots across the flat. "You got a fish, mon? Yes, Yes, that's a fish!"

The fisherman sees the newcomer holding his rod up high. He sees the arc, the pulsing of the tip. He sees him steering something, perhaps a clump of grass, toward him through the shallow water. Now he sees him reaching down into the water, with the rod held high. Both he and Nelson Mingo are bending over. And the fisherman realizes the young man has caught a fish.

The newcomer has fought her for fourteen or fifteen minutes. Stopped her three runs. Turned her away from the gates of freedom. And now she lays motionless, defeated, wallowing in ankle-deep water at his feet. She is brilliant broadsword of a fish with big, defiant, angry, yellow-rimmed eyes. An object of awe and adoration by the newcomer, Mingo ... and the fisherman.

"God, look at that fish, look at that beautiful fish," the newcomer says, seemingly mesmerized by the sight of her.

"God, just think, when I got up this morning, I almost didn't come. My pal said it was no use; forget it, he said; the wind is too high, the water too cold. Damn, I can see him there in his jockey shorts, rolling over in bed and going back to sleep."

"That's a big bone," says the fisherman. He hands his rod to Mingo and reaches into his chest pack for a tape.

"Twenty-six and a half inches, he says as he lays the tape from the tip of her chin to the fork of her tail.

"What do you think it weighs?" asks Mingo.

"Looks like seven/eight pounds, maybe more. Maybe even nine. Big fish," says the fisherman.

"Wow! She was right where you said she'd be. I saw her. Actually saw her. Right where you said to look. And it was just a short cast, thirty feet. She was lying right along the edge of the grass. Just like you said."

"Mon, oh, mon," says Mingo, turning to the fisherman, "you put dis young mon right on dat fish, I think that's the first fish caught this whole month, the first for sure. Mon. you really know de game." Mingo is squatting, touching the fish affectionately and looking up at the fisherman as he speaks.

"Would you mind taking my picture?" The newcomer wrestles a yellow and black Minolta Weathermatic out of his pack. Hands it to the fisherman.

The fisherman takes it and turns it vertically, and presses the zoom button and moves until he has the sun just right.

"Tip the fish back a little, to catch the sun. That's it," he says. And he snaps the picture.

"Want me to take a picture of you with the fish," asks the newcomer.

"Nope. That's OK"

"Hey, mon. we keep this fish? Huh? Take it back to show your sleepy-head friend? He will be mighty sad." Mingo looks up at the newcomer. The newcomer looks at the fisherman,

"Sure, why not? That's not a skinny three-pounder. That's one helluva bonefish. Keep it. This isn't some stocked trout stream in Pennsylvania. This is the ocean, the Bahamas, Eleuthera. There are plenty of bones out there. Plenty more. Besides, she's a trophy for this season and these waters, that's for sure. Go ahead, keep it."

"Oh, mon. yeah. I know how to cook that fish. You stretch him like this and that line up the bones. Sweet meat. Yeah, right, we keep this one. Show it to your friend." Mingo looks up at the newcomer.

"OK we'll keep it."

Mingo beams as he carefully washes the sand off the fish, scoops her up and cradles her like a baby in the crook of his arm.

"Hey, mon. you really one helluva a guide. I see it. I see the whole thing. You one helluva a fisherman. Let me shake your hand." He shifts the fish under his arm like a loaf of French bread and offers his big hand to the fisherman.

The fisherman shakes Mr. Mingo's hand and then the hand of the newcomer.

◆ ◆ ◆

For a while the fisherman and the newcomer fish side by side almost in each other's shadow. Then they drift apart.

While they fish, Mingo takes the prize up the road to David, one of the conch fishermen who has a set of scales. She weighs exactly eleven pounds, eleven ounces.

By noon, the fisherman is alone again. He is resting, sitting on the wooden bench on the edge of Savannah Sound, drinking a warm Kalik, smoking a thin Mexican cigar and staring out across the smooth waters. He is a small man and he's stretched his legs full length along the bench, resting his back against the arm. He's taken his cap off and the wind blows through his short white hair. He thinks that if Ireland has forty greens there must be forty blues here in the Bahamas.

Around one o'clock, maybe a little after one, a van pulls up, not Mingo's but another, a white van, and two tall gentlemen get out. They both have neatly trimmed white moustaches and deep tans. One, he will learn, is a retired surgeon from Harvard. The other, the younger one, doesn't say. Both are regulars, they have been coming to Eleuthera every winter for years, staying at Ten Bay.

"There he is, that's him," the surgeon says as they walk up to the fisherman.

They tell him how they heard he caught a giant bonefish on the flats that very morning. Many bonefish, in fact, all big ones. Nine-pounders and better. And how he guided a young fellow from Club Med and put him right on a trophy fish. A thirteen-pounder. A monster. And, he, they said, had pointed right to the fish like Babe Ruth pointing to the fence in center field. Showed the young man how to get it with one cast. One short cast. Stood right there at his elbow while he cast, and played the fish.

Now they wanted to know where the fish were, what fly he used, how he made his presentation, how he strips his line, fast or slow, long or short, what size and brand is his rod, how long and what weight is his leader. They came here just to find him, to speak to him, to get his advice.

◆ ◆ ◆

That afternoon the fisherman is walking beside the break water in Governor's Harbour and Dwight Pindar and a friend drive by, licking ice cream cones. They stop the car in the middle of the dirt street. Dwight leans out the window and says, "Hey, mon, we hear about those big bones you catch at Savannah Sound. Hey, some fishing! You some fisherman. Nobody catch bones but you. Not all week. Not even Gladstone. Hey, mon, no fish I think not all month. What you know they don't know?"

Later, when the fisherman goes to the liquor store for a cold Kalik, the counter man calls him by name and says "You know they not even catching fish up at Harbour Island. Not even the old pros and the millionaires at Pink Sands, no siree. The Petty's, they not even goin' out cause of the wind and rough water. But you do good. Right? You some fisherman. Don't even need a black mon to guide you. Lone ranger, no? Don't need a Tonto. And who go to Savannah Sound, Ten Bay where they go. Hey, mon, tell me, how many you catch today? How big?"

That night he drinks rum and lime and eats dinner at Mate and Jenny's in Palmetto Point. When the waitress takes his American Express card up to the bar, the bartender sees his name and says, in a loud voice, "Hey, look here, ladies and gentlemen, we got a genuine celebrity. What we got here is the best white guide in all the Bahamas. He catch the bones in good weather and bad, cold water, high wind don't matter because he catch them when no one else can. And he catch them where no one else does. He know the game."

The next day two fishermen from Darien, Connecticut, go to Savannah Sound. They find David, the conch man, and ask him has he seen the fisherman today.

David says, "No, not today. No one really <u>sees</u> that mon, least ways not fishin' less, of course, he want you to. Less, of course, he take pity on you. Oh, but early on a morning sometime, I do see his footprints only once in awhile though here in the sand. They always go up there toward the narrows. They always bare footprints. He wears no shoes, no wading shoes. He step in the holes the bonefish leave. That's so he can tell by the feel of the sand where the fish be and what they be takin'. He always come alone. In the winter. He always catch fish, always the big ones. Some time he rest on that bench over there. See? He smokes big Cuban cigars, Montecristos, Cohibas, you know, big thick ones like the fish he always catch and he always sits there on that bench looking out over the water, chewin' on a lime, smokin' and drinkin' dark rum right outta de bottle."

One day at Club Med a guest asks Nelson Mingo what this man, this fisherman, looks like, and Mingo says," Oh, this is a very big mon, a tall mon. He got long silver hair, I mean silver as the bonefish. A white mon. that for sure, but very, very dark by the sun. And he uses a long, wooden rod, very dark brown many, many years old."

When asked, Dwight Pindar says he thinks the fisherman has left the island by now. Others think he actually lives somewhere on the island. Alone. Back in the bush. In a very big house.

Seems like everyday, especially in the winter months, fishermen come down to Savannah Sound, sit on that wooden bench and stare out across the smooth sapphire water. From time to time, they look over their shoulder, up the sand road. Up to where that goat lives. Up by David's. They bring fresh limes. And pink Crazy Charlies. Some smoke fat Cuban cigars. They wait. And wait. Long as they can. Hoping to see the fisherman.

◆ ◆ ◆

Not a single fish, but that one, was caught that week when the cold front sat so stubbornly astride Eleuthera. And, now, even with the coming of gentler winds and warmer water, Mingo, Pindar, yes, the Petty's, too, and Andrew Bethel (who now, by the way, has a Browning noodle rod that he claims the fisherman gave him)—these and all the others, from Southeast Point to The Bogues and beyond, even way up there on Harbour Island—they still talk of the tall white man, the fisherman with long hair as silver as the sides of the bonefish and an ancient cane rod as dark as mahogany, who appeared that cold and windy week, stayed up there on the bluff at Heron Hill and fished alone on the flats. Catching many fish. Many big fish. A generous man who once shared his considerable knowledge of the ways of *Abula vulpes* with a nameless young fisherman on the flats one chilly day down there at Savannah Sound.

4

THE TOOLBOX

You can take the measure of a man by looking at his tools. The way he selects them, cares for them, uses them. It's true. Look into a man's toolbox and you can tell the archbishop from the acolyte. Why, back when this century was very young, many tools were what you could call works of art. Handmade with handles shaped and shined as skillfully as major league bats. Polished ash and oak sometimes even black walnut or dark lush mahogany. These were the kinds of tools that the pioneers used to shape America. And their own lives.

Back then, it seems, no tool escaped the craftsman's touch. Once I saw a small shaft of polished wood and gleaming brass dangling on a rawhide thong from the belt loop of an old-timer's sky-blue Levi's. He said it was called a "priest." Used it to give the trout he caught their last rites. In other words to boink them on the head in a final act of mercy before laying them to rest in his creel on a soft bed of damp leaves and meadow grass.

The old-timer's "priest" was seven inches long; three-quarters of an inch in diameter; notched out at the end to a diameter one-and-one-sixteenth of-an-inch thicker than the shaft; fitted over this notch was a brass cap one-eighth-of-an-inch thicker in diameter than the shaft. The other end had a notch, too, and was drilled through and fitted with brass collars so the rawhide thong could pass through. The shaft was honey-gold oak, as smooth as a leaf of Connecticut shade-grown tobacco. The brass was engraved with the words "H.L. Leonard, Maker."

The old timer cradled his priest softly in his hands as he spoke, a smile of remembrance on his lips. When he walked away, it swung to and fro like the pendulum in an old Regulator clock, counting out the years.

THE TOOLBOX

Yes, men have always, and will always, take pride in their tools and in their ability to use them. Out here, out West, it is even said, with more seriousness than mirth, that you'd be wiser to steal a man's wife than his toolbox. And this brings us to Gustafus Adolfus Putzinger. And his dearly beloved wife, Glum.

It was more than five decades ago when Gus cinched a length of hemp rope around his toolbox, tied it with a granny knot, hefted it onto his wagon, said "Giddyup!" to Esmerelda, his mule, and headed east from the shores of the Pacific up into the coastal highlands, following the steep banks of the North Umpqua, a river born high in the snow-melts of the Cascades, its waters flowing lime-ice green over the black bedrock spines of middle Oregon.

Gus had set out looking for a new life in an old land.

He made a camp just above Famous Pool, just south of Steamboat. And one night he came down from that camp to fill his cup of loneliness at Three-Fingered Jack's. He sat at the bar contemplating the whiskey in his glass, puffing on a cheroot. Behind the bar, in a blue calico frock, stood Elizabeth Glumdalklitch Wertzenbacker. Her beauty a striking counterpoint to her name. The blue calico parted below her throat revealing the deep, smooth valley between her breasts. A valley that widened enticingly whenever she leaned over to wash a glass or pour a drink. The lanterns hung on iron hooks in the ceiling would seize these opportunities to bathe her luscious landscape in lecherous light. Gus thought how remarkably like large ripe peaches were her breasts. And, to steady his thoughts, he slipped his fingers down around the whiskey glass and tightened his grip as if he were holding the handle of a hammer.

Dear, dearest, calico-frocked Glum. On their wedding day, she would be resplendent. She would never again wash a glass, wear a calico frock of any hue or give lanterns an opportunity to bathe her round and peachy bosoms in lecherous shafts of light. And in time, the grandchildren Putzinger would call her Glummy.

Gus tended to business, acquiring bigger and better tools. Bought the patch of land above Famous Pool. Built a home there. And opened a lumber mill down in Glide and trucks migrated down the Umpqua highway and through its gates like a never-ending gaggle of geese. In time, like a ceaseless drumbeat, the demands on Gus both at home and at work would grow louder.

"Gus, darling, my dear. My shawl is in the drawer, the pink one, darling. Would you be a dear?"

"Gus, could I have a cup of tea, the persimmon tea in the pantry, with wild flower honey, and, oh, please, a tiny piece of lemon peel? Twisted, dear. You know. In the china cup, not the mug. Would you be so dear?"

"Stop that nonsense, Gus. Stop whining about going fishing. For God sakes you just want an excuse to get out of the house. To go down there to Jack's and ogle that barmaid, Miriam. Do you know what you are? You are a stinking old lecher."

"Oh, yes, yes, you built the lumber mill. And, yes, we have money in the bank. But look at me, look at me; you've neglected me all these years. Going fishing. Spending money on, God! Of all things, 'tackle'. And me with a shabby winter coat. Oh, sure, you bought that fur coat for me in Portland knowing full well that I am allergic to fur. And you bought it just to show 'the boys' how successful you are. Well, that's not a coat, Gus, that's a dead animal."

"I have told you one thousand times, no, one million times no, you absolutely cannot smoke those vile 'ceegars', those dog turds, in this house. Never. Never. Never. You know I'm allergic to smoke. You do it just to aggravate me."

"Gus, if you are going to sleep in that filthy, smelly chair of yours, then, peelee-ase, do it with your mouth closed."

"Good God, Gus, I don't even know you anymore. You reek of tobacco. Your clothes reek of tobacco. Your chair, it reeks of tobacco. And whiskey. And that chair, like you it <u>was</u> old and cracked and stank. Yes, <u>WAS!</u> <u>WAS</u>. I had the man from Purple Heart Veterans haul it away, this very morning. It's gone! It was a goddamn eyesore and you know it."

"Your fly rod? What did I do with it? What did I do with that? The same thing I did with that chair. Gave it to Purple Heart Veterans. Yes, I did. Serves you right. I have told you time and again not to leave your fishing rods in the living room. How many times? So, yes, yes, it is <u>gone</u>. <u>Gone</u>. <u>Gone</u>. Gone, too. Gus's little rod is g-o-o-n-e. Bye-bye, little rod. God knows you seldom caught a fish anyway and you have, what, a dozen of the damn things. A dozen! Who would believe that?"

"Go ahead. Glower at me. Do you think you scare me, you sniveling son-of-a-bitch"?

And, so it was that Gus, now retired from the lumber mill, lived his life and bore his torment slumped in his brandy-colored leather chair. At least until Glum gave it away. After that he mostly just sat in the new orange and purple nubby-weave Lazy Boy, one of two—his and hers—that she had bought at the Sears Homelife store. He smoked cheroots once in a while but way out in the backyard way down by the river. And, Glum, like a woodpecker from hell, pecked away ceaselessly at the very eaves of his life.

One night in August when the Umpqua was nothing but a whisper under a full moon, Gus stirred softly in his Lazy Boy. He looked out the window. The moonlight lay like frost on the pines. He rolled his eyes across the room. Glum was asleep, her mouth agape, snoring wetly with her head tilted back. The Sony TV was flickering fitfully as a Toyota commercial danced across its surface. "Why do they always yell at you like that," he thought. Then Gus picked up the remote and extinguished the TV. Now, except for the moonlight, the room was dark.

In the rare, savory silence that followed, he let his mind wander to thoughts of the steelhead in the river, to thoughts of the generations of fish who come, as he had come, from the Pacific to the highlands, up through the green waters of the Umpqua, up, up to Steamboat Creek and beyond to spawn. Just like he had done.

He rose slowly and shuffled across the darkened room. He went out through the den and into his workshop. On the bench sat that old toolbox which had come with him in the mule wagon up to this place. He touched it. Felt the smoothness of its corners. Opened it.

His old collection of tools, they were all still there. Under the workshop light, he thought they looked almost, well, happy to see him. Among them was a handsome ball peen hammer. Its polished oak shaft as strong and smooth as a river stone. When his eyes fell on it, it seemed to move like a dog whose master has entered the room. At this thought, he smiled and reached in the toolbox and lifted it, and, admiring it, stroked it gently. Held it up, turned with it toward the window and let a blue spark of moonlight wink off its polished ball.

Now he tightened his right hand around the handle, cradled its head in his left. And lost himself in images of the past: thoughts of steelhead never caught, places never gone, ceegars never smoked, whiskey never drunk.

"Gus, Gus, Gus! Where are you? Gus! What are you doing? Gus! Come here. Come here. Now. <u>Now</u>. I mean <u>now</u>. Why the hell is it so dark in here? Who the hell turned off the television set? You know I want the TV left on. <u>On</u>, damnit. <u>On</u>. Gus, you son-of-a-bitch, where are you? Come in here. <u>Now!</u>"

Gus came. And with him came that artfully crafted ball peen hammer.

◆   ◆   ◆

It wasn't really much of a trial. Fact is, no trial at all. Least ways not in the true and usual sense of the word. District Judge Thurgood Titus had known Gus for nearly all of Gus's eighty years. And he just made a little speech. It was about spitefulness, mean-spiritedness, patience and long suffering. Those who heard it shook their heads sadly and they remember, near the end of his little speech, that Thurgood said something about "The patience of a saint."

At the end of his speech, Thurgood said that Gus was to be put on probation for the rest of his life. The rest of his life. A harsh sentence, indeed, said the judge, yes, putting a man on probation for the rest of his life. Then he had the bailiff return the ball peen hammer to Gus. After all, it was just a simple tool he said. Not a weapon. Least ways not in the true and usual sense of the word. And certainly not a threat to anyone. Neither the hammer nor Gus. So be it, he said, and he shook Gus's hand with magisterial solemnity and warmth.

Gus still lives in that old house perched above the whisper and the roar of Famous Pool on the banks of the North Umpqua. And a tranquil life it is. He gave the Sony TV and both of those nubby-weave Sears Homelife Lazy Boys to the Purple Heart Veterans Association. Got a receipt and took a modest deduction on his tax. Got his fly rod back in the bargain, too. The Purple Heart driver had just left it in the back of his truck.

Gus then went all the way up to Portland, hadn't been there in years, and bought one of those Ralph Lauren leather chairs, a rich brandy color, one of the ones that's all distressed and scarred up the very day you buy it, like it's old and used without ever being old or used. And right there in that chair, he smokes cheroots and sips whiskey right there in that same living room, three cheroots a day. Yes, sometimes four.

His toolbox is still on his workbench right off the den. It is tied up with a length of hemp rope and a big granny knot.

And Glum? Dear Glum? Peachy-bosomed Glum? She lies in the soft creel of the earth, at last silent and content.

Not too long ago, Gus, he caught a steelhead, a ten-pounder, by God, in the Famous Pool with his favorite rod. Had it mounted by old Bill Carson down at The Blue Heron, down there in Glide. Hung it over the mantelpiece. And, below it, on a honey-gold, highly polished piece of oval oak—he polished it himself with rotten stone and oil—is a very artfully crafted ball peen hammer. Beneath it is an engraved brass plate. It reads: "Peacemaker. By Black & Decker."

Note: This story is the only version of the Putzinger saga that is authorized by the Ball Peen Hammer Society of North America and is the exclusive intellectual property of its charter members.

5

FIRST TROUT

Robert Traver, aka John D. Voelker, wrote in his "Testament of a Fisherman" that he loved to fish, not because he regarded fishing as "so terribly important," but because he was drawn to and loved the beautiful places where trout dwell; because trout, unlike men and women, "respond only to quietude and humility and endless patience … because only in [those places wherein trout dwell], he writes, "can I find solitude without loneliness."

I first visited one of these places deep in the mountains of West Virginia.

My father went there on a business trip early that summer and he took me along. We drove up into the mountains in his sleek black Pontiac and checked into in a big, white hotel with Victorian gingerbread and gargoyles on its eves and teak lounge chairs lined up on its porch. The hotel was a wonder to me: it was hung on the side of a mountain and when you got to your room and walked out onto the porch and looked over the railing; you felt as if you were soaring, completely free of the earth, high above a mist-filled valley.

The next day, while Dad went about whatever business he was about that particular day, I went fishing. Dad had arranged this with the people at the front desk. And he had specified, "Fly fishing in one of the mountain streams." So, that morning after breakfast the waitress gave me a brown paper bag with two ham, cheese and mustard sandwiches, 4 chocolate chip cookies, an apple and a bottle of Coca-Cola. Dad walked me out onto the porch and told me to wait there. A man would come to take me fishing.

I sat down on the top step, cradling my lunch bag in my lap. There were men in green and yellow and raspberry pants, in white shirts and saddle oxfords coming and going so I sat over to the side to be out of their way.

In a short time, a dusty old four-door Ford pulled up. There were two men inside. One young, the other old. The old man next to the driver got out, pushed back his beat-up gray felt hat, saw me on the steps, motioned and yelled, "You there. C'mon, son, time's a wastin', we're goin' fishin."

Right away I could see that this tall, loose-limbed man was as comfortable and uncomplicated as an old broken-in moccasin.

He opened the back door and I slid in. "I'm Henry. This here's my son, Jack."
Jack said, without looking back, "'Lo, son."
"Morning, sir."
The old man turned around in his seat and said, "Got lunch in that bag, son?"
"Yes, sir."
"Better be enough for all three of us. Waddaya think?"
"Ah, yeah, I guess so."
They laughed and off we went.

They both smoked Camel cigarettes and chattered about the weather. I heard them say it would be a good day, "the moon is right," they said.

When we got to the stream, Jack pulled the car off the road. And Henry got out and said, lowering his voice to a whisper, "Here 'tis. Shush, now." And while Jack opened the trunk and started to pull his gear out, the old man motioned and he and I crept in silence like Indians along the edge of the road above the water. After we'd walked down the bank a few yards toward the water, he gave me the Indian sign to stop.

The stream was narrow and fell down from the mountain in a series of waterfalls and swirling pools. Step pools, Henry called them. "See that there pool down there, son? The one right below? That's the famous Rainbow Pool. Well, now, you listen close, there's this here mighty big trout lurkin' in there, a rainbow, we call him the Monster of Rainbow Pool, now gonna take patience to git 'em, but iffaya got the patience and the dee-sire I'mma gonna tell ya how ta do it."

We eased back from the stream and walked back up to the car. Jack had rigged his gear and was leaning against the fender. "I'm goin' downstream, Dad."
"OK, Jack. I'll be along rightly."

Then Old Moccasin reached into the trunk and pulled out the extra rod and reel they'd brought for me. It was a fly rod. A nine-foot two piece split-bamboo Shakespeare with a Pflueger Medalist fly reel model 1492 (made in Akron, Ohio U.S.A.) attached to it and loaded with bright yellow fly line. He set it up for me, tied on a fly and gave me a few lessons flicking the line out. Then he handed the rig to me.

"Here, you try it."

After a few tries I seemed to be getting it right. At least right enough to satisfy old Henry.

"That'll do fine, just fine," he said.

Then he grabbed the fly and held it up." This here's a Royal Coachman, number 10, that's what it's called. This here one's the 'wet' kind, means it sinks, means you fish it under water. Now do what I say. Go down there. Right to that ole famous Rainbow Pool. Set yourself on that ole flat rock yonder 'bove th' pool. Do as I say. Have patience. Swim your fly in the water. We'll come back to fetch ya 'roun' three o'clock."

"Yes, sir."

He started off, stopped and looked back. "You got a hat?"

"No, sir."

"Well ya gotta have a hat. Cain't be a fisherman without a hat. Let's see if I got an extree one." He came back and rummaged through the trunk of the car and came up with a crumpled red baseball cap.

He stepped over and pulled the cap down on my head to my ears. "There, keep the sun outta your eyes." And he turned and disappeared down the trail above the stream.

I was a little afraid. It was awfully quiet and all. But I stuffed the lunch bag into my shirt, buttoned it up tight, held the rod up high and carefully lowered myself down the steep bank toward the edge of the stream. When I got there, I hopped out onto that big, smooth gray table rock above the pool. The pool looked deep. The water dark. It was surely one of the biggest pools on the stream—as big as a living room. Almost perfectly round. The water came in on the upstream side in a boisterous waterfall, which spread tan bubbles across the surface of the pool. It went out down stream between two gray boulders in a broad, humped shoulder of current. The pool looked like a giant, overflowing bowl.

Although I'd been taught to swim, the pool, I think, scared me a little bit. But I settled down on the rock; sat there cross-legged, pulled the lunch bag out of my shirt, set it aside in a small shallow depression in the rock. Then, doing what Old Moccasin had shown me, I tried to flick the fly out onto the water.

The first time I tried, it caught in my shirt and it took me five minutes to work it loose. Then it caught it in my cotton sock. Another five minutes to work it loose. And all the while that red baseball cap kept falling down over my eyes. So I took it off and set it on top of the lunch bag.

Finally, I managed to get the fly into the water and once I got it in, I left it there and let is rotate slowly in the current. Then I relaxed and looked around. It sure was quiet. All around me it was green. Above there was a periwinkle blue sky. And it was warm. Just warm enough.

I moved the fly up and down, rhythmically. Then I eased it slowly out of the water, pausing, moving, lifting. Then I pulled it out of the pool and flicking it in again. I seemed to be getting the hang of it. Again and again, just like the old man told me. Never once did I get tired. Never once did I get thirsty—good thing because I had no opener for the Coke. Never once did I have to remind myself to be patient. I was instinctively being patient.

In time, the pool seemed to reveal itself to me. It seemed to accept me. To begin to show me things. There were swirls, lazy ones in the center and deep shadows along the edges of the rocks. And I realized that it wasn't so quiet. Squirrels and chipmunks chattered. Birds chirped. Insects buzzed. I think I had never really heard all these things before. As time passed I imagined that I could see further and further down in to the depths of the pool where the darkest shadows were, where that big old monster trout dwelled.

After a while I had no trouble at all flipping the line out into the pool. I had been, in effect, practicing for hours. And I'd flip it out and concentrate on the line floating on the water and the very end where it sank. I'd let the fly sink and swim along the far edge of the pool, swinging out beneath the thin procession of bubbles fleeing from the falls. The old man said to watch, be patient and to "feel for a tap." He had demonstrated what this would feel like by tapping his finger lightly on the back of my hand. It was exciting, waiting for that to happen.

When I got hungry, I ate the sandwiches, leaving the line to trail in the water. I managed to open the Coke by scraping the cap off on the rough surface of the rock. I'd seen some big boys do that once by hooking the cap on the side of a picnic table and hitting it with the palm of their hand. I washed the cookies down with Coke, wrapped the empty bottle in the paper bag and placed it back in the small depression in the rock. I knew they'd be mad if I wasn't wearing the hat so I picked it up and put it on, pulling it down to anchor it over the tops of my ears. And went back to fishing.

The line was swinging out along the far edge of the rock when I saw it stop and dip down. Then I felt the *tap*. Instinctively I snugged the line against the rod at the handle and raised the rod tip just like the old man said. Immediately I felt a strong, wild tug and the line went straight and taut. I was amazed and scared. Some unseen, unimagined thing had taken the fly. And then a big rainbow trout burst into the air out of the center of the pool. It cartwheeled through the air—I thought it looked like a porcelain plate glistening in the sun—and dove deep down along the edge of the rocks. It was startling." What do I do now?" Moccasin hadn't told me.

The long rod and the strong tippet cushioned all of his twists and turns, forgave me for all my mistakes. I could feel him shaking his head back and forth. Then he'd kind of rest and swim powerfully around the far edge of the pool. Then he'd dart at full speed toward the broad shoulder of water spilling out at the bottom of the pool. And I'd try to pull him back.

I was sitting on the rock when I hooked the fish. So I had fought him seated, raising my hands above my head. Now when I tried to stand up my feet went out from under me. When my butt hit the rock I thought for sure that I'd broken my teeth. And then, as if I were on a sliding board, I slid feet-first into the dark waters of that deep and famous pool. As I fell, I held the rod as high as I could.

Henry would be mad if I broke it. I knew that. I went into the water over my head. My feet did not touch the bottom and that was really scary. I mean really scary.

When I came up, I was shivering and hatless. I kicked and paddled my way to the edge of the pool on the downstream side to the right of that big shoulder of out flowing water. Then I elbowed myself up onto the rocks, slithering across them like a commando, getting my chest, stomach and then my legs out of the water. I lay there on my belly, still holding the rod and still shivering. I had lost Henry's hat … and the fish, too. But I didn't break the rod. Boy, I'd be embarrassed when they got back. Ashamed to tell my Dad that I had fallen in and lost Henry's hat.

I stood up and started to reel the line in. "Oh, no," I thought, don't tell me I've lost Henry's fly." Suddenly something pulled back on the line. That trout was still on. He was swimming deep down around and around in the pool, holding near the bottom and still shaking his head. I turned the crank on the reel very carefully and instinctively held the rod tip high.

Finally, he came to the surface and rolled over on his side. I backed away from the pool, up the flat rock. I was pulling him across the surface of the water, pulling him slowly toward the edge of the flat rock below me. When he touched the rock, he flopped several times and when I loosened up he fell back into the water. That's when I worked my hands up the rod, just beyond the grip, dropped it, grabbed the line and over-handed my way down until I got to the fish. I was on my belly again now, head out over the water. In one desperate move, I grabbed for the fish with both hands. He squirmed and wiggled but weakly now, and, holding him as tightly as I could, I reverse wiggled back up the rock clutched him to my chest, hugging him as if he were my baby brother.

I knelt there cradling him with one arm and worked the fly out of the side of his mouth. I was afraid to let him go, so holding him with one hand I used the other to gather some rocks and with them I built a little corral behind the flat rock a safe distance from the water and laid him inside. Then I took off all of my wet clothes, except my Jockey shorts, and spread them out on the big flat rock to dry in the afternoon sun. I prayed they would dry before Henry and Jack got back. If I could get them dry, then they'd never know that I had fallen in.

I sat there in my wet Jockey shorts, getting up every once in a while to walk over to look at the big fish. He was silver and red with spots all over him except on his tummy.

Just as I'd hoped my clothes dried out, even my Jockey shorts and I was dressed by the time I heard Henry and Jack coming back. Jack was up on the path above the stream and Henry, I could hear him, was bushwhacking his way upstream through the alders directly below me.

"Well, son, did you enjoy lollygagging all the day in the sunshine? Looky here, son, at the big trout me and Jack caught downstream." Henry reached down and lifted the stringer hanging from his belt. Four ten-inch rainbows, slit and gutted, were hanging from it.

"Don't you feel bad now, son. Everybody can't be this lucky. Wal ain't so much luck as skill. Naw, whattaya say?" and he looked up at Jack, "waddaya say Jackeroo? This ain't luck it's pure-tee skill."

The old moccasin, with a Camel hanging out of the corner of his mouth, was standing in the center of my flat rock when he said this. And that's when he saw my little corral.

"Watchya been doin? Collectin' river rocks? That's when he looked down.

"Jackaboy! Jackaboy! Looky here. Know what he done? He done caught the damn monster of Rainbow Pool. Well, I'll be a good-for-nothin' … come on down here Jack. Git your scrawny ass down here. He got the big bugger on a damn *fly*, on my damn store-bought fly, onlys one I ever bought, and ain't never been afishin' in his whole life. Damn, damn, damn. Double damn. Hell fire and damnation. And he landed the sucker without a net. From atop at rock. Beats all I ever seen. Jackaboy, git you're sorry ass down here, boy."

Henry knelt and looked with awe and genuine reverence at the big rainbow trout lying there in his corral. The sight seemed to relax and calm him, to fill him with, well, satisfaction. He reached down and picked up the big fish, cradled it in his arms just like I had and pursed his lips. Jack was now by his side.

"God-a-mighty, look here Jacky boy, ain't this the most beautiful thing you ever did see?'

"Shore as hell is," said Jack. "Shore is. Biggest, too."

"What do ya think? Twenty inches, naw more."

They both turned and looked at me.

"Son! Ah … what's you're name, son? I forgot. Truth is I never knew."

"It's Ed, sir."

"Well, Mr. Ed Sir, gotta tell ya this, you done got yourself some ole fish here. You got yourself a big rainbow trout—this here's what we call the Monster of Rainbow Pool. Ain't nobody in these parts what ain't fished fur 'em. I'd say with worms, dough balls, min-ners, shiners, hell, chicken livers, corn, I'd guess. And looky here, there he lies. Caught on a goll-durn store-bought fly. Hell, look at that big fish, let's see here, waddaya think, Jackaboy, twenty one inches, twenty three, twenty four inches long?"

"I'd say so, Pop."

"Say what? How long?"

"Well, twenty four, Pop. That's my guess."

"And weigh? Waddaya say, Jack, four pounds."

"Naw, Pop, I'd say five. That or more."

"Look id 'me. Too damn purrty ta gut. He's goin' back with my ole buddy, Ed, here, Mr. Ed Sir here, goin' back in all his glory." And he held the fish with one hand around the tail and the other cupped under its chin and he leaned over and handed it to me.

"Damn, Jack, we shudda had a camera here. Ed, son, your Daddy gotta camera?"

"Yes, sir, he has."

"Well, here, let's keep this fella fresh. Unbutton your shirt." He bent down and pulled some ferns and long grass out of the ground, wet them in the stream and said, "C'mon over here. Put that fish in your shirt." Then he stuffed the grass and ferns down between the fish and my stomach and piled the rest on top of the fish. "Now button up your shirt."

"When we get back at the hotel, your Daddy can get a pitcher of you with this here baby. Ed, son, Eddie, Eddie, I can't believe it—you caught the Monster of Rainbow Pool. On a fly! Damned store-bought fly. Hell, I ain't never used one in all my whole life. C'mon, ole pal." He draped his arm over my shoulder and the three of us, Henry, Jack and I—I was marching in the middle holding that bundle of fish and ferns tight to my belly—together we walked back to the Ford.

Dad was standing on the porch smoking a cigarette when we drove up. He was talking to some other men. "Hey, Dad, Dad, Dad look at this! Wait 'til you see this!" I held up the fish with both hands. Dad came down the steps and walked over to the dusty old Ford. And even though he had on his straw hat and his crisp, tan cotton poplin suit, he held out his hands to take the fish. (I thought, "Oh, no, it'll get all over his suit ...")

"Edward, you son of a gun, let me see that. Wow, now that's a fish. A big rainbow trout. Hey, fells, look at this," he turned and held it up so all the men on the porch could see it.

Then he turned to Henry and Jack. "Where'd you guys catch this?"
"We didn't catch it. Your son caught it. Ed did it. Down there at Rainbow Pool. And that isn't no ordinary trout, mister, no siree. What he done got—and he done got it 'fly fishin'', is what we call the Monster of Rainbow Pool. Got it all by hisself. On a fly rod with a goll-dang store-bought fly, by golly."

"Dad, Henry said you should take a picture of me with the fish."
"Good idea." He turned—still holding the fish—it was dripping all over his poplin suit—and yelled up to the porch. "Hey, Joe, Joe, do me a favor, get the bellboy to go up to my room, 456, and get the camera. It's on the desk. Have him bring it down here right now. Make it pronto."

Dad handed the fish back to me and wiped his hands on his pants. By this time all the men on the porch and some who had been in the lobby had drifted down to admire the fish close up. They stood in a semicircle around me and the fish. And the men coming back from the golf course, they joined in too.

"Wow, look at that. One helluva trout."

"That what it is? A trout. Hell, it's as big as a salmon."

"What did you get him on, son?" someone asked.

"On a Royal Coachman, sir. A wet Royal Coachman."

"Pretty fish, son."

"Real nice fish, son."

"Great fish, son."

"Thank you, sir."

The bellboy came running down the steps with Dad's camera and Dad took pictures of me with the fish. I couldn't wait to show Mom.
When he finished, he stuffed the camera into the side pocket of his suit coat, reached for his wallet and walked over to Henry. And Henry said, "Thank you, sir. That's very generous. Very generous. Thank you, sir."

"Your name's, what, Henry? Well, Henry you deserve it. Helping Edward catch that fish and all. You earned it. I think he'll never, ever forget this."

That evening Dad and I went down to eat dinner in the big dining room. We were joined by one of Dad's business friends and his wife. We didn't order from the menu. Something special was coming. And it came on one of those serving trolleys on this big silver-edged platter covered with a silver dome with a handle on top. The waiter wheeled it up to our table and the chef, in his white jacket and white hat, came with him. A really pretty girl, she was a blonde with curls and she was just my age, and she was sitting with her parents at a nearby table, she looked over and smiled at me. Right at me.

The chef raised the gleaming dome. And there, beneath it, on a bed of steaming rice and sprigs of parsley lay the Monster of Rainbow Pool, as big and pink as a prize salmon. The chef picked up the platter in two hands, tilted it slightly and swept it left and right for all in the dining room to see. Then he set it down on the table, turned toward me and bowed. Jeez, can you imagine, he bowed to *me* like I was some potentate or something. Everyone clapped. Even the curly blonde and her parents, too.

Then he stepped aside and the waiter stepped forward and with miraculous ease he boned the fish, and laid a generous portion on my dinner plate. He did the same for Dad, his business friend and the friend's wife. Before we picked up our forks, my father poured a splash of wine into my glass, filled the other glasses and made a toast—"May the Monster of Rainbow Pool swim in our memories forever."

The next day the blonde (I've forgotten her name) and I had lunch together by the pool. I wore my white pants and blue blazer. Her parents sat at a separate table. My Dad was off somewhere on business.

6

HULK HOGAN

Alaska. A fisherman's dream. Why out there in Alaska you can pack a whole lifetime of fishing adventures into a week. You can do that by choosing from a thick anthology of rivers, lakes and streams. And a whole taxonomy of fish. Broad-backed, acrobatic rainbows—the Hulk Hogans of their breed—flame-red, hook-jawed hump-backed sockeye salmon, blue-green neon-gleaming spinnaker-finned graylings up to twenty inches. Fill in what I've left out.

Alaska. I had long dreamed of going there to catch a ten-pound rainbow on a fly in the chilly glacial melt of an Alaskan stream. As a freelance writer, I had the time to go. But not the money. It ain't cheap.

My chance came one day in Los Angeles. I'd been flown out there from New York on an assignment for an advertising agency. One of their clients was having their national week-long convention in L. A. and I was assigned to be there on stand-by in case they needed some last minute writing. Like last-minute changes to the officers' speeches. Or last-minute fixes on the agency's new-campaign presentation to the board.

J. Harrington Cotton, a polished Princetonian, and number three man in the agency, was acting as the account executive and one afternoon he collared me in the hotel lobby. It was around 3 o'clock in the afternoon. There was a crisis he said. (There was always a crisis.) The executive director, he explained, needed an entirely new speech to offset an unanticipated challenge to his position. He had to change his whole approach. That meant a new speech. From scratch. And it had to be written, reviewed by the director, revised, loaded into the teleprompter and be ready to go by 3 P.M. the next afternoon.

Harrington filled me in on the background right there in the lobby. When he finished, he gave me the key to his suite. Before I went up, I stopped by the concierge desk and asked them to deliver a PC to Harrington's suite as soon as possible—within the hour. (This was in the days before laptops.)

I was in the suite making notes when the bellhop arrived with the PC and I had him set it up on the table in the dining nook. Harrington, a master of detail, already had provisions spread out on the bar—a half dozen Montecristos (long, smooth Cuban-made Churchills), a virgin bottle of Dalwhinnie Single Highland Malt, 15 year's old, a basket of fruit, and a crystal bowl of pretzels, another with ice cubes, tongs on the side. There were a dozen Heinekens in the fridge. And six Cokes for caffeine and sugar. Harrington arrived about an hour later.

Thus equipped, Harrington and I "pulled an all-nighter." The new speech was written, and delivered by Harrington to the executive director's suite. He was back in about an hour with the director's comments. I made the revisions, revised and polished it according to more give and take and by mid-morning the next day, we were downstairs in the auditorium watching the tech guy load it into the teleprompter. As with all Cinderella stories, the speech was a rousing success, making the challenged director more secure and happy, and making Harrington and the agency certified heroes.

"Nice job. You deserve a bonus," said Harrington, circling his arm around my shoulder. "Just name it."

Harrington himself was a well-traveled sportsman (African Safaris, no less, and jaunts to New Zealand, and even to the Seychelles to chase bonefish long before it was added to the lexicon of exotic, bragging-right waters), and I knew he would understand my yen to catch a big rainbow in Alaska. Besides we were almost there. So I said, "Hey, how about sending me up to Alaska for a week's fishing?" "Done," he said.

And "done" it was. Two days later—the last day of the week-long convention—a manila envelope was waiting for me at the message desk. It contained a brochure for a place called Iliamna Lodge, a confirmation of my booking there, along with round-trip First Class airline tickets, L.A. to Seattle, to Anchorage to Illiamna and back to New York. Enclosed was a typed note saying that Mr. Cotton had arranged to have a fresh box of Monticristos, a bottle of Dalwhinnie, a brand new

Orvis fly rod, all purchased at agency expense, and all Fed Exed to me at the lodge. His secretary called my wife in New York and told her to dump all my fishing gear into a duffle bag and Fed Ex that out to the lodge, too.

Although I used to call him "Captain Chaos" usually behind his back, but sometimes, under the influence of Dalwhinnie, to his face, Harrington was the epitome of the completely polished "can do" guy. He never seemed to miss a detail. And he remained completely unflappable under the most intense pressure. You had to give him that: he knew how to get things done no matter what the circumstances. And done in style. No matter what the cost. No matter how little time was left. Even at the last minute, which was always when he got around to things.

I embarked from Los Angeles, trailing clouds of glory, and headed up north for my long-dreamed-of Alaskan fishing adventure.

I arrived at Iliamna Lodge on a Friday. The new Orvis rod, the Montecristos, the scotch and my duffle bag were already in my room. The next morning, feeling like a millionaire sportsman, I awoke to the luxury of having my own pilot, Larry, and my own guide, Dave, and shazam! We're aloft over a puddled carpet of greenish brown tundra in a carrot-colored Cessna 206. I'm sitting up in the co-pilot's seat, hands folded in my lap like a good kid in Sunday school. Dave, my very own guide, is in the back. The skies are robin's egg blue and we're winging our way toward a rendezvous with Alaska's Copper River. The Upper Copper, to be precise.

Can you believe it? A guide and a pilot all to myself. How did I end up this close to heaven? Well, by the luck of the draw, I happened to arrive at the lodge too late to fit into the regular rotation of guides and guests. I had missed the so-called switch-over day. So, now, it was my turn to catch up and that's why I have Larry and Dave all to myself. All day long, of course.

Larry swoops in over the tree tops and lands the Cessna on a three-acre lake nearby the main branch of the Copper where the outfitter has stashed a broad-bottomed aluminum boat with a jet outboard engine. That means its engine has no conventional screw propeller; instead it uses a suck-in-the-water-and-spew-it-out propulsion system. In other words, you can navigate in really shallow water, a few inches is enough. So, off we go, jetting down the Upper Copper.

Now this place is, well, it's like flipping through a rack of jumbo postcards all devoted to the most heavenly fishing holes on planet earth. Take your pick.

Larry, he's got a Missouri twang like God gave him banjo strings 'stead of vocal chords. "Mind if I fish?" says he to me. "Hell no, buddy," say I. (I'm in a very generous mood.) So now he's in the middle, standing there between us, rigging up. Larry's going to do some fishing too. Fly fishing'. It's new to him. The guys back at the lodge are trying to convert him from Missouri River bait fishin'. "We're tryin' to make a gentleman outta him," they say.

By the way, when it comes to riggin', as I'll later learn, nobody can do it as fast as that sport back at the lodge, that pipe-fitter from Bridgeport, Connecticut, "Motion Morrissey" I christen him—hell, if he'd been with us, he'd be all rigged up by the time the plane landed on the lake. But, slow as I am, I do beat Larry who's slower than a three-fingered tailor—and when Dave beaches the boat on the edge of a likely spot, I'm the first to shuffle out onto the gravel bar. Dave's hunkering and hovering right at my elbow.

I'm hearing the words from that old Frankie Lane song, yeah, I mean really old, called *Swamp Girl:*
She will call you to come to the water,
Where it's cool and calm and serene;
She will call you to come to the water
To a world made of emerald green.
I have heard that call before....

I had now answered that call and I am standing here on a gravel bar in a world made of emerald green. Below me there is a broad, green tongue of water flowing thirty-feet wide between two straight banks. There's not a ripple on the water's surface for a city block. After that you can see the white whiskers where the rapids begin. The banks are overhung with bangs of bright green grass. Dave says it's lime grass and then he points to the subtle wavelets and the thin line of bubbles flowing underneath it on the right edge of the pool just below the bar. "See how dark it gets in there, on the side? There's an undercut bank there."

I've rigged my brand spanking new Orvis 9 foot 8-weight graphite. It's beautiful. Just beautiful. Dave admires it and reaches for the naked tippet dangling out of the tip-top. My leader's one of the ones that I have hand-tied myself, tapering it down according to a formula with sections of diminishing diameter mono tied end-to-end with barrel knots. The last section, 21 inches long, is eight-pound test.

Dave takes the tippet end and ties on what he calls an Electric Leech. Size 8. It is made with soft, sooty blue-black dyed rabbit's body fur. The fur is tied down along the shank matuka-style and extended two inches beyond the curve of the hook. In the water, this extension of fur wags like a happy puppy's tail. Tied in on each side at the cheeks and trailing back to the end of the tail are two strips of purple metallic Flashabou. With the fly secured, Dave puts a .22 caliber split shot on the leader, slips it down and snugs it tight against the head of the fly. Finally, he squeezes two more same-size shots on the leader and snugs them tight against the last barrel knot just above the 21 inches of tippet. Then he tells me to cast slightly across and down stream toward the left hand bank so the fly will swing through the pool below the bar and drift deeply into the dark water under the right-hand bank. The undercut bank he'd pointed out earlier.

I'm standing at the end of the gravel bar in four or five inches of clear, cold water. The sun warms my back. I roll cast. The leech flips up and caroms into the water. The split shot at the fly's head goes, "Plunk!" Then the double shot flips in and goes "Kur-plunk!"

I feed out a few feet of line. The lemon-yellow portion of the line straightens out in the current and the dark brown sinking tip ahead of it follows the flow curving out into the center of the pool and disappears downward in a graceful arc. The electric leech is now dead-drifting, drag-free and deep through the center of the pool.

When the line straightens out, the fly swims into the dark water along the bank. Dave says, "Now strip." He's still hunkering and hovering close beside me, bent over, peering downstream. Nothing happens. I retrieve and cast again.

I make three identical casts, stripping after each when Dave tells me to. Then he decides to change strategy: "Try one up into the grass on the right." "Right up into the grass?" I say, "Up into the grass?" "Yeah, that's what I said." "OK"

I flip the fourth cast up and over into the grass on the right bank. The stream catches the trailing line and pulls the leader through the grass toward the water.

Plunk! Kurplunk! The leech sinks and starts its drift in the shadow of the overhanging grass. The line straightens as the current takes it down stream. The sink tip, drawn by the split shot, sinks quickly, and the floating section of the line overtakes it, bellying away from the bank into mid-current. I flick the rod tip in a half circle to mend the belly out of the line. The mended line now swings out smoothly and straightens in the flow. I waggle the rod tip to make the rabbit fur undulate as if it were a leech struggling or swimming in the current. "Strip!" says Dave. With my left hand, I make two quick six-inch strips. And that's when I shook hands with Hulk Hogan.

The coils of line hanging from my left hand disappeared like Budweiser at spring break. My venerable Hardy Princess reel lets out a sound like someone was tearing a brand-new-hundred-yard-long starched Spring Maid 410-threads-to-the-inch bed sheet. The virgin Orvis rod arcs into a capital "C." Instantly my right bicep burns like I'm doing curls with a dumb bell. My deltoid bulges. My left hand releases the disappearing line as if it were hot wire. ZZZZZZZZip. Next thing I know the nail knot joining my backing to my fly line pings through the German silver tiptop. The white Dacron backing melts off the Princess spool like grease off bacon in a red-hot skillet.

Way down stream now, just above the whiskered rapids, I see a flash—a bright silver flash—and out of the water comes a Hulk Hogan of a rainbow. When he turns his side to the sun, it looks as if somebody had thrown a sterling silver Frisbee and bounced it off the water and it was now somersaulting through the air—three feet off the water in a splash of sparkles.

The old Princess, now screaming like a lady frightened by a mouse, stops screaming and I start cranking on her faster than a banjo player dueling with the devil. Next thing I know, my arm starts to burn like, well, like I'm locked up with Hulk Hogan in an arm-wrestling contest.

The fish is now deep down, way down, up under the left hand bank, shaking his head bump, bump, bump; then he pulls real hard and swirls at the surface, dives, and takes more line—I mean he's in the backing and he takes twenty feet more—and then he holds, resting in the current. I lean forward, then back, then crank. Click. Click. I ease the rod tip down, raise it up slowly, slowly with both hands, steady, slow, and crank—click, click some more. Ole Hulk is wrestling against the pull of the current, the weight of the line, the flex of the rod and the burning muscle in my arm.

Soon, they all take their toll. And with a lot of heaving and cranking, Mr. Hogan is only twenty yards below me. My right arm, my shoulder, too, aches. Dave tells me to move my right hand up on the cork grip and brace the handle against my forearm. That feels much better. More secure. More control. More leverage. Then, like a corner man, he calls out the strategy: "Lower your rod, move it to the left. Bring it down parallel with the water. Put a bend into it. It won't break. Put the wood to him. That's right. Now, slowly, switch the rod over to the right side. That's it. Down parallel with the water. Keep him off balance. Easy. Now hold. Bend the rod. Easy. Eaaasy. Be smooth. Take it easy."

I do everything my corner man tells me except I forget to breathe. Dave notices that. "Take a deep breath for God's sake!" The fish moves off again, slowly but powerfully, downstream. Bump, bump, bump. The line, the part in the air leading from rod tip to the surface of the water, waggles back and forth. I crank the Princess. Click, click, click. I pull back on the rod with both hands. I take deep breaths. Click, click, click. Breathe. Crank. Breathe. Thirteen minutes now since the lightening struck.

Finally, I have all the lemon-yellow floating line back on the Princess. Now I start to reel in the dark brown sinking tip. I hear and feel the line-to-leader knot "tick" through the tiptop. Oops! That's dangerous. Then I hear "tick, tick, tick" as the barrel knots in my hand-tied leader move through the tip top. Yes, dangerous, so I strip line off the reel, let some line out to give me more leverage and get the tip top back on the smooth fly line. Hulk takes this as an invitation to pull harder, to swirl and then to wallow just below the surface. His dorsal fin now shows above the water. And his big, broad, black-green back. Now he's lollygagging not more than fifteen feet below me out in the shallow water just below the tail of the gravel bar Dave and I are standing on.

"Ease his head up," says Dave as he moves forward and positions himself just below me on my right. "You want to ease him up on the gravel. Easy," says Dave. "He could make another run." "What?" you've got to be kidding. He's finished. Whupped." Hulk's broad side shows now, speckled, peachy-yellow-silver-bright like an ancient broadsword. Ten feet away now, just at the end of the leader and now in barely eight inches of water. I see his head. His mouth. The electric leech.

His eye. Why, for God's sake, it is the size of a quarter! And his head is as big and shiny as a new garden spade. His cheeks are rouge red. Metallic rouge red.

Fifteen minutes now. Dave moves closer. Bends at the waist. Cautious. Hands outstretched. (Hands outstretched! *Hands!* Where th' hell's your *net*?) "For God's sake, Dave, where's your net?"

I'm holding the rod tip as high as I can now, both hands over my head, and I'm trying to drag Hulk up onto the gravel bar below me. But he's still tugging, feeling heavy and he's now managed to right himself and get his head turned back down stream. I see his wide tail flapping in the shallow water. Then there's an explosive splash as if someone dropped a cinder block into the water. An enormous splash and a mighty surge downstream, followed by a rapid bump-bump. Then nothing. Only silence. The kind of silence when even the birds forget to chirp. The bugs forget to buzz. The breeze forgets to blow. And you forget to breathe. And the only sound is the beating of your heart. The silence that you hear when you've just lost the biggest fish you ever hooked.

Had you been there, you would have seen three men standing on that gravel bar in that surreal silence, heads bowed as silent and forlorn as mourners at a graveside.

Dave is the first to speak: "It broke at one of the barrel knots in the leader, see the pigtail here." Dave holds the line up toward the sky. I see a pitiful little crook in the end of my naked tippet. The electric leech is gone. I look down at the top of my boots. I have removed my hat and I am holding it against the rod in both hands at my waist. Dave says, "Ed I wanted that fish as much as you did." I feel like a popped balloon. His words sound as weak as far off whispers. "He'd go over ten, maybe eleven or twelve pounds. Shit, he coulda been thirteen, maybe. Damn. One of the best fish I've ever seen in here."

"Dave. I've got a question. Is there a law against using a long-handled net on the Copper River? Some sinister Sierra Club conservation thing. Some SPCA ordinance. Some frou-frou Trout Unlimited regulation? Like you gotta grab 'em barehanded or get arrested by the fish and game officer? Huh, Dave, huh?"

"Yeah, the net, yeah. Ah, think I left it back in the Cessna. Or, maybe, back at the lodge."

You know, maybe another time, in another life, I shall go back to that pool, to that undercut bank with its bangs of green lime grass curving over the edge of the Upper Copper for another chance to shake hands with Hulk Hogan. But this time I'll be damn sure to take a net. You see, the next time I'd truly like to take the Hulk to dinner. Now that's not a crime, is it?

7

THE BUTTERFLY TATTOO

Silva and Lyrette had begun their task three days ago at dawn. Now, they worked in the swamp along the edge of the beaver dam. They were cutting trail and behind them lay a narrow miniature cemetery of poplar stumps.

Silva swung his chainsaw rhythmically like an artist's brush, cutting each tree precisely four inches from the ground as if each tree had been measured and marked. Lyrette followed, casting the cut trees off to the side.

They rested, too tired to speak. Besides, the growling of Silva's saw has temporarily deafened them both. Lyrette pulled a little pouch of tobacco out of his shirt pocket, reached into the other pocket for papers, rolled two cigarettes and handed one to Silva.

It would take them another two days to clear the trail along the margin of the swamp, climb the slope and reach the stand of birch and pine at the top.

Once there they would make a clearing. And at the downside of the clearing, they would strip the limbs from a big poplar, leaving one to stick out from the trunk as a hook. The next day they would come back on an all-terrain vehicle and hang a burlap bag bulging with raw, rancid garbage.

At first, when he left the logging road, Christian could barely see the trail because it began so faintly in the woods above the swamp. Of course he knew it was there. Silva had told him the way. Then, further along, with the little poplar stumps beneath his boots, he was reassured. Only once in the muck of the swamp where the trail seemed to lose its way was there any doubt. Only a moment's doubt. For once the trail emerged from the swamp at the bottom of the slope; it was virtually a tunnel, carved with Silva's artistry through the underbrush woven as tightly as the backs and bottoms of wicker chairs.

Silva had mentioned the beaver dam, as a landmark, but nothing he had said prepared Christian for what he saw. He had never seen or imagined anything like it: fifty yards or more of white, barkless sticks, piled like a jumble of pick-up-sticks, a thousand tooth marks on each, mortared willy-nilly one-by-one with mud and swamp debris, stood there holding back a vast, smooth apron of dark, tea-colored water. A half-acre of water.

Christian now balanced himself on the edge of the dam, peering across the dark water at the beaver's lodge, a pile of sticks in the middle of the pond.

He reached down and picked up a long narrow stick as straight and as smooth as a broom handle. He poked it into the water. "Must be five feet deep," he thought. Then he looked at his watch. It had been sixty minutes since he left the logging road.

In spite of the late afternoon chill, he was sweating when he reached the end of the swamp and started up the slope. No horizon was visible. All he could see was an intricate tracery of young trees against the sky with branches just beginning to swell with bright green buds.

He paused to loosen his coat, adjust his hat and rub the back of his hand across his forehead. It was four o'clock. The sky was slate. There was a lull in the wind. Silence in the woods. Christian felt an alien, primitive apprehension as he followed Silva's trail deeper into the woods.

He had now walked for well over an hour. Silva said it would take ninety minutes. But, then. Silva, half the size of Christian, walked twice as fast.

The stand appeared like an apparition. It was much higher than Christian had imagined it would be. And much older. So old in fact that its railing and platform had weathered as gray as a grandfather's hair. And where the nails were, there were stains. Long black stains. They reminded Christian of the dark stains beneath the nails on the cross atop Golgotha.

Again, Christian paused to wipe the back of his hand across his forehead.

The stand was in a big tree at the top of the slope. Below, there was a thick thatch of poplars and birch. Silva had cut a narrow clearing in these trees to form a narrow field of fire. At the end of it stood the bait tree. A big, old stark white birch eight inches in diameter.

For three days, Christian would walk to the stand, climb up the steps nailed to the trunk of the tree, and sit there with his rifle across his lap. Waiting. He would walk in each afternoon and out at dark each night, growing more familiar and comfortable with the trail each time, even managing to cross the swamp on the last day in the darkness with no trouble.

He would often set the rifle aside and hang his arms over the railing and stare down at the bait bag with his feet dangling over the edge of the platform. Then he would lean back against the tree and doze. From time to time, the wind would come up from the northwest and roar through the forest like a locomotive. First, there would be a little rustling far off, and then he'd feel a breeze on his face, then hear a great long "whoosh" and wake to find the stand rocking like a cradle.

It was early May and Christian woke one day to find snow sprinkled like powered sugar on his arms and the toes of his boots. Then the sun came out, melted the snow and spilled brilliant yellow light into the clearing. Christian would look at the buds, imagined he could see them actually swelling in the warmth of the sun, and imagine that he could see little leaves unfolding like toddlers waking from their naps.

Once, asleep in the stand, Christian dreamed of the butterfly tattoo he had seen on the tummy of one of the dancers at the Algonquin Lounge where they had stopped before going into the bush. Its tiny wings were a delicate blue against the dancer's peach-velvet skin. In his dream, the butterfly sprang to life, flew off her tummy and landed on his nose like a fairy in a Disney film. He could actually feel it there.

When he woke, the sun had come out again. The clearing now reminded him of a page from his daughter's coloring book. He was stiff. He stood up on the platform to stretch and to warm himself in the sun. Then, sat down again and put the rifle across his lap.

Suddenly, from the corner of his eye, he saw something quick and small. A hummingbird had come to see what Christian was. It came with no warning. No sound. It hovered not twelve inches from Christian's nose and looked into his eyes. Where did it come from? What was it doing here? God, how beautiful! How small! How fast!

Never, ever, in his life had Christian seen a living hummingbird. But he knew instantly what it was. And he had never seen a living bear either.

Through the woven underbrush it was hard to see anything—unless it moved and even then it was hard. But somehow he saw the bear. Perceived it, far away at first. A hundred yards. A black thing among all the grays and greens. A big black thing. Way off, beyond the hummingbird. In fact, had it not been for the hummingbird, Christian would never have seen the bear.

The bear moved forward with a bestial nonchalance, his head swaying rhythmically like a chainsaw in Silva's hands. He moved slowly.

For forty-five minutes, Christian watched the bear appear and disappear. For forty-five minutes, the bear browsed leisurely below the clearing; now he raised his nose to test the air and circled to the right just below the bait tree itself. Then he stopped. He raised his head again and stood up on his rear legs, standing motionless with his short bowed front legs dangling like Christian's arms had dangled over the railing of the stand. There was a vivid patch of white on his chest between his dangling front legs.

There was no sound. What was left of the sun was now at Christian's back. It had turned pale rose, had painted the clearing pale rose.

The bear dropped down, lowered his head and came to the bait tree. Noiselessly, just as the hummingbird had come to Christian.

Now the sun was gone completely and when it left it took all the color from the woods leaving nothing but shadows behind. It was as if the lights in a room had been extinguished and a small candle had been lit to take their place. The candle was the moon.

Christian was kneeling below the bait bag. He looked up wearily. He could see every star in the Milky Way, if they were fluorescent appliqués stuck on the ceiling of a planetarium. He was tired. He knew the walk out, especially through the swamp, always took much longer in the dark. So, he'd better start. They would be waiting for him.

Silva was surprised not to find Christian waiting for him there in the dark where the trail begins at the edge of the old logging road. So he switched on his flashlight and started in.

When they met on the trail, Silva said, "Ho, *mon ami*. Why you walk so slow on such big legs? Why you make me come to you?"

Christian, big as a bear himself, wrapped his arms around Silva's shoulders. On both his sleeves were long dark stains.

"Ah, Chris, your friends, they have cognac. They drink by the fire. They laugh and talk of sweet girls, of the *tatouage papillion*. Come, we join them." Silva hugged Chris back.

"Silva, you son-of-a-gun, have you been drinking my vodka?"

"No, no, no. No-no-no-no."

"Hey, Silva, listen. I saw a hummingbird in there, right at the stand. Right up in the stand. My first! He flew like this, right up to my nose. A foot away. Looked me in the eye, hovering there—you understand me?—like a tiny helicopter. Like Tinker Bell. Silva, I swear, her wings were as thin as smoke. Came right up to me. Silva, have you ever seen a hummingbird, I mean up that close? Like this?" Christian reached out and fluttered his hand, big as a bear's paw, in front of Silva's small red nose. "Oh, Silva, back there in the clearing, at the bait tree, I killed a big black bear. Field dressed him. That's what took so long. You'll have to go fetch him for me in the morning."

8

THE THIRTY YEAR DEER

Thirty years ago, dressed like Rambo and armed with a Bear "Grizzly" 45-pound laminated recurve bow concealed in its own mesh camouflage sleeve, a black leather quiver bristling with cedar-shaft broadheads slung over my shoulder, I ventured stealthily into the crisp predawn darkness of the early December woods.

My destination was a wooden tree stand perched thirty feet up an oak tree growing beside a deer trail overlooking the Croton Reservoir in Westchester County, New York.

It was my first time.

When the rising sun finally began to pink the sky, my feet, which were double-socked and stuffed into felt-lined hunting boots, were as cold as champagne bottles in an ice bucket. I could suffer no longer, and lowered myself stiffly from the stand, crossed the trail and stalked slowly down the slope deeper into the woods. It was 9 A.M.

The sun had by now topped the ridge. When I turned toward it, I saw a deer. Just its head and neck were visible through the tangle of branches. It was a buck with perfectly symmetrical eight-point antlers. He was on the trail that passed below my now empty tree stand. He had paused. His neck was arched. He was looking calmly straight ahead.

I raised the bow, and sighted down the arrow's shaft through a narrow opening in the tangle of limbs between us. The sharpened edges of the broadhead threw off a spark in the brightening sunlight. I centered the point on his neck, pulled the bow string back to full draw, pressed it against the corner of my mouth and released the arrow. Its flight was intercepted by an overlooked limb and it ricocheted into a tree trunk. When I looked up, the buck had disappeared. The woods were silent.

For the next thirty years, when deer season opened in the fall, I would sneak into the woods at dawn with bow and arrow or rifle and in all those years, I never saw a deer like that or got another shot like that.

◆   ◆   ◆

Deer hunting? A friend of mine calls it "slaughter" with a towering disdain born of his intimate knowledge of the literature of Bambi and the wildlife populating his spacious suburban lawn—namely squirrels and deer.

"They eat out of my hand," he says. "Come when I call them."

But anyone who has ever stalked wildlife in the deep woods meets a very different breed of animal. And plays a very different game.

Here the animals are alert and elusive. Cautious. Nervous. To imagine that here one can dance with wolves and feed wild animals from the palm of one's hand is an illusion. Besides, in the wild, animals are protected by a society of vigilant and numerous sentinels: crows, squirrels and even bratty little chipmunks who give away your presence like squealing smoke detectors in a hallway. Have I forgotten to mention the crunch of Vibram soles on frosty leaves and brittle twigs?

This different game is played principally at dawn and in the early morning. That's when it begins because that is when deer, having grown nocturnal as an adaptation to the incursions of man into their habitat, leave their feeding grounds in the open fields and return to their bedding grounds in the deep thickets, dark swamps and high ridges.

Dawn is always a portentous time. Filled with possibilities. But, truth be told, when it spreads its possibilities across the awakening land, I'd rather be in bed. Most especially if it is a cold, wet, gray dawn, which it always seems to be when the post-Thanksgiving deer-hunting season opens in the Northeast.

The hunter's dawn creeps like Sandberg's fog into the woods on the back of mists that arise like ghosts in the creek bottoms and swamps and ascend to the ridges above. Next, it is like twilight in reverse as a blush spreads across the cheeks of the dark gray sky. Then, gradually, there is a yellowish brightening as if the fingers of some unseen hand had slowly turned the dimmer up.

There is what you could call a sort of thermocline effect in the woods at dawn, a turning over of the air as cold and warm breezes awaken, shift around and exchange places. It is this mysterious transition from night to dawn that fascinates and fuels the expectations of early risers. Most especially deer hunters.

At first light, sitting alone in the silence of the early December woods, you begin to see an intricate three-dimensional tapestry of twigs, trunks, limbs, the delicate arms and elbows of red-tinged thorn and berry bushes twinkling with diamonds of dew, and leaves dangling like little rusty bells and mute wind chimes, all woven together into an essentially vertical herringbone of charcoal blacks, muted rosy grays, soft chalky yellows, weathered-copper greens, pale rust oranges, and the whispers of pastel violet. The colors of a Harris Tweed.

I say "essentially vertical" because the deer hunter is taught not to look "at" but "into" this multi-colored, 3-dimensional tapestry. He must try to see anything that is monochromatic and horizontal, anything that breaks up the verticality—like the back or belly of a deer. Searching out horizontals is difficult in the deep woods because you will see nothing dwelling among this tangled intricacy unless or until it moves. Absolutely nothing. No matter how close it is. Because lack of motion in the woods confers invisibility. Even a squirrel spied climbing up the gray trunk of a white oak will disappear when he stops. Look away. Look back. And he will simply not be there. This is why the hunter searches for a stand that affords him a field of fire: an opening in the tapestry.

I talk of "silence" but that word needs qualification. Unless you are deep in the "real" wilderness—northern Canada, for example—there is no true silence in the woods. Even in the wilderness you will sometimes hear jet planes flying overhead. See their con trails.

Here in the pre-dawn woods surrounding rural Pennsylvania's farmlands you will hear the chug of an old McCormick tractor on a distant field, see the twinkle of a car's lights as it navigates a distant road—at first you will think it is another hunter heading through the darkened woods with a flashlight toward his tree stand. Later, you will hear the squeaking brakes and exhalation of a school bus.

The barking of a dog, the distant crowing of a cock, and at first light the chirping of small birds, the coughing of crows, the chattering and scrabbling of unseen squirrels. Sometimes, you will hear a predawn rain falling on crisp leaves, snapping and crackling like Rice Krispies in a breakfast bowl.

After you select a stand and settle into it, you realize that now you have at least three hours to just sit there. To amuse yourself you will move your eyes like tiny roller coasters up and down and across the intricate warp and woof and weft of the woods around you. You will listen. Listen intently. You must not clear your throat or sneeze or swat a winter moth that alights on your nose. You must play a serious game of statue.

The early morning woods do strange things to the imagination of a hunter. It fuels exaggeration and self-deluding wishful thinking by turning nearby stumps into wild turkeys and black bears. Branches into antlers. That's why, at nine o'clock or thereabouts, when you meet up with fellow hunters and form a conspiratorial circle, they will whisper, telling you tales of the five deer they saw, does, oh, how big and fat, followed by a buck, huge and majestic—the biggest buck they have ever seen. They will tell you that all those animals walked "right behind you ... when you got up to pee." "Didn't you hear them? Didn't you see them?"

One morning, standing in the darkness, my companion told me, looking back over his shoulder as he zipped up his son's quilted fluorescent orange jacket, to pick a stand above and precisely to the left of the windowless, roofless ruins of a small, one-room cinderblock building near the main ascending trail. From there, he says, I can see the trail in the moonlight. It's easy to find it. Once "there," I should sit motionless, he say, until eight o'clock. At least. His son, he says, pointing into the darkness, would go to that rock pile over there. To the east. He, the father, will go down into the swamp.

"Where will *you* be? I ask.

"Down the swamp."

That's what happens when you hunt as a guest in someone else's territory. They always take the best places. But they always assure you, "Now, here's the best spot. You sit here. Harry and I will go down through the swamp and flush some critters up to you."

It is especially so when they bring their son along. The lad will be placed on the trail above the uncut corn, just where several fresh trails converge among a scattering of dark, damp, fresh scrapes, and gleaming yellow rubs on the sides of thick saplings too numerous to count among the piles of dewy, still-steaming deer droppings.

So, on this morning the son is sent up to that unseen pile of lichen-dappled rocks that the glacier kindly left in the woods above the uncut corn. It is a regal spot. A veritable throne, a catbird seat overlooking a narrow corridor strewn with oak leaves and acorns stretching through the tapestry of the woods to the edge of the field. I shall call it Sonny's Perch.

At 7:25 A.M. I heard the first shot, a single pow! It came from down the ridge to my left. Far off. I heard another, a double pow! pow! Again far off. This time in the valley.

It is now 7:45. Pow! Pow! Whenever I hear a shot echo through the woods, I tense, hunker down, raise my rifle in readiness and listen for a deer in panic to come crashing through the brush.

In other words, I feel anticipation and a touch of fear. I comfort myself, however, with the rationalization that it would be improbable for a bullet to find me through all these trunks and limbs. Surely the oak I am hiding behind will shield me. Unless, of course, another hunter has mistaken me for his quarry and taken direct aim. Or, I think of a friend who told me about a hunter who shot a deer standing behind a six-inch tree with a high-velocity Winchester .270. The caliber rifle that I now have cradled in my lap. The bullet went through the tree.

An asphalt road defines the lower boundary of the territory we are hunting. On its far side are corn fields rolling in gentle undulations across the valley floor all the way to the mountains. On the inner side, beginning at the edge of the road is a nearly impenetrable black-water swamp. Above that is a two-acre stubble field sloping up to the tree line.

Getting into this territory is easy. You just turn right off the asphalt road, bump across a half buried drainage pipe, nose your car up a muddy opening and park on the edge of the field where two tractor trails diverge. One branches to the right, crossing a tiny spring-fed brook. The other to the left. The first ascends straight up and then two hundred yards above the brook, it curves to the left around a high, natural pile of rocks (that's Sonny's Perch). Then it dwindles into a narrow walking trail. The other hugs the side of the field along a hedgerow and ends at the tree line. From here on it narrows into a foot trail that enters the woods and ascends the ridge. Along the spine of the ridge is a power line straddling a grassy clear cut. On the high side of the clear cut, the trail continues through thick thorn bushes and into the far woods.

The property we are on is rented by the owner to a man who boards horses. Therefore, it is posted with bright orange and white signs along its entire perimeter. We are the only ones allowed to hunt here.

For the purpose of storing hay, the horse-boarder has hauled an old panel truck body up and positioned it near the end of the tractor trail in the left hand corner of the field. He has also spread manure around on parts of the field. (A delight to those of us with Vibram soles on our hunting boots.)

The top boundary of the field is defined by an old, tumbled-down stone wall with a twenty-foot-wide opening positioned just off-center to the right. That's where the trail enters the woods. To the right of this opening is a fallen tree. Its top pokes out into the stubble field for about thirty feet forming what canoeists call a "sweeper."

It is now full light. We've left our original spots, had our early morning rendezvous, exchanged exaggerations, and left for new stands. The one I have chosen is to the right of the truck body, the fallen tree and the opening in the stone wall. I set my pack-chair up catty corner, with its back to the wall, facing the fallen tree, which is about twenty-five yards from my position and screening me from where tractor trail goes through the opening in the stone wall at the tree line.

I don't usually set up the back-rest on my pack-chair because fiddling with the metal inserts is time-consuming and noisy. But this time I do. Then I clear all the leaves from beneath my feet and use my Buck knife to cut the branches in front of my nest to ensure an unobstructed yet narrow field of fire.

To preview possibilities, I shoulder the rifle, swing it in an arc, again stopping to cut any twigs that obstruct the free movement of the barrel, and practice releasing the safety, and sighting the scope on objects at various distances and various angles. Dress rehearsal over, I think of moving my pack chair down the slope away from the rock wall to give myself a clearer view of the trail. But that would expose my position to the bottom border of the field. Besides it is too late now. It is nearly 9 A.M. The sun is warm, high and bright. The sky is a cloudless Carolina blue. My coat, down vest and red wool blanket are all now stowed in the pack chair beneath me. And with reconnaissance and rehearsal completed, my position rationalized, I settled down to wait.

What I had hoped was that, when the deer left their feeding grounds in the fields across the road, they would come up the tractor trail on the left of the field—to the right of my position—and instead of following the branch that crosses the tiny brook and curves up to skirt the pile of rocks; I hoped they would follow the other trail along the edge of the field and enter the woods where it goes through the break in the wall. This way my shot would be a slightly up-angled broadside taken just before the deer were screened from my view by the tangled branches of the fallen tree. Or, if they were to come up the right edge of the field, turning left at the wall and walking along it toward the opening, that would take them in front of me and before they got there, I would have a shot either head-on and slightly down-slope or when they were opposite me, broadside.

In the hunter's woods, deer always seem to materialize like ghosts. Soundlessly. Especially when the morning dew muffles their footsteps. This morning was no exception.

As I swiveled my head to the right, I saw something rising like campfire smoke. The image slowly took shape—the shape of a deer, a buck, standing sculpture-still with the sun at his back. Head raised. Almost imperceptibly he swiveled his head, as I had, until he was looking directly at me through the branches of the fallen tree. He appeared relaxed, alert but not tense. Not perceptibly afraid, just curious or I hoped just cautious. He had stopped a short distance below where the trail enters the woods through the opening in the wall ... only a few feet below where the trail began its journey to the sanctuary of the high ridge.

Without my seeing him, he had walked either diagonally across the field, screened from my view by the truck body, or across the road, through the swamp and up along the edge of the field taking the path I had hoped he would.

When our eyes met, I froze even though I did not believe that he could see me, hidden against the darkness of the stone wall and screened by the branches and trunk of the fallen tree. No. It was impossible for him to have seen me. But, then, perhaps the sun has glinted off my glasses. Perhaps he had winded me. But had he done that, he would have snorted, pawed the ground and bolted into the woods.

Now his head moved again infinitesimally lower and toward me, a subtle focusing maneuver. I knew I dared not blink. Or breathe. An old-timer once told me, "You are sitting in their living room and just as you would notice if a small chair were moved or added to the room, the deer knows that something has changed in his living room. Something is out of place. Something is there that was not there before."

The new morning sun had turned his antlers to gleaming porcelain.

There was about him an atavistic calm, an almost mystical awareness, and, in the moment our eyes met through the branches of the fallen tree, we both seemed to understand that the denouement of our meeting would be his death.

He shifted his head, turning away, lifting his black eyes and raising his black nose … not to test the wind so much as to exhibit hauteur.

As I watched him through an opening in the branches, he seemed to flex and arch his neck. It was beautifully shaped, swollen with the muscles he would need for the battles of the rut. He stood there smooth, solid and flawless. In that microsecond, a kind of resignation appeared to settle over him. His body language seemed to say, "I am discovered. Something is watching me. But I am not afraid. I am invincible and too proud to raise my tail in panic and lunge up the trail. I am here. I accept what the next second brings."

The safety on the Winchester Featherweight, which locks the trigger *and* the bolt, is a horizontal lever that must be thumbed forward until it lines up with the red word "FIRE" stamped on the top of receiver. When it is pushed forward, it makes two metallic clicks, which I muffle with my gloved hand.

When he looked away, I had raised the rifle, framed him in the scope and chosen a narrow field of fire through the branches of the fallen tree. Because of the branches, I could not move the aiming point down to where it should be for the traditional heart/lung shot—just below and behind where his front leg intersects his body. All I could see was his head and neck in an incredibly clear three-dimensional picture the size of a postage stamp. He was 35 yards away.

The crosshairs were bright red, like a branding iron just lifted from the fire. I thought no thought. Felt no tightness in my muscles, no flutter in my belly. No tremor in my hand. I do not remember pushing the safety forward. I do not remember putting my finger on the trigger. Nor do I remember any sound. Or any recoil.

He simply disappeared from the scope.

I waited a minute or two then rose from my pack-chair and carrying the rifle with both hands held in front of me, I stepped out from the shadows into the stubble field. Slowly, I walked over to him. He lay on his side like a dog on a hearth. He twitched once. His hind leg. Like a dog dreaming. Then he lay completely still on a sun-warmed carpet of stubble and oak leaves. His black, bright eyes were open. Life had left him quickly. A small tear, thick and dark as vintage Amarone, wept from the center of his broad neck. There were no sounds in the woods. None at all.

The circle back to that trail above the Croton Reservoir was now unbroken after thirty years.

His head is mounted European-style on a walnut plaque, like the stags' heads and horns displayed along the halls in Scottish castles. His skull is bleached a stark white, his antlers polished with pumice, rotten stone and oil until they gleam like porcelain. He is, as it were, a replica of Georgia O'Keefe's painting, Summer Days. There is about him, still, that air of bestial hauteur and invincibility.

9

MUSKRAT AT THE BAR

The Beaverkill is a wide and winsome river flowing through New York's Catskill Mountains. It makes legends of its own and it draws its many lovers from all manner of men. Charlie Allen among them.

It was Doug Bury, then owner of the Antrim Lodge in Roscoe, who first told me about Charlie Allen, that manner of man who limits-out on every opening day before noontime and looks upon mostly all other fishermen, especially the city fellers up from New York, with, well, let's call it a casual unamused disdain.

The subject of Charlie Allen came up one night at the Antrim Bar when Doug was showing us a Daniel-Boone-type hat minus the tail made, not of 'coon, but muskrat. He told us how Charlie had trapped the 'rats in the damp lands bordering the Beaverkill, had given him a half-a-dozen pelts which he then sent up to Canada to be cured, cut and sewn into this hat now sitting on the bar as if it were a soft, lustrous Russian sable muff.

"Muskrat! Real muskrat," I said, stroking the hat. "No kidding." And I asked Doug if perhaps I could meet Charlie, to ask him if he might give me, or sell me, a muskrat pelt, no, not for a Daniel Boone hat, but for fly tying.

Doug said he didn't know if that would be a good idea. Charlie, after all, was a kinda to-himself fellow. He looked on everyone from the city, most especially New York City, as greenhorns and interlopers, and, he, Doug, doubted that Charlie would even discuss his pelts, much less sell one to a city feller. Case closed.

The next night, it was about five o'clock, George, my friend, and I were drinking Manhattans at the far end of the Antrim Bar when through the door—that one right there, the first one at the end of the bar—comes this man, skinny as a spade handle and wearing a green-checkered billed cap with fold-up ear flaps.

This man hiked himself up onto the bar stool, adjusted his hat like a pitcher on the mound, pushed his sleeves back, put his elbows on the bar, turned his palms upward, looked into them, dropped his head and rubbed his whiskered cheeks. Les, the bartender, brought him a Budweiser draft without his even asking. The man looked down into the glass momentarily, hands now cupping his chin, fingers now rubbing his lips, and then he slowly reached for the glass, brought it to his mouth and turned it up. He wiped his mouth with the back of his hand, and, again without asking, Les brought him another.

His face was deeply lined like all men who work outdoors in the sun and when he settled back, he turned his eyes down the bar, hardly moving his head and I looked straight into them. They were the brown eyes of a muskrat, glinting out of a thicket of wrinkles, out of their own tiredness and completely empty of curiosity. They were the eyes of Charlie Allen.

He was into his third unasked-for beer when Doug came out of the kitchen to wipe his hands on his apron and survey the house. We were sitting at the opposite end of the bar as I said, near the kitchen door and I motioned Doug over. I asked him, "Who's that?" "Well," Doug said, "that's none other than Charlie Allen. But don't you be bothering him now. He comes in after work. Got a highway job. Has a few beers then goes home. Don't like to be bothered."

But, being a city feller, I just couldn't help myself. Here was Charlie Allen, a muskrat dressed up like a man, by God! Sitting right here at the Antrim Bar. A muskrat who knew the river and her fish, whose eyes had seen all the secrets of all the deep holes, all the broad flats and chattering runs ... and, so, I moved down a few stools with the caution of a man easing closer to a wild animal in a clearing. Charlie stirred. It was like you were trying to put the wrong ends of two magnets together.

"Evening," I said, attempting to mask the city-feller inflections in my voice. He didn't move. I cleared my throat theatrically. He counted the bubbles in his Budweiser. Then I thought I knew a way to tempt this wise old muskrat out of his hole.

"Les," I said, "another beer." (Didn't want to reveal my origins by ordering another stemmed glass of city-feller juice.) When Les brought it, I said, "You know, Les, fishing's bad lately. Real bad. Must not be any fish left in the ole Beaverkill. That's what they say, you know, all fished out. Hell, I can't catch 'em in the morning; no luck at dusk, dries, wets, doesn't matter, all fished out for damn sure."

Out of the corner of my eye, I saw the old muskrat stir cunningly. And as Les turned away without a comment, I mused out loud, looking up at the gigantic brown trout above the bar, "No, only the old timers, I guess, know what it was like to fish this river when it was full of trout like that."

Then George moved down beside me and picked up where I left off. "Hell, I must have used every fly in my vest." And George and I started to trade comments back and forth until, again out of the corner of my eye; I could see that Charlie was moving to and fro, ever so slightly like a brown trout with a Royal Coachman floating over its nose. And, when I thought he was ripe to rise, I twitched the fly—I turned to him and said, "Say, you ever fished this river?"

The old muskrat turned his head slowly, tugged the brim of his cap down and echoed my question, "Ever fished this river? Mister, I can't remember when I haven't fished this river. And that fish up there, he pointed to the monster hanging over the bar, he weren't caught in the river. He was caught on a shiner in the reservoir, Pepactin, at night."

He had risen to the fly. I bought him a beer and we talked about the river. Rather George and I listened to Charlie talk about the river and tolerated his telling us that everything we did was wrong. Then Charlie made a most curious statement, said he fished the river with only one fly. That was all. And that fly was the Light Cahill. Number 12. He fished the dry Cahill and the wet Cahill. He fished it in the spring, through the summer and into the fall, all seasons, all the time, rain or shine, high water or low.

Thus, from the old, wise and careful mouth of the man who limits-out on opening day before noontime, that's what he told us. And, after a few more beers, he said, truth be told, the only time he doesn't use a Light Cahill is on opening day when he uses worms and split shot. But, he confided with a smile melting across his face like butter on warm toast, that's only so's he can limit-out to impress the greenhorns. (Charlie was now finishing his fifth Budweiser and talking like a Trappist monk who has just renounced his vows.)

I asked him if he ever heard of the Muskrat Nymph. Some guy out in Oregon, I said, name's Roseborough, he ties them. Real shaggy. Lots of guard hairs. His eyes lighted and caught mine and held tight for a full second; then he looked into his glass, shook his head and said, no, he hadn't. Never heard of Rose-whatever either.

So I reached into my jacket pocket pinched one out of my little Perrine box and showed it to him. He twirled it in his fingers, spit on it to see how it looked wet and pursed his lips. Looked interesting, the muskrat said. Yep, sure did. That Rosy tie this one? he asked. No, I did, I said. And, I said, I heard he trapped muskrats roundabout these parts and that if he had a scrap of fur around, well, I'd like to buy it to tie up some more nymphs, or better yet, if he had a pelt, I'd like to buy it and I'd tie him all the muskrat nymphs he could use. He could try them for me. Let me know how they worked.

Before he could answer, some friends of his came through the door, said "Hullo, Charlie," and the conversation turned to other things. George and I drifted back down to our end of the bar and then to a table where we ordered steaks for dinner. Charlie left. He had finished his after-work beers and now it was time to head home.

Later that evening, George and I were still sitting at the table oiling our jaws now with Grand Marniers when Charlie came through the door again. That old muskrat had shaved, slicked his hair down and changed his shirt. He bent over to prop a piece of plywood against the legs of that last bar stool by the door and then, as before, settled on the next-to-last. Les brought him a draft. Again, unasked for. He twirled the glass in his hand and glanced down the bar. Then he swiveled around on the stool halfway and looked straight over at us.

"Hi, Charlie!" I said. He nodded his old leather face. "Join us," I said and motioned to one of the two empty captain's chairs at our table. He came over with his beer and sat down. Soon as he sat down he cocked his head a little and asked me if I'd really like to have a muskrat pelt and if I had one would I really tie him up a dozen of those muskrat nymphs.

I said, yes, I did, and, yes, I would. I could just see it. A pelt! A real pelt. Sweet smelling and supple and as lustrous and soft as a piece of Russian sable. Just like that hat of Doug's. I confess, I was drooling.

Charlie got up, walked back to the bar stool, reached down and picked up that damp plywood board he had left there. He brought it over to the table and propped it up without ceremony in the empty chair. Well, every tinkling spoon and dish in the Antrim Lodge fell silent. One of the waitresses put a hand to her mouth, the other to her stomach. I remember hearing a muffled scream behind me to my right. To my left, I heard someone gag. Directly in front of me cruelly crucified with a circlet of nails was a steam-roller-flat, shaggy-edged, salt-encrusted, stiff-as-parchment, gamy and gooey as bear bait, yellow and blood red skin-side-out muskrat deboned and disembodied.

That's right. Charlie Allen had served up a freshly skinned muskrat right there at our table in the dining room of the Antrim Lodge's. For dessert.

I reached across the table, picked up the board and held it like you'd hold up and admire a fine painting, brushed back the sticky guard hairs on the edges, reached under and plucked out some damp fur from the middle and twisted it, rubbed it, preened it, spit on it to see how it looked wet, plucked out some more, then placed the board back in its chair, skin side out for all to see, and said "Charlie, we got us a deal." Then I bought him a beer and a shot of Jack Daniels. Les had to bring it over to our table because the waitress wouldn't. Charlie made fast work of both, and when I reached for my wallet he said "Money's no good," got up and left.

Doug came over and said, hey, guys, I'll buy you both another Grand Marnier if one of you takes that board outside. Like right now. Good deal, I said.

Two weeks later I carefully wrapped a strong, little cardboard box with crisp brown paper, sealed up all its seams with 3M transparent tape, took a felt marker and addressed it to "Charlie Allen, Antrim Lodge, The Bar, Roscoe, New York." And I took it to the post office. In that little package were two dozen very carefully tied, luxuriously shaggy Muskrat Nymphs. Tied in an assortment of sizes on the very best X-L genuine Mustad hooks. The deal was done.

10

THE ANGLERS' APOTHECARY

Twenty-five years ago when I was a panther in pinstripes stalking the canyons of Manhattan, there was a strange little fly-fishing emporium located "ten blocks from Tiffany's, three flights up." It was called The Anglers' Roost. I'd go there sometimes after a two-martini lunch at P.J. Clarke's to pick up odds and ends for fly tying—then, a newly acquired hobby of mine.

That year, 1976, in Fly Fisherman *magazine, volume 7, Number 3, cover price $2.50, I published a piece about the rooster who nested in that roost.*

Now, back then, you could buy the hardcover edition of Ernie Schweibert's Nymphs *for $12.95; Nick Karas's* The Complete Book of the Striped Bass, *hardcover, for $5.95; a Hardy reel for $49.95; a chamois-cloth shirt from L.L. Bean for $12.50; and, if you needed a "complete" fly-fishing outfit, the rooster would get a guy up in Kingston, New York, to oblige. The Kingston guy would use a Fenwickglass blank to make the rod. Then, he'd package it up with a reel, a double-tapered line, two tapered leaders and five dry flies pack everything neatly in a plastic bag, box it and ship the whole kit and caboodle to you for $19.99. There was no mention of "shipping" costs.*

Back then I didn't realize the distinguished company I was in when I published my little piece, this little piece, in Fly Fisherman *magazine. As I look at the masthead of my yellowing copy, I see that the Contributing Editors were Jim Bashline, Nick Lyons, Charles C. Ritz, and Dave Whitlock. Charlie Fox was on the advisor board.*

The feature articles were written by the likes of Ernest G. Schweibert. And there are excerpts from Negley Farson's "relatively obscure angling work," Gone Fishing. *It had been published by Harcourt Brace in the '40's—heck, I worked for Harcourt at the time and never heard of the book. Today I have two copies in my collection. The "Tips on Tackle and Techniques" featured the bylines of Art Flick, Al McClane, M. Charles Ritz (he's referred to as" Charles C. Ritz" on the masthead. In this very same issue, a "New Feature" was introduced. It was titled "The Seasonable Angler." It was written by contributing editor, Nick Lyons.*

Illustrating my article were two photos. First there was a picture of the old rooster himself surrounded by an unbelievable clutter of, well, stuff, including in the foreground a helter-skelter pile of unopened mail. The second illustration revealed the chaos of the place—what the caption called, "One of the more photogenic corners of the Angler's Roost."

With that introduction under your belt, I hope you enjoy my little portrait of Jimmy Deren just as it appeared way back then:

◆   ◆   ◆

I know an unlikely man, a famous man, a man whose name is gold-leafed onto the lore of trout fishing in the East. He's a rooster and he lives in an Angler's Roost. His name is Jimmy Deren.

The Angler's Roost is a walk-up apothecary shop specializing in relief of the fisherman's malady. You have to sidle in, and then turn sideways to the left, then sideways to the right, then drop your left shoulder, and then move up to the counter. Yesterday's mail, and the day before's, and the day before the day before's mail is piled there and you are standing in the most incredible disarray of angling equipment that could possibly be imagined. It is a veritable angling kaleidoscope. Creels and boots, rods and reels, and flys [sic] and flashlights and knives and books and lines and ointments and oils and wings and beaks and barrels full of feathers and behind the counter, always in a kind of soft, reposing anger, is Jimmy Deren, reading something.

Jimmy's glasses ride on the tip of his nose. His face is weathered like the western wall of Linville Gorge. He'll look over those glasses with little shopworn eyes and show only the most subtle hint of hello and howdy. He'll make a sound and go back to his reading.

You look around for a while and then with some timidity you approach the desk. It's like advancing toward a judge who's found you guilty.

"Jim, I need some things for fly-tying."

"Mm-hmh."

"Uh, do you have any yellow floss?"

"Now what are you going to use yellow floss for?"

"Well, I was going to tie some Dark Edson Tigers."

And Jimmy will give you a scrap of floss tied in a bow which he has found somewhere and somehow without moving from his stool....

"And I'd like some hooks. I'd like some #10's, extra long shank."

"And what do you want those for?" Jimmy growls like a dog at his bowl.

"Well, I thought I'd tie some nymphs."

"You don't want that kind of hook. Here's what you want." And again without moving Jimmy tosses a little packet of hooks on the desk with "ten-n" neatly printed on the packet. You call out the rest of your order while being growled at and corrected on each item until you're done. I remember once trying to buy a flashlight he had in the glass case on the wall.

"You don't want that goddam thing," he said. "It's not worth a damn." And no matter how much I pleaded, he wouldn't sell it to me.

So this is Jimmy Deren, old rooster, who badgers, reprimands, instructs and cajoles every customer who sidles into the Angler's Roost. The old rooster who sits there with his thinning crewcut comb, making noises at you deep in his throat, and you love every minute of it because you know you're talking to Jimmy Deren.

And there's one more thing about him. He has an infernal machine. It's an old adding machine, the crank-handle type, and it sits passively on his right hand. Now what's infernal about the machine is that no matter what you buy it always rings up to a total over ten dollars. For example, you'll buy some waxed thread, a bottle of head cement (no bigger than a thimble), two 20-inch strands of yellow chenille, and say, a bobbin. Jimmy will pull a brown paper bag out from under the counter, pull the handle of the machine, pick up the head cement, drop it into the bag, punch the machine twice with his finger, pull the lever, pick up the strands of chenille, drop them into the bag, punch the machine twice, pull the lever, and when he pulls it the last time, somehow you always own him $10.56. You can own him more but you can never owe him less. And if I knew less about fishing and fishermen I'd think that Jimmy had an adding machine that was rigged.

And when you leave you know you've visited an oracle—and as you are leaving he calls out in sounds you almost mistake for his clearing his throat—"Have fun!" There's a small inflection of real interest and sincerity in the call and you know that the man who invented Deren's Fox would almost like to latch the door and leave his roost on 41st Street to join you at the stream.

The editor's note reads:
"Tis all true. We're not going to give Deren's address or phone number, let alone what town it is that he roosts in, because he doesn't advertise with us. He doesn't trust anyone who charges more than $10 for anything. Editors.

11

BAD DOG

My old friend and hunting buddy, Wayne Earp, says, even when not asked, "I'm a hunner purcent West Virginian and fifty purcent Cherokee Indian." So, to borrow a tobacco-stained leaf from Wayne's book, I should tell you that I'm one hundred percent Pennsylvanian and fifty percent North Carolinian. That's right, I was born in Pennsylvania, out on the Main Line, but I was raised in North Carolina. Lived as a kid in Lenoir, North Carolina, then Hickory, "Furniture Capital of The World." Grew up in Charlotte. From there I went to a Benedictine prep school in Belmont, North Carolina, where most of my classmates, the day students mainly, were Southern Baptists, the rest were from NY, NJ, PA, VA, MD and such exotic places as Cuba (pre-revolutionary), Puerto Rico and Panama.

Down south I started using a bamboo fly rod to stalk trout in the mountain streams of western North Carolina, up around Asheville, in the Great Smokey Mountains on the edge of the Appalachians. But not far from the prep school campus, in Duke Power country was the great Catawba River named after an Indian tribe that once lived along its banks. The river rises up there in the Blue Ridge and flows east and then south for 220 miles to Great Falls in South Carolina.

Now if you have never seen a North Carolina river like this one, you need some orientation. First of all North Carolina soil is famously red, as in potter's clay, and the river waters flowing through it are khaki-orange—something like redwood stain in a paint pail. So it's low to no visibility water.

Down here on the piedmont, this is bass country. Largemouth bass country. Besides water skiing and drinking moonshine enlivened Cokes and chugging beer, near everyone on the Catawba water, least ways in these parts, is there for one reason—to fish for bass. The tackle of choice is the Texas-rigged plastic worm (purple preferred) and subsurface plugs like the Flatfish and the Rapala minnow and surface plugs like the Hula Popper. Not to mention live baits—worms, crickets and shiners.

I never had the time or the inclination to fish those muddy waters until I graduated prep, went to college, and got a job traveling around the South selling college textbooks for a New York publisher. That ... plus the fact that I married a Southern belle I'd met in the seventh grade at Oakwood School in Hickory brought me back to the piedmont for mother-in-law visits. Now there's nothing like visits to a mother-in-law to intensify one's yearning to go fishing.

On those visits I'd sometimes drive up into the mountains and fly fish some of my old haunts near Asheville and some of the rambunctious streams tumbling through the wild laurel and rhododendron-choked gorges and deep ravines of the Daniel Boone Preserve. But that was sort of an expedition, and, anyway, right down the road from my mother-in-law's in Hickory, right there in Catawba County, in west-central Carolina, just east of the Appalachian foothills and the Smokeys about 60 miles northwest of Charlotte, was the good old Catawba River. And that's where it was dammed to form Lake Hickory.

I decided that's where I'd go for short getaways. And that's when I developed this obsession to catch a Carolina big-mouth bass. So, on one of my mother-in-law trips, I paid a visit to Mr. Abernathy at Hickory Sporting Goods and had him outfit me with a spinning rod and reel, a selection of plastic worms and a couple of Hula Poppers, a white popper as big as a man's thumb with a yellow plastic skirt. Truth be told, if I was to catch a bass, I really wanted to catch it on the surface.

Once rigged up like the locals, I'd drive over to the lake, cross the bridge, buy a three-day license and rent a boat and motor at Chitter's Crossing and putt-putt out onto the muddy waters.

Most of the boating and water skiing were done on the weekends, so my weekday jaunts were rather peaceful. I'd cast the popper into the bank and chug-chug it back to the boat, again and again. Then I'd switch to the purple worm, cast it out, let it sink and walk it along the bottom. Real slow. But I couldn't get the strike right. Being a trout fisherman, I struck as soon as I felt a tap. In bass fishing that's wrong. After you feel the tap, you let the line go slack. You let the bass take the worm and swim off with it. Wait. Then strike like thunder. But I just couldn't get it right. So most of the time, instead of a plastic worm, I used that Hula Popper.

Up along the river bank here and there were what they called Pepsi shacks. Ramshackle wooden shelters, some nothing more than lean-tos, set up by the locals to sell soft drinks, snacks, bait and cigarettes to passing fishermen. The center piece of all of these Lilliputian establishments was a big, square steel, tin-lined cooler with Pepsi logos on them and blocks of ice and bottles of Pepsi and Nehi ("a big orange") floating around inside. Since I usually provisioned myself with a cooler of beer, I had never stopped at a Pepsi shack. But one day I puttered in to shore and climbed up the bank to visit one.

The proprietor, tall, lank, skinny as a mop handle and white-whiskered, was sitting there in a rocking chair. He reached up and tipped the brim of his baseball cap back and said, "Howdy." His dog stood up and barked, then gave out this low rumbling, toothy growl. The hair stood up on his back. And on mine, too.

Now this was one strange looking dog. About as big as a Jack Russell terrier and about the color of the river. Had these real pointy ears and a really small head. "Won't hurt ya none," said the man reaching out to pat the dog's tiny head. The dog was chained to one of the legs of the rocker. "Howdy," I said and pulled a cellophane package of peanut butter crackers off the rack on his make-shift counter.

"Whar you be from?" he asked.

"Up north."

"Knowed that first I seed ya. How'd I'd know that right off?"

"Can't guess. But I lived in Hickory as a kid. Went to school for a couple of years at Oakwood."

"Carpetbagger, then. I think that's the key-rect name." He picked his nose, inspected the result, then wiped his finger on his pants.

"Say, what kind of dog is that?" I asked.

"Knowed you'd ask that. Everbody does."

"Well he's got an unusual look. Real small head for his body."

"City fellas, specially Yankees, ain't never see'd a dog like this. And he ain't nothin' real special. Just one of them Mex-i-can chee-wa-was."

"Come on, you gotta be kidding."

"Nope. Not kiddin'. Don't kid none with strangers. Ya see some people gets holt a small dog and feeds 'em small food. Kibbles 'n Bits er somethin'. Store bought stuff. Not me. Got this little dog here and he *was* mighty little when I got 'em, And from the time he's a pup, I feeds him just like I feeds my hounds. Raw meat. Rabbit, deer, groundhog, possum, squirrel. Natchal stuff. 'Cept I added me some gun power."

"Now I know you're pulling my leg."

"Ain't got no time fur that. You asked the question and I'm answerin'. Like I said, this here dog was raised on raw, red meat, natchal meat, wild meat, and gun powder. Ever hear'd a 'black powder?' Don't suppose so. What I does is grind the meat and sprinkle it with the powder, black powder. Like seasoning with pepper ya know. Look here, that dog don't *know* he's supposed to be *small*. Pup's don't know that. And that raw meat, it grows him. And the gun powder, it helps his add-e-tude ta grow, which ta start with, was meant ta be as small as his hide. Yes, sir, that there's a gen-u-ine Mex-i-can chee-wa-wa. Ya cin believe me or not. No matter ta me. And he's meaner than a black snake. Meanest little sun-a-bitch you ever did see. Wanna see?"

"No. Not really."

"Well, son, ya see what that proves? Do ya? Proves ya *can* learn somethin' ever day. Hell, even a carpetbagger can learn things. Don't you want a Pepsi to wash down those crackers?"

"No, thanks."

"Thin why th' hell ya stop here and take up my time? Shit-fire, one pack o'crackers ain't worth my time. How about a pack of Luckies? The matches is free. Or how about a jar a shine, like this here?" He held up a Mason jar filled with a liquid as clear as star shine.

"What's that, spring water?"

"Water," he laughed, rocking back in the chair. "Yeah, yeah, this here's water, son, *fire water*. Want some?"

"Naw, think I'll have a Pepsi though and be on my way."

"Watcha doin'? Fishin? Damn, son, ta me ya look like y'air goin' ta a weddin'. Your momma wash and iron that there shirt this mornin'? How ya gonna catch fish smellin' like a bar a laundry soap? Whatcha got fur bait? Ya all need some bait. Want some real flippy-floppy shiners? Got some real lively uns over yonder in th' tub."

"No, thanks, got no bait bucket."

"How 'bout some worms then? Comes with the coffee can."

"No, I'm using plugs and plastic worms."

"What? You a-feared ta git your hands dirty?"

"No, not really."

"Son you're a pure-tee mess. If you weren't so scrubbed up, I think I'd sic this here ferocious dog on ya." He reached down and rattled the dog's chain." But I want ya to go back up north and tell 'em how nice we treat strangers down here … and how well we treats our dogs. Guess't I learned ya sumpen. And I gonna bet a can a worms you'll be tellin' this story 'fur one long time 'cause that's all you'll have ta tell. You sure ain't gonna catch a bass big enuf to brag about."

Turns out the amiable Pepsi-shack guy was right. I've been telling his Mex-i-can chee-wa-wa story for years. But he was wrong about the bass: In spite of smelling like a bar of Ivory detergent, I did catch a bragging-sized Carolina bass. A bucket-bellied female five-pounder. On the surface, on that Hula Popper. If it hadn't been getting dark, I'd have gone back to collect my can of worms.

Note: According to urban legend, as related to me by Mike at Cigars Unlimited, Pit Bull handlers will feed their dogs small amounts of gun powder to "tune-up" their fighters' dispositions. Maybe Mr. Pepsi was on to something.

12

ANGLING ATTIRE

Clothes make the man. Naked people have little or no influence in society.
Attributed to Mark Twain

How well one dresses for an event or an endeavor—getting married or going fishing—is a subject of importance because others form opinions of us often solely on the basis of our attire. Books *are* judged by their covers.

Often, equally important is *where* one buys one's clothes. Gentlemen I should think do not often shop at Wal-Mart, Penny's, or the Dollar Store.

I realize that today, when young men and women—and Boomers arrested in their adolescence—wear a uniform of faded jeans and an untucked shirt to dinner parties, it may be hard to believe that in the past far more care was taken in the selection of clothing appropriate to the occasion.

Years ago, when I was a young man working in midtown Manhattan, there were several well-known outfitters who catered to the refined tastes of well-heeled anglers. For example, one such place occupied a helter-skelter room in a midtown office building on 42nd Street across from the side entrance to Grand Central. It was called The Anglers' Roost. Farther downtown was the famous Mills emporium. On Madison Avenue was the illustrious Abercrombie & Fitch, where, if you wanted to try out a rod, you took the elevator to the roof. Of course, if you didn't have time to visit these places—although it was an interesting way to occupy your lunch hour—there was always the inestimable Orvis catalog.

My generation, that is, the young professionals of that era, would do both. We would stuff the Orvis catalog into our attaché cases and pore over the pages on the train up to Westchester. On our lunch hours, we would go to the aforementioned urban outfitters. At Abercrombie's, we'd buy vests with a plethora of pockets from an original design by none other than Lee Wulff. At Mills we'd buy a pair of waders that reached all the way up to our armpits by Hodgson of England; and Winston rods, Hardy reels, khaki shirts with epaulettes, twill pants and all manner of gadgets superfluous and essential. Not to mention a genuine wicker creel to dangle from our hip.

When we went astream, we would bespangle ourselves with this stylish apparel, practical paraphernalia and impractical geegaws. In the pockets of our Abercrombie vest—with a Theodore Gordon Flyfisher's patch sewn on—we would stuff multi-compartmented fly boxes made by Wheatley of London with their spring-hinged mica windows covering each Lilliputian compartment. We would festoon the D-rings on the front of it with such essentials such as hook-sharpeners, knot-tiers, clippers, small flashlights with flexible necks, gunk to sink our wet flies and goop to float our dry flies, and, of course, a gleaming pair of real surgical hemostats for removing miniature hooks from the lips of trout. Some of us would even purchase one of those five-inch-long-half-inch-in-diameter oak-handled, brass-over-lead-headed "priests" for administering a *coup de grâce* prior to slipping a supper's trout into the creel. Finally, we'd top it all off with a dark brown felt hat with a pheasant-feather band.

I never thought much about the impact this attire might have on trout let alone less discriminating fishing pals or our non-fishing brethren, that is, until one day while I was exploring the Manatawney, a meandering meadow stream near Boyertown in south central Pennsylvania.

On this particular day in early June, I had crossed a stone bridge beneath which the stream, overgrown with briers and alders, ran narrow, dark and deep. On the far side of the bridge was a serious wire fence guarding the upstream portion of the brook. Also behind the fence, across the meadow on a hillside, stood a handsome farm house. As I stood there debating whether or not to climb over the fence, a man appeared and walked toward me through the meadow.

When he got to the fence separating us, he said, "Nice stream, don't you think?"

"Yes, it is. Yes, sir, my thought exactly."

"Would you like to fish it?"

"You mean upstream there, across the fence, beyond the meadow? Well, yes, yes, the thought *had* crossed my mind."

"Well, walk up the road to the gate there, and come up to the house. We'll have a talk."

When I got to the gate, two Doberman pinschers appeared like arrows shot from unseen bows. They started barking madly, lunging like horses under Ben Hur's whip. Thank God for the gate! The man yelled at the dogs, came up and grabbed them by their black leather collars. They looked up at him apologetically. And stopped barking. They were glossy, well-muscled black beasts trimmed with touches of copper and brown. They stood nearly, or so it seemed to me, three feet at the shoulder and weighed, I'd say, 80 pounds. Trim, agile, alert. Salivating. Yet obedient.

Over the man's shoulder, I saw a sign that indicated he ran a kennel, a place to breed and board dogs. Apparently he did well at this because there were two late-model Cadillac convertibles nosed into the shed underneath the sign. One pink. One white. The man was a rather squat, broad-shouldered specimen with a luxurious black moustache suspended beneath his small crabapple nose. He wore a red-and-black plaid shirt and blue jeans held up by a broad leather belt with a huge oval sterling silver and gold buckle. Cowboy boots, of course.

With the dogs under control, I entered at the gate and together the man and I walked up to the porch.

"What kind of business are you in?" he inquired.

"I'm in the publishing business. An editor. And a writer."

"Now that's very interesting. Very interesting. A writer, huh? My wife will want to meet you. Here, sit down. I'll get her."

I sat on a green Adirondack chair, placed my rod across my lap and my creel at my feet. The dogs sat at the bottom of the porch steps with their tongues hanging out like pink ribbons blowing in the wind.

The man returned with his wife. She was an astonishingly gorgeous woman endowed with a Dolly Parton bosom. The buttons on her white blouse—the top three were unbuttoned—strained to hold the treasure of her chest from spilling out. I recall that she had long, curly blonde hair. I have no idea what her face looked like. Beautiful, no doubt. The pocket on her shirt bore the embroidered logo and name of their kennel, which I don't remember. She too wore khaki pants (they looked as if they had been painted on her shapely legs) and a leather belt with a silver buckle identical to her husband's. Her cowboy boots had toes so pointed that they looked as if they had been sharpened in a pencil sharpener. She smelled like a lavender bush in bloom.

"My husband tells me that you're a writer," she said. "How very interesting."

"Well, an editor and a freelance writer. That's true."

"I am a writer," she said. "So we have something in common. How did you get into that line of work?"

We chatted, sitting there on the porch under the watchful gaze of the Dobermans. Her husband had left us after the introduction and gone over to the garage. When he returned, he said, "I have to tell you that I am proud, well, I *would* be proud, to have a man like you fish my little stream."

"Well, I'd be glad to oblige you. It's a great-looking stream."

I could tell that he was intrigued by my profession, if not also, impressed by my fly fishing regalia.

"Man, I have to tell you, you are dressed to kill. And that's a beautiful bamboo rod. I've never really seem one of those up close. Is it an Orvis rod? I've heard they're the best. Very expensive."

I handed the rod to him and after waggling it gingerly and giving the reel a turn or two, he said, "Well we're wasting your time. You want to fish my stream. And I should tell you that we only allow a few people to fish it. A very few. Now, you should know, they prefer to leave it wild with all the brambles, alders and briars and overhanging branches. I offer every year to prune all that back but they said, no, they want it that way. Makes it more challenging."

Then he pointed to a faint foot path leading up and across the meadow. "Follow that path upstream. It will lead you right into the brook. You'll find a series of pools there. A big deep one right where it ends. We've got big browns in there. Natives. Born and bred right here in my stream. No hatchery fish. Now go ahead, have a go at it. And, remember, don't mind the dogs. They're your friends now. Oh, and keep what you catch. I'll want to see them."

He had assured me that "my friends" were instructed not to eat me. They would not interfere with my fishing. They would, however, he noted, accompany me. This was their custom with visiting fishermen. So, with not an inconsiderable amount of fear and trepidation, and with the two sleek, salivating dogs following not far behind, I set out on this path less traveled. The man and his wife watched me from their porch,

At the end of the path, I met a formidable Hawthorne tree, a Tolkeinian tree with a rather mean disposition and crooked, cranky limbs. Its scimitared, inch-long thorns pricked and caught my khaki shirt as I struggled past. To avoid them, I had to bend over and bushwhack my way commando-style along the now overgrown path, which ended abruptly, as he said it would, right at the water's edge. And, there it was, the pool.

True to the owner's word, no one had bothered to trim any of the thorny tree branches or the briars or the bushes that guarded its banks. Damn, those other fishermen and their foolish and unnecessary affectation. This pool was, indeed, *severely* bunkered.

It was also unexpectedly deeper and larger than I had imagined, twelve feet long by six or seven feet wide. Maybe five feet deep. On either side, the dense, low-bending willows intermixed with gnarly alder branches hanging down into the water.

I fought my way upstream to the top of the pool. Once there, I had to force my way by backing into the branches to gain a position from where I could manage a cast. In fact a proper cast was impossible, so I tied on a large Hare's Ear nymph, heavily weighted and when set, flip-cast it downstream to the lower edge of the pool.

I let it sink and then worked it back with a very slow, hand-twist retrieve. Inch by inch by inch. It was now swimming through the lower center of the pool. Instantly there was a tap and a tug. Hung up on the bottom, I thought. But then my line moved and sank. My Hardy reel clicked.

I was using my nine-foot Orvis bamboo rod and when I raised it to strike, the tip tangled in the overhanging branches. I wrenched it free and rolled my wrist to the right and strip-struck with my left hand, and managed to set the hook. The fish immediately surged toward me and dove to the bottom of the pool, where it shook its head like a dog with a sock in its jaws. Speaking of dogs, my friends, the Dobermans, were sitting unseen back there where the path entered the underbrush like lions at the gate.

This was a very large fish and when I tried to move him, he turned and ran into the tangle of roots under the bank. I put both hands on the cork handle and steered him out, carefully straining to move him back upstream into the center of the pool. But I could not get him out of that tangle of roots. So I stepped into the water and stripping in line, edged my way down stream toward him.

That's when the line-to-leader knot caught in the tip-top guide. I was using a twelve-foot leader. The rod was bent double and the fish rolled on the fouled line showing his thick black back and buttery yellow sides with hot-orange speckles. His side was at least six inches wide. He was a truly huge brown trout. No less than five pounds. An amazing fish for such a small stream.

At the end of his roll, he surged and dove again. That was that. The last thing I saw was a whale of a tail slap the surface like a beaver. The line popped back. Went slack. I had lost him. He had broken me off.

After this encounter with Big Brown, I worked my way downstream toward to the bridge flipping my nymph in each and every likely spot without feeling another tap or getting another take. When I emerged from the jungle and started to follow the stream across the meadow, I saw the Dobermans following along at an indiscreet distance. Each time I stopped to cast, they stopped and took up positions behind me.

Finally I gave up and walked sullenly across the field to the house. My companions came along. It was late afternoon.

The man was sitting on the porch smoking a cigar and drinking a Budweiser. He stood up to greet me.

"Any luck?" he asked.

"Nope. None."

"What do you mean, none? Nothing. Nothing?" He seemed agitated.

"Yep, nothing," I said.

"Now I can't *believe* that, can not *believe* it. It is not possible."

He sounded well beyond disappointment.

"No luck? Good God, man, good God, I have to say you are the best-dressed fly fisherman ever to set foot on my property and you could not catch a fish, not one, even in that big pool upstream? Nothing? Nothing? Tell me you're kidding. Show me the fish. C'mon."

"It's true. The briars. That formidable Hawthorne tree. All the overgrowth. It's hard to cast up there. But, but I did hook a fish. You said there was a big one in the pool and I hooked him. But lost him. He broke me off."

The man made no attempt to hide the fact that any disappointment he felt at first had now turned to downright disgust. He had put his faith in me and I had failed. He lowered his head and shrugged his shoulders. Looked at the ground. Our conversation was over.

"Ah, thank you, thanks a lot." I said. "It's a great little stream. That fish was huge. Hell, I think it was a five-pounder. So, ah, well thanks, thanks again, very much."

The man, head hung low, turned slowly, walked back to the porch, up the steps and into the house. Before he disappeared, I saw him shaking his head and chewing on the end of his cigar. Wow! Talk about taking fishing seriously, this guy was a case.

I tucked my tail between my legs and walked past the two Cadillacs, through the gate and up the road to where I had parked my car. The Dobermans followed silently but stopped at the gate and sat on their haunches posing like sentries at King Tut's tomb. I sensed that "my friends" and I had built some rapport by going up there to fish together. Camaraderie. Now I sensed they genuinely felt sorry for me. You can tell.

Truth is, I actually felt guilty about letting this man down. I had no idea his expectations were so high. For my part, however, I must confess that my major disappointment lay not so much in losing that huge fish, hell that happens, but in the realization that had I landed that lunker, I would have had the opportunity to see his gorgeous wife again.

Just imagine the celebration. He'd call her. No, he'd yell to her: "Betsy, Betsy, come out here. You gotta see this!" She would come out on the porch. She would bend over to admire the trout in my creel. They would ask me to stay for dinner. Offer me a glass of 18-year-old Macallan and Betsy and I would chat about the writerly life late into the night.

But you tell me. What do *you* think? Would his expectations have been lower, his disappointment less if I had been unshaven, wearing a baseball cap, a threadbare shirt, shorts and sneakers and carrying an old fiberglass Fenwick? Hell, had I been a plumber or a house painter (both of whom make more money), he would probably never in the first place have invited me to his fish his prissy, precious, prickly little stream.

Oh, I can hear him now: "You should have seen this city dude. Stepped right out of the Orvis catalog. Hell, he couldn't even catch that big brown in my Briar Patch Pool. I put that fish there myself. Know what? These fancy city fellas; they're all style, no substance. I shoulda let him hop that fence and watched the dogs drag him off."

13

PAINTED LADIES

Sir Isaac Newton was sitting under an apple tree when he was conked on the head by a falling Red Delicious. That event, according to highly reliable witnesses, led to Sir Isaac's discovery of the law of universal gravitation.

So it is, when you examine the genesis of great discoveries, you find that serendipitous events, combined, of course, with devoted study, often play a key role. I cite this Newtonian example to lend gravitas to the story I am about to tell, the story of my own personal discovery of a scientific principle, a discovery that has far-reaching implications for the scientific underpinnings of the art of fly tying.

Since the devil dwells in the details, I tell the story within its entire contextual ambiance. It is a story that illustrates the value of studious observation combined, of course, as noted above, with a dash of serendipity. In other words, it is the story of how a seminal contribution to the art and science of fly fishing was made under circumstances far removed from the pastoral field and purling stream.

The story begins years ago when I was a young man on the cusp of thirty, a panther in pinstripes prowling the canyons of New York City where I was employed as an editor for that venerable publishing house, Harcourt Brace, which in those days was known as Harcourt, Brace, Jovanovich. (That's another story.)

I was what was called a "procurement" editor, in fact, a Science Editor in Harcourt's college textbook division. This means that my job was, first, to interview professors in such citadels of scientific thought as MIT, Caltech, Stanford, Yale, Princeton, and, yes, out in the hinterlands, too, Kansas, Iowa, Indiana, Illinois, Nebraska—in an attempt to discover academics that were likely textbook authors, and, second, to persuade those thus identified to write their books for my employer, HBJ.

In those days most of the Harcourt boys (some years later there would be Harcourt girls) wore the uniform of the day: a Brooks Brothers, or J. Press narrow-shouldered three-button suit—the more flamboyant and affluent among us—usually the bachelors—bought their uniforms at Paul Stuart. Some even had theirs tailored on Savile Row while abroad on their annual manuscript and rights-buying trips to London.

The suits were dark blue or charcoal gray with pinstripes or a lightweight tan/brown herringbone, or cavalry twill. Our silk ties were small-patterned, paisley or regimental-striped and tied in a tight half Windsor, deftly dimpled. Our shirts were light blue or creamy white button-down Oxfords, again from Brooks (only Brooks Brother's collars had that just-right roll). Our socks—over-the-calf, of course—were made of British ribbed wool. Some of us ensured that they never fell to half-calf by using garters. Our shoes were either black leather-heeled wing tips, or lustrous, cinnamon-and-honey-colored calves' skin cap-toes, British-made, Peal & Co., of course. We carried attaché cases, discretely branded with our initials. They were dark green inside and guaranteed for life—I still have mine. They were, of course, made in Britain exclusively for Brooks Brothers.

My world back then was punctuated by collegial two-martini lunches (on-the-rocks, please, Beefeaters, with a twist of lemon peel) at places like P. J. Clarke's where we dined on volcanic mounds of moist, crimson steak tartar with a raw egg floating in the center encircled by a necklace of capers looking like old, puckered and pickled peas, finely chopped onions on the side and a glorious green sprig of parsley crowning it all. The parsley was eaten first, picked up ceremoniously between one's fingers, a pause to admire its freshness and then devoured in one bite.

For lunches with authors or prospective authors who'd come to New York, we'd choose more formal surroundings, places like the Four Seasons, and, if their book was a bestseller, to places like L'Argenteuil on Third Avenue for three-hour lunches, all paid for with our unlimited expense accounts.

Once in awhile, your boss would invite you to lunch. There was, of course, some agenda (perhaps your last expense account was over the edge). In these cases you'd go to someplace a little more, well, serious and quiet, like The Bull & Bear at the Waldorf Astoria—the hotel where, by the way, HBJ kept a suite to accommodate visiting authors. There you would dine at a table covered with a starched, blindingly white tablecloth in an atmosphere of gleaming brass, polished walnut, oak, mahogany and thick maroon gold-edged carpeting. You'd be served by waiters of a certain age in crisp white shirts, black bow ties, black vests and black pants. (In those days women were not allowed in the Bull & Bear at lunch time.) My boss, a redoubtable Canadian named Paul Corbett would have a Rob Roy, and, to show restraint, I would forego the Beefeater martini and order a Bloody Mary.

In the evening, when you were entertaining authors or hobnobbing with colleagues or friends from another publishing company or one of your own salesmen from out of town, you'd go to the bar at the Pierre, the Waldorf, or the St. Regis and have cocktails and snack on the canapés and hors d'oeuvre arrayed on sterling silver trays.

In the lobbies and cocktail lounges of those grand hotels, you could feast your eyes on a flock of elegant, sophisticated ladies and deliciously attired younger women. An activity not unlike paging through the latest issues of *Vogue* or *Cosmopolitan*.

In fact, that's why we went to such places, so we could enjoy observing all those delectable morsels of New York femininity that floated through their lobbies and lounges like a hatch of *Dollimentia sophisticata*. Out-of-town authors would especially be delighted and entranced by the spectacle. Why, I remember a mathematician from Oklahoma State, for example, who sat there slack-jawed and speechless for minutes at a time as he gazed at this plenitude of pulchritude.

Among these elegant ladies, every so often, there would appear a working woman, a woman of easy pleasure, a painted lady, not too, too different from the rest. Her difference lay in small things. Perhaps she would be slightly more enticingly dressed in colors a bit more assertive, with hair coiffed like all the rest, but perhaps a little more cunningly curled; with carriage and manner like the rest, but perhaps a little more flirtatiously conceived, and on her face there would be perhaps a little friendlier, broader, easier, more welcoming smile.

These women were, in other words, *almost* exact copies of the women around them; but the eye of the experienced observer could perceive something different, some slight exaggeration, subtle though it was. Some slight exaggeration of the things that men notice, the things that trigger desire and attraction. Perhaps the lipstick would be a little darker, a more daring shade of scarlet. The blue eye shadow, the black mascara a little, just a little, more generously applied. The décolletage just a little deeper, the color of the dress just a little bolder, its length perhaps just a little shorter.

We'd try picking them out. It was a game. Sometimes you'd think you knew but didn't know for sure. That increased the tension. Was that delectable little darling waiting cross-legged, thigh enticingly revealed, on the flowered brocade couch, was she the daughter of that ambassador to the United Nations whose limousine just arrived ... or, could she be a painted lady?

One evening while at the Waldorf, engrossed in my study of the costumes and conduct of the hatch of beauties surrounding me, I thought, suddenly, inexplicably, of the Green Drake hatch on the Beaverkill.

In my mind's eye, I saw a confetti fall of *Hexigenia* settling on the water. I saw the trout gently plucking these canapés from the silver tray of the calm evening waters. And in my reverie I made a cast—with a rather clumsy self-tied Green Drake imitation, a Coffin fly with an extended body of porcupine quill and a moose mane tail. When it alighted on the water—on its side—amid the naturals, a big brown trout slashed at it and took it unhesitatingly with a head-turn-tail rise. And it was as if I had been conked on the head by a falling Red Delicious.

Often I had wondered what it was that makes a trout rise to an artificial fly with more gusto than they exhibit in rising to a natural.

That night, the answer was in my mind before the question was asked. Because, (why had I never realized this?) when an artificial fly floats into the trout's narrow window of perception, he sees an object that artfully exaggerates the "trigger" characteristics of the natural—and it is this slight exaggeration that excites and unleashes his predatory instincts.

That's because the artificial fly presents an elegant caricature of the natural fly's color and silhouette. The wings and legs are perhaps slightly more pronounced. And, when, during a hatch, the trout, confronted with a parade of nubile edibles, all exactly alike in form and figure, his attention is drawn to the artificial. An artificial that stands out from the rest. An artificial with wings whiter, browner, bluer or blacker than all the rest. An artificial cunningly coiffed by the fly tier's art to appear more flirtatiously, more deliciously different, yet alike. And, unable to control the primordial instincts that drive his predatoriness, he pounces.

Perhaps you think I am only talking about "attractor flies" or "stimulators." Or even "cripples," other phenomena, by the way, that supports the theory that it's the difference that makes the difference. But all flies, even the most "exact" imitations are, in effect, exaggerations, albeit some more subtle than outright attractor patterns.

All flies, you see, to one degree or another, are painted ladies.

Take that most famous of artificial exaggerations, the Royal Coachman. It is a caricature of insect-ness with all the triggers artfully in place: a drip of scarlet red, a flash of white, a luminous chestnut hackle collar, the sparkle of peacock herl. What red-blooded trout could resist such a temptation?

Take all the stimulators and attractors—some, by analogy, come from the sophisticated pages of *Vogue* and *Cosmopolitan* others from *Playboy* and *Hustler*, some prowl around Times Square, others lounge in the lobby of the Waldorf, but all are painted ladies nonetheless. And, in fact, the more naturalistic exaggerations—those designed to closely resemble the real fly—are more lethal on occasions for being more subtle in their style, color and form. Perhaps they have more appeal to female trout.

All flies, therefore, are impressionistic imitations of the real thing. All are crafted to attract. This is why a trout will sip a natural with gentlemanly nonchalance as if sipping a martini at the Waldorf but will gulp an artificial with gusto, because, like any painted lady, it appears more tantalizingly real than real.

This explains why the painstakingly tied exact imitations of stoneflies, or those molded plastic or rubber bugs are so often not as effective as the more impressionistic imitations made of fur and feather. Because they *copy* but do not *exaggerate* the trigger characteristics—the luminosity, flexibility, and delicacy of the naturals. This is what makes all painted ladies, at first sight, arrestingly more desirable, more approachable.

So strong are the trigger characteristics in proven artificials that they bring the essence of buggy-ness to the foreground and push into the background such distractions as the hook and line. Trout, you see, being sentient beings, are not unlike us: they tend to see what they want to see. And ignore all the rest. Yes, perceptions are colored by desire. And that is why in fly fishing as in life, lust and love and appetite, are blind.

14

DIVINE PROVIDENCE

They stood in the center of a humpbacked fieldstone bridge, Mick O'Brien, his bedraggled border collie and his tousle-haired, blue-eyed six-year-old son. Mick had lifted the boy and perched him on the broad top of one side of the bridge safely encircling him in his arms. They peered down into the water. The dog sat at Mick's heel, watching the narrow road.

Below them the waters of the Culdaff River—the color of long-brewed black tea—flowed through beds of watercress on its way to the sea at Culdaff Bay. This little river, not far from Malin Head, the most north-westerly point on the Irish mainland at Bloody Foreland on the Inishowen peninsula, is 10.5 miles long and drains northeastern Inishowen in county Donegal (Irish *Dún Na Ngall*), which lies in Ireland's far northwest bounded on the west and north by the Atlantic Ocean, on the east by Lough Foyle and Northern Ireland. It is one of the nine counties which together comprised the ancient province of Ulster. The Culdaff meanders through Donegal's bog and meadow lands with banks so steep and slippery and thickly overgrown in places and in others so wet and marshy that access, let alone casting a fly, is difficult. O'Reilly's *Fly Fisher's Guide* gives this advice: "Local knowledge is essential."

According to O'Reilly, the Culdaff "affords a good stock of sea trout in July and August ... and ... salmon come on the first flood in late summer along with fair numbers of brown trout.... Poaching is a big problem." The fishing is "free" and open season runs from the 1st of March to the 12th of October.

I had rented a cottage named Carrowhugh from Mary O'Conner. It is perched on a windy promontory above the town of Moville. And, seated at the kitchen table eating streaky bacon, toast and tea, once the morning mists dissolved, through the picture window I could see nearly the whole slate-gray expanse of

Lough Foyle (Irish *Loch Feabhail*). After breakfast I could sweater up, tug my new tweed cap down to my ears, pull on my rubber-bottomed shoes, grab the walking stick beside the cottage door and make my way down a steep-sided hill ("the greenest green you've ever seen") and across a rugged little golf course to the edge of the lake itself.

Once there I would be standing in the Republic of Ireland looking east across the lake at Northern Ireland's district councils of Limavady and Londonderry. To the south lay more of Northern Ireland and County Leitrim, Ireland. The lake is 16 miles (26 km) long and from 1 to 10 miles (1.6 to 16 km) wide. The narrowest points are to the southwest, where the River Foyle enters the lake, and at the northeastern end just opposite Magilligan Point standing there on Foyle's Shores, in the distance, I could hear pa-pa-pa, pa-pa-pa's echoing across the lake from the military camp at Magilligan in the North and ponder how politicians can turn such tranquility into alienation and torment.

As far as the fishing was concerned, Mary O'Connor had told me to ask the grocer, the barber and the haberdasher in Moville. All three are avid fishermen she said. And they would know. I visited each and to a man, at this time of year, July, given this weather, they all advised that the best place to fish was not far west of Moville, in Lough Fad, a smallish lake as I imagined. According to them, it contains char and brown trout eager for the fly. They did not mention any rivers.

So, early Monday morning, I loaded my fishing gear into the trunk of the rental car and set out on the narrow, dusty roads in search of Lough Fad. Not an easy task especially since—as I learned when I asked for directions at a tiny post office—some local hooligans had reversed the sign posts. The prank amused the postmistress—"Brings more tourists by this way," she said. "And if it's Lough Fad you'd be lookin' fur, why it lies far west o' here but if it's fishin' you're after, there's a little river just up the road."

Thus it was at her direction that I came across the humped-backed bridge, Mick O'Brien, his son, his dog and the waters of the Culdaff.

When I spied Mick standing on the bridge, I pulled onto a close-by gravel turn-around and parked. There were two pastures on either side of the bridge through which the river ran. The upper one was lush with long meadow grass and thickly hedge-rowed along both sides of the river. The lower one was quilted with hummocks of meadow grass and puddled with pockmarks from the hooves of cows, four of which now stood in the middle of the pasture.

Mick's collie greeted me with a friendly bark. And Mick with a "hello."

"Hello," I said. "Is this the Culdaff? What's the fishing like?"

"Difficult," he replied. "But come along, I'll show ya." I followed him, the dog and boy across the turnaround and into the upper pasture. The hedgerow, which obscured the river bank, appeared to be impenetrable. But he motioned me forward and pointed to a break in the thorn bushes not more than a foot wide. "Ya kin nudge your way through here and stand down there and git a cast. Flip it out you know. Right there. See? There's a good, deep pool. In the season, a month or so from now, there'll be salmon holdin' there. You'll see 'em by the flash o' their sides."

The pool was black as licorice, no bigger than a Jacuzzi and bunkered on both sides by the overhanging thorn bushes. The spot where I'd have to stand slanted toward the water and glistened with tar-black mud.

Then he led me back across the road to the other side of the bridge and showed me how I could climb down to the water's edge to get within casting distance of another pool—the same size as the first.

"Scramble down here, see here? Then ya kin stand down there. See down there? And git a cast." He was pointing to the foot of the bridge abutment, 7 or 8 feet below, and a mere twelve inches wide and semicircular. It was covered with moss and only two-inches above the water's surface.

He straightened up, walked off the bridge and now pointed to the field with the four cows. "You kin walk across there and git to that lower pool. See there, 'crost the field?"

I could see a broad run as wide, flat, smooth and black as a newly paved asphalt road. It was bordered on the near side by the muddy pasture—no bushes—and on the far side by a thick stand of trees and thorn bushes. "Now there's a handsome pool, don't ya tink? Thad a be likely fulla sea trout, " he said.

"Should I ask the farmer for permission? I said looking toward the white house in the far corner of the field. "And will I need a license of any kind?"

"Not a need fur neither. Fishin's free hereabout. Take my word."

"Thanks for the tour, Mick. Can I buy you a drink? I said pointing to the pub sandwiched among a row of houses on the far side of the village circle.

"Sure, and that would be me pleasure."

When we entered the pub, the bartender looked surprised and then a bit perplexed. He and Mick did not exchange a greeting or a glance. The bartender just fixed his eyes on me in a not too friendly manner and asked, "What'll it be?"

"A pint for my good friend here, Mick, and a pint for me, and a Coke for the boy." I'd of said "and a biscuit for the dog," but he didn't look like the kidding kind.

We sat at a table by the front window. Mick's collie lay down by the leg of his chair. The boy said nothing, just nursed his Coke, holding it between two hands. We drank our pints and talked about the hereabouts, the river and the fishing ... and America. A place, Mick said, where he'd like to go someday.

After three rounds I was too dizzy, I knew, to navigate that thorny, slippery river bank, besides it was nearing dark, so I told Mick I'd come back on Wednesday to fish the little river. I thanked him for his advice, bade them all farewell at the pub door and tottered back to the car. Now all I had to do was find my way back to Carrowhugh before dark. Then on Wednesday find my way back to the bridge and the Culdaff.

On Wednesday, before I left Moville, I bought a bottle of wine for Mick. On my way I noticed that someone had returned the signs to their proper position and I had no trouble finding my way back to the Culdaff. I parked in the turnaround, parked and geared up. I started fishing at the pool above the bridge, making my way through the narrow break in the hedgerow just above the pool where in season, according to Mick, the salmon would be lying.

The thorns bit my arms and tugged at my wool shirt as I sidled through the break. The mud at the end of the narrow opening was slipperier than I had imagined. Standing was difficult. Casting impossible. All I could do was hold a branch carefully in one hand and flip the fly downstream with the other. I was using an Orvis Battenkill, bamboo, six feet eight inches long and a #12 Henryville Special—a peacock herl body palmered with a grizzly, a red-brown hackle collar topped with a swept-back gray Mallard quill.

On my second try, I got a fair drift and a dainty rise. I twitched the fly and hooked an energetic little trout. But in the ensuring battle I slipped in the mud and descended up to my armpits into the dark waters of the Culdaff. With the rod held high, I struggled out of the water and slithered on my belly up the bank. The fish? Well, it looked like a brown trout for sure but was no bigger than a minnow; four inches long and an inch wide. I unhooked the little tyke and tossed him back, then waddled to the car.

I took a swig of Scotch from my flask, peeled off my vest, removed and opened the fly boxes and spread them out on the car's hood, took another swig of Scotch, removed and emptied out my chest-highs and changed my shirt.

After recess, and another swig, I suited back up and decided to try the pools on the other side of the road. The abutment pool first. The idea of lowering myself over the side of the bridge onto that narrow, moss-covered footing did not appeal to me but, what the hell, I knew for sure that here in this ingeniously bunkered pool a five-pound lunker must lie waiting to welcome me to Ireland. So over the side I went.

I made it. Now I was standing on the narrow footing with my back against the clammy side of the abutment wondering how to get my fly (still the Henryville) into the water. There were dense, prickly bushes to my right. And dense, prickly bushes stood on the other side of the narrow stream ready to snare a fly flipped too close. But somehow I did manage to get the fly on the water. It floated drag-free for a few inches, and I was rewarded with another dainty rise. In fact almost every time I managed a proper flip I got the same result: a miniature trout not much bigger than those pewter pins you buy at the fly fishing shows. After a little more of this Lilliputian sport, I quit and clawed my way back up and over the side of the bridge.

Now I looked across the road to the right. I had saved what appeared to be the best for last—that long, flat pool that ran, unbunkered on its near side, through the cow pasture.

On my journey across the pasture, I tried to place my feet as squarely as possible on the damp hummocks of long, lush grass while avoiding direct eye contact with the curious cows and direct foot contact with their numerous cow pillows strewn like land mines throughout the field. When I failed, which was frequently, my foot either broke through the cover of a cow pillow with a result not unlike stepping on that proverbial banana peel, or it would sink into the maniacal mud. When that happened, the more I struggled to extract my foot, the more yummy sounds the mud would make, sucking me deeper into its maw. In a demonstration of the law of opposite and equal reactions, the act of trying to extract my ensnared boot drove the other deeper into the mud to a distance equal to the depth of the first. Fortunately, it appears that in county Donegal, the tectonic plate lays a mere 13 inches below the surface. Thus there would be a bottoming out effect: my leg would not descend any deeper than that, which means up to my calf.

When I finally got to the river—damp with sweat and hyperventilating—I realized that I was where the cows come to drink. Here the mud, albeit shallow, was of the texture of mallet-pounded meat and it was almost impossible to stand upright on its surface. But at least here on this precarious shore, if I could manage to stabilize my feet, I could cast more or less normally.

As before, on nearly every cast, I caught a trout—but again and again a miniature trout. They were, it appeared, all of a generation. All the same size, none any longer than my index finger. I laid one in the grass, put a coin beside it, wiped the mud and moisture off the lens of my Konica and took a picture. Then I switched to streamers # 8s in the hope that bigger bait would attract bigger fish but alas I still caught only the miniatures that seemed eager to bite anything of any size thrown near them either on or under the surface.

I quit and navigated my way back across the field to my car. I took a swig of Scotch from the now almost empty flask and used a stick to clean the mud and cow dung off my wader boots. I had a notion to wash them off in the stream but did not want to again risk the dangers of its slippery bank. It was now around 2 in the afternoon.

The farmer's house stood serenely in the upper corner of the field behind a white-washed waist-high wall. There were overflowing flower boxes below each of the windows. I left the car where it was and walked along the road and down the gravel path to the front door. Before I reached the door, it opened and the owner appeared. He was a bent-over old-timer in a green tweed cap, red checkered shirt, gray wool pants and rubber-bottomed boots. A pair of clean, black Wellingtons stood beside the door. He supported himself with a long walking stick and smoked a pipe.

"And what is it I can do for ya? he said.

"Excuse me, sir, but could you tell me where I'd find the home of Mick O'Brien? I met Mick and his son the other day and I wanted to pay him a visit."

"And what would you be wanting with the likes of Mick O'Brien?"

"Well as I said I met him the other day and today I'd be paying a visit and bringing a gift," I had inadvertently picked up the Irish lilt of his voice, which made me sound as if I were, I supposed, mocking him.

"A gift ta deliver, now would ya?"

"Yes."

"Well you'll likely find him back over there." He scowled and motioned with his hand and the pipe toward the left, pointing in the direction over and beyond the rear of his house.

"Back there?"

"Seems to me that's what I said and where I pointed. So I'll say it again. Back that way." Again he motioned with his pipe in hand.

It struck me as unusual for the Irish to be so abrupt with strangers, with Americans especially. It had not been my experience so far, not in Moville and not anywhere along the two-day ride up into the far northwest. This must be just a grouchy old man suffering from heartburn and arthritis. Besides that, he is probably upset that I walked across his field and fished his stream without asking. But, against my better judgment, I had taken Mick at his word when he said permission was not necessary. I should have known better. I did know better.

"Thank you, sir," I said. And because the lane looked extremely narrow, I asked, "Ah, I suppose to get back that way I take the road, and turn down that little lane over there. In the car? That's OK is it?"

"Well if ya got a car and you know how to drive it and you can see the lane, I suppose that's as good a plan as any."

"Thank you, sir. Oh, I, um, walked across your field and fished that pool over there early in the afternoon …"

"And caught no fish, none at all I'd say."

"Well, I did catch some actually. Very, very small fish. Trout. Fingerlings we call them, and I was just going say that I appreciate being able to do that. To cross your field, I mean. And fish the stream."

"All you got to do to do that is be able to walk and if it's appreciation you be handin' out I'd think the gift, whatever it may be, you got for that O'Brien fellow ought to be a gift for me although I can't believe I'd be want'n anything he'd fancy."

"Oh, it's just a bottle of wine. That's all. I just bought him a bottle of wine. He showed me where to fish. Pointed out the pools, you know. I'd be glad to fetch it from the car and give it to you … and get another one for him."

"Don't drink wine, too sweet. Don't think O'Brien does either. And I ain't lookin' for a gift." He turned, shuffled back into the house and shut the door softly.

I knew I had made a mess of that and walked dejectedly up the path and across the road to the car. I drove out of the turnaround and stopped in front of the pub. I went in and bought a bottle of whiskey, Jameson's Irish. Before I turned into the lane, I pulled over, got out and with the bottle in hand walked down the path to the farmer's house. I left the bottle by the door, over to the side next to the Wellingtons so he wouldn't knock it over next time he swung the door open.

The lane was not much more than a goat path. It wound down and around toward a cluster of cottages. They seemed rather haphazardly placed. At one, on the left, a little boy was playing with a stick in the yard—it was Mick's boy. The cottage looked like one of those ramshackle cabins that you see in the Catskills in upstate New York—summer cabins hunkering down behind weed-filled lawns. In front of Mick's, peering at me from behind tall weeds, was a gallimaufry of discarded objects—warped and weathered boards, a dented, rusty bucket, a broken sink, and a weathered tricycle with the front tire missing.

I stopped the car, rolled the window down and said, "Hey, lad, is your Dad home?" Without answering, the boy turned and ran into the house. So I grabbed the bottle of wine, walked up to the door—such as it was—and knocked.

Mick came around from the back. He was shirtless, pink from the sun, barefooted, his hair matted as if he'd just got out of bed.

"Well, hello! The fisherman from America. Come in."

I was startled. If the lawn, for lack of a better word, was a gallimaufry of discarded objects, the living room was, well, it looked like the bedroom I had once seen at a fraternity house—all manner of underwear, T-shirts, pants, skirts, slips, sweaters were strewn about as if someone had just emptied a dozen laundry baskets helter-skelter on the floor. And there were plates with half-eaten food, glasses with half drunk drinks, newspapers, magazines—enough litter to fill a dumpster.

Mick shuffled through the disarray and yelled toward the kitchen, "Ay, love, c'mere, got company, that fisherman from America. The one I told ya 'bout."

The collie burst out of the kitchen and barked. His wife—a slim, wan-looking strawberry blonde with freckles sprinkled on porcelain cheeks—appeared holding a daughter, a few month's old baby cradled in her arms. She wore a soiled white blouse open nearly to the waist and tucked into a pair of periwinkle shorts. She, too, was barefooted.

"Hello," I said. She looked sleepily bewildered, smiled weakly and said nothing.

"Comere, sid down, sid down," said Mick, as he cleared some laundry off the couch.

"Can't stay. Just stopped by to bring you this bottle of wine. And to thank you again for showing me the river, the pools and all that."

"No trouble, no trouble at all." He reached out for the bottle of wine. "Oh, look how nice. Mary look at this." He held the bottle up to the light. "We'll save it for an occasion, right, Mary? For an occasion. Here sid down. Sid down. Did ya fish today? How'd ya do?"

I said, "For a minute only," and I slumped onto the couch. It was warm and Mick's cottage smelled of sour milk and mold.

"How'd ya do? Git any trout?"

"Well, Mick I caught trout but little tiny ones. What we call fingerlings or parr. Not bigger than my index finger." I held my finger out.

"Ah, and I guess that's no surprise to me. None at all. Here let me show ya something. Come on. Out back here."

He got up and walked toward the kitchen motioning me to follow. We went through the kitchen and out the back door. There were three wooden barrels lined up in a row on two side-by-side planks just outside the door.

"Look here," he said motioning to the barrels. He had rigged a spigot on the end of a pipe which stuck out of the ground. A clear, cold trickle of water ran out of the spigot to feed a trinity of pipes. One ran into each barrel. And each barrel was filled to the brim, indeed, overflowing with fresh water. And fresh fish. Trout. And all of them were, I'd say from the ones on the top, two-pounders. All were incredibly bright, cool and fresh.

Mick plunged his hands into the first barrel and brought forth a glistening sea trout. A two-pounder. He held it out for me to admire like a baker holding a loaf of fresh-baked bread.

"Now there's a sea trout for ya. Don't ya know? Mary, Mary," he turned and yelled into the kitchen, "fetch me them plastic bags, Mary, the big ones in the box on the counter there."

Mary came out still holding the baby in her arms and handed Mick a box of clear plastic 2-quart bags. He handed the box to me and told me to take out a bag and hold it open. He dropped the trout in.

"Now how many trout would you be needin'?"

"Tell you what, Mick, since you have so many, I'll take—if you can spare them—three for my friends in Moville and one for me. Is that too many? Can I pay you for them?"

"How could it be too many beings as I got so many and by givin' me that bottle o' wine ya already paid the down payment? Add a wee five pound note and I cin fill your order, no trouble a t'all."

I dug a five-pound note out of my pocket and he turned and scooped another fat trout out of the barrel and dropped it into another outstretched bag … and a third and a fourth. Then for good measure he went to the barrels on the end and scooped out a bright Pollack 18 inches long and dropped it into a fifth bag.

"That one's on the house. That'll be ya dunner for Thursday night. And a samplin' of me Irish generosity."

"Where the hell did you get these fish?"

"Why from the waters of the Culdaff! From the bounty of the sea."

"What? How the hell did you get *all* these fish? So many?"

"It's no mystery that my luck as an angler is better by far than yours, you see," he turned his head in a conspiratorial way and lowered his voice to a whisper, "I am the local poacher. Me net is at the mouth of the river, set there waitin' for the spates to come, the rains you know, which bring visitors from the sea. And it's me net what greets them."

And so it was, struggling under the weight of four bulging clear plastic bags—four trout and one Pollack (the latter I threw into a hedgerow, to conceal the evidence of intrigue)—I retraced my steps to Moville arriving late that sunny Wednesday afternoon.

First I stopped at the barber shop. Had to pass right by anyway. There was one customer in the chair, otherwise the shop was empty. The barber looked up and greeted me with a wide smile. "Ah, the American fisherman. And have ya been to Lough Fad? And how did ya do?"

"Truth be told, I never did find Lough Fad. Made a wrong turn."

"Never did find … Oh, the pity. The pity o' that."

"But I did find a little black water river northwest of here, the Culdaff."

"There's where ya fished? The Culdaff ya say?"

"Yup."

"Oh, the pity. The pity o' that. Come all this far he did." The barber looked mournfully into the face of his customer. "All this far, by God from a world away he come."

"Well, my friend, " I said, "don't pity me. Instead be kind enough to accept a gift, it's yours in appreciation for your advice and friendly counsel," I pulled a plastic bag from behind my back.

"Lord above! Would ya look at that." They both appeared awestruck. "From the Culdaff, ya say?"

"Yup."

"What was ya fishin'? What bait?"

"I was fishing flies, dry flies. What we call, the Henryville Special. This fly." I took one out of the Wheatley box in my shirt pocket and handed it to the barber.

That's yours, too." Then, since they appeared to have been struck dumb, I turned and rode off into the sunset.

My next stop—had to pass right by anyway—was the haberdashery. And upon the haberdasher I conferred the same dual honor of giving him the second two-pound trout from the waters of the Culdaff, and, from my Wheatley fly box, one of my Henryville Specials.

Finally I stopped at the grocery store and gave the third fish and a third fly to the grocer. He was even more incredulous than the others.

"The Culdaff. This trout. This here trout? You don't mean to say. Don't seem possible. No offense to your skill. But it hasn't rained in four days. Four days! And the Culdaff, why that's a spate river. Got fish in it mostly only on the spate. After the rain, you know, flushes her out to sea. And you, you caught how many fish like this? Three, four ya say?"

"Well 'caught' I think is not the proper word. There needs to be another word to describe the events of this blessed day. I would say, since fishing has so much to do with luck, mind you, I would say that it was by the hand of Divine Providence that three or more beautiful sea trout came into my possession this day. I would say that Divine Providence chose to share with me a small portion of the endless bounty of the sea."

"Ah, Lord above, there's near a poet in ya. Bless us all but it does stretch the bounds of faith and belief. But this here I'll tell ya twice. Come Sunday after Mass, rain, shine, fog or smoke, every man, woman and child, every mother, father, uncle, aunt, nephew, cousin, bosom friend, priest and nun in Moville will be leaning over that little stone bridge over the Culdaff with a pole in each o' their hands praying to Divine Providence. And you can bet I'll be chief among 'em, if not the first to get me spot on the bridge."

As I motored up the hill toward Carrowhugh at sunset, my resplendent sea trout sitting comfortably beside me on the seat, I knew that I had just learned something about what it means to have Irish blood trickling through one's veins. And I wondered if Divine Providence would provide me now with a quarter pound of butter and a well-seasoned iron skillet big enough to hold my good fortune.

I'd say that to this day not a week goes by that the pub talk in Moville doesn't turn to the story of the American fisherman and his blessed day upon the little Culdaff.

15

WITH PENELOPE ON THE MINIPI

Years ago when I took my first trip to Coopers' Minipi Camps in far off Labrador, Canada, I was guided on my first outing by a young woman named Paulette. (I immediately invoked poetic license by calling her "Penelope" for the sake of rhyme.)

Now all the guides in Labrador must complete a six-week in-the-field and in-the-classroom course in guiding, so I had no doubt that she knew her stuff. But I found it intriguing nevertheless to be out there in the wilderness on the vast Minipi river-lake with a girl guide.

This is not to mention that I found her accent about eighty-eight percent undecipherable. She was not alone in this because most, if not all of the Minipi guides spoke with the same curious inflections. And I thought that it would be interesting to let you "hear" what this Labradorean speech sounds like by attempting to reproduce it in a dialectical poem. Like the speech itself, some readers have found my attempt as undecipherable as the speech itself. Therefore, following the dialectical poem, you'll find a translation.

By the way, the following describes my experience in catching what was the very first of many giant Labradorean brookies. So, here goes ...

◆ ◆ ◆

Way oop dere in Lab-a-door whar Arctic breath blows frew da trees,
I found me woot turn oot t'be d'purdiest guide y'ever did see.
Her name, least ways ta me, wus 'nelope.

Now one misty munnin' oot inna boot we goos, jus' she an' me.
Wus lookin', we wus, fur 'atches a boogs 'a fur trot on um feedin'.

So, way oop da Minipi, 'nelope an' me, we goos some speedin'.
Now, at woot dey cull d' Bar, floatin' on d'wadder, we fine a hunner boogs.
An' quick, shay stoops d'mooder an' at m'sleef shay toogs.
Well, feedin' on det 'atch a beeg grain drake flies I spies one trot det's fadder
Done ya cooda pud onner two-fud-wide servin'pladder.
An', fass as I cane, I trote m'fly ta d'furry spoot ware 'e be raisin
An' 'e tuk det fly wid a savage splash 'en fass ta d'rooks 'es racin'.

Now det fad trot, 'e did toog an' pool an' sheck 'is 'ed
An' bend m'rude in 'alf a tryin' det 'ook ta shed.
Why, 'e tuk me near tweddy mins ta drug um ta da side a d'boot
Ware m'preddy Penny wus reddy wid d'ned ta tack'em oot.
"Ged d'ned unner um, Penny," says 1, a quiverin', "an' scoop um oop!"
"An' how'm a gonna doer," 'plies 'nelope, "ef ya naw kin ged em oop?"

Wid det, I lifts m'rude so my-dee high an' det beeg trot e's fairly beat.
An' det sweet 'nelope, shay deps d'ned in d'wadder, ahhh, sa neat
An' scups um oop an' doomps 'em flippin' an' a floppin' et m'feed.
An' 'nelope, shay snoops a pitcher a jus' dat fad brook trot an' me,
An' den I poses fur anudder wid dat purdy Penny stan'in' furry, furry close ta me
Wid lodda blue sky, black spruce, an' silver wadder so's all a ya cane envy me.

And now the translation …

Way up in Labrador where the Arctic's breath blows through the trees,
I found what turned out to be the prettiest guide you ever did see.
Her name, least ways to me, was Penelope.
One misty morning out in the boat we goes, just she and me.
Was looking, we was, for hatches of bugs and for trout on them feeding.
So way up the Minipi, Penelope and me, we goes speeding.

Now, at what they call The Bar, floating on the water, we find 100 bugs.
And quick, she stops the motor and at my sleeve she tugs.
Well, feeding on that big Green Drake hatch, I spies a trout that's fatter
Than you could have put on to a 2 ft. wide serving platter.

And fast as I can, I throw my fly to the very spot where he is rising.
And he took that fly with a savage splash and into the rocks he goes a racing.

That trout, he did tug and pull and shake his head,
And bend my rod and in half trying that hook to shed.
Why, it took me near 30 minutes to bring him up to the boat
Where my pretty Penny was ready with the net to take him out.
"Get the net under him," says I quivering, "and scoop him up."
"Now how can I do that," replies Penelope, "if you cannot get him up."

With that, I lift my rod so mighty high and that big trout he's fairly beat.
Then my sweet Penelope she dips the net in the water, oh, so very, very neat
And she scoop him up and dumps him, flipping and flopping, at my feet.
Now Penelope, she snaps a picture of just that fat brook trout and me,
And then I pose for another with pretty Penny standing very, very close to me.
With lots of blue sky, black spruce and silver water so all of you can envy me.

16

THE TRUTH ABOUT FALSE ALBACORE

The place is coastal North Carolina, Harker's Island,[1] off the Outer Banks bracketed by Cape Hatteras National Seashore to the north and Cape Lookout National Seashore to the south. It is early November. The predators, man. The prey, false albacore, *Euthynnus alletteratus*. Baby-sized tuna. But, wait, these fish are not, in the biological sense, "true" tuna, hence they bear the designation "false." Come to think of it, if they are tuna, why are we calling them "albacore."

I know you want to get on with the fishing, but give me a moment to attempt to make sense of this confusing nomenclature.

Here's the question. Is albacore just another name for tuna, or is tuna just another name for albacore? Evidently not, because you can find cans of both albacore *and* tuna sitting side-by-side on your grocery-store shelves. Nevertheless, have you ever heard anyone order an albacore sandwich? Or, for that matter, you only seldom hear of anyone sport fishing for albacore?

---

1. Originally known as Craney Island when it was inhabited by Tuscarawas Indians, Harker's is four miles long and half a mile wide at its narrowest point. In 1714, the island was ceded by the Colonial Government to Thomas Sparrow, who in 1750, sold it to a Bostonian named Ebenezer Harker. He and his family moved to the island, which soon became known as Harker's Island. At the turn of the century, not more than thirty families lived here. In 1941, to supplement the ferry service, a wooden bridge was built connecting the island to the mainland and today Harker's is home to 2,000 permanent residents.

I suppose, judging from his book *The Founding Fish* on shad, that John McPhee would have all the answers to questions like this right up there in his head. I had to look it all up.

According to the latest electronic *Britannica,* there are seven different species of tuna: bluefin, albacore (*Thunnus alalunga*), yellowfin, southern bluefin, bigeye, blackfin and longtail. They are all related to mackerel and have great commercial food value. Because they vary both within and among their species, tuna classifications may differ from one authority to another. One example of intra-specie variation is their considerable variation in size. The largest, the bluefin tuna, sometimes called albacore, may grow to 4.3 m (14 feet) and weigh as much as 800 kg (1,800 pounds). The yellowfin reaches a maximum weight of about 180 kg (400 pounds) and the albacore grows to about 36 kg (80 pounds).

There are three species of "little tunas," *Euthynnus alletteratus.* The one I am writing about in this little recollection is the "false albacore," sometimes called "bonito." The oceanic version of the bonito, by the way, is the skipjack tuna, which grows to about 90 cm (3 feet) and 23 kg.(50 pounds).

The false albacore is an incredibly swift, predatory, schooling fish found worldwide. They have distinct black sergeant's stripes on their backs and silvery, iridescent sides and bellies. They grow to a length of about 75 centimeters (30 inches) and, those we caught off Harker's weighed up to 17 pounds. I am told that those caught off Montauk are generally much smaller, weighing only three, four and five pounds. The world record, 35 lbs. 2 ounces, was caught in 1988 at Cap de Garde, Algeria.

Like tunas, they are built for speed. Their tail base is extremely narrow; the tail itself is deeply forked and sharply tapered at the ends. They have a row of small finlets behind their dorsal and anal fins. Look closely and you will discover that the fins are capable of retracting into cavitations in the body like the wheels on a jet—an adaptation that makes this fish, indeed, a creature capable of mind-boggling bursts of speed. For example, while out on the water we noticed that pelicans could keep up with our boat traveling at 30 knots. These fish, on the other hand, could not only keep up, but they could overtake and pass us at that speed and higher speeds. This means they must be capable of bursts of speed up to, if not more than 50 knots.

I cannot leave this subject without injecting one further comment about the biological use of the word "false." Biologists use the term to identify both plants and animals that closely resemble the "true" version of a given species. In other words, it becomes part of the name of animals and plants, which look almost but not quite like the "true" bearer of the species designation. There are, for example, false sunbirds, false cypress, false scorpion and the false vampire bat.

Now let's get back to the truth.

At dawn, fog, as thick as Grandma's pea soup, hides the docks at Harker's Island Fishing Center. The sun itself was barely visible, appearing as if it were a mere tablespoon or two of melted butter dribbled on the horizon. We'll have to wait.

"How about we drive down to Steak & Shake?"

Good idea. We'll have a non-traditional breakfast: a strawberry shake, topped with whipped cream, a cherry, and a pink stand-up straw; a famous Frisko Melt—two layers of burger beef with chili in between, a slice of American cheese on top, all sandwiched between a sliced burger bun and grilled to a golden brown in a pond of bubbling lard.

I've been invited on this trip by Lanier Woodrum, a Southern gentleman from Roanoke, Virginia, whom I met on a Canadian fishing trip. With us is his son, Bo, a master carpenter, in fact, a movie-set builder whose credits include *The Silence of the Lambs* and several Stephen King movies. Just to name a few. He's studying architecture on the side. And Wayne Grayson, a fifty-something general practitioner and sportsman also from Roanoke, Virginia. Wayne's just back from salmon fishing on the Kamchatka River in far eastern Russia, his third trip there. Before that he and his English setter, Molly, had been grouse hunting in Minnesota.

Lanier is in his late forties, lean and loosely built. He's an early-retired lawyer who has set up his retirement schedule to include one week of serious, far-flung fly fishing every month. Every month! His dedication to the sport is evidenced by the message on his answering machine at his home in the hills above Roanoke. It goes like this: *You have reached the home of an old fisherman who lives here with the greatest catch of his life ... his wife Beverly.*

Now when I was a kid I had my own special fishing hole just down the road. Most fishermen can remember having the same. But as we grew older—and hopefully more prosperous—we went further down the road to fish. Farther and farther down the road. For some middle-aged fishermen, men of means, the world has become their fishing hole: Paraguay, Patagonia, Argentina, Chile, Mexico, Russia, Norway, Iceland, Scotland, Ireland, Islamorada, Boca Raton, the Abacos—wherever they want to go, whenever they want to go however far.

That's the life that my friend Lanier and his friend Wayne have achieved for themselves. Naturally they have all the gear to go with it. Why not? Nothing but the best—$600 reels and $600 rods. High rollers. And we are now rolling down the road in the comfort of Lanier's well-appointed, sky-blue Chevy Suburban, down the road to Harker's Island—seven hours from Roanoke heading southeast through North Carolina—Greensboro, Raleigh, Goldsboro, Kinston, New Bern, on to Newport, Morehead City then across the bridge and into Harker's.

The conversation consists of fishing stories and jokes. I remember Lanier recounting stories he's picked up from the Darwin Awards website, a site that gives mostly posthumous awards to persons who have given up their lives, or nearly done so, as the result of their own stupidity. For example, one winter two fishermen pile into their Ford pickup put their dog Emily in the back and head out to a nearby lake. When they get there, they discover it's frozen solid. Got an idea says one. He reaches under the seat and digs out a stick of dynamite. They can use it to blast themselves some open water. One lights the foot-long fuse and throws it out onto the frozen lake. Emily leaps out of the truck, races across the ice, picks up the dynamite and trots back toward the truck. In a panic one man grabs his shotgun and tries to shoot the dog. He misses. The dog makes it back and runs for cover under the truck. Ka-boom!

Here's another one: Two guys are hunting ground hog. They shoot at one. He runs into a culvert pipe. They can't get him out, so one guy decides to smoke him out. He goes to their truck and gets a spare can of gasoline. He takes off the cap, makes a fuse of rolled-up newspaper, stuffs it in the gasoline can and crawls into the pipe. Once well inside, he flicks his Bic. Ka-boom! The explosion propels him down the pipe like a human cannonball into the other guy who had knelt down behind him in the pipe to watch the action. R.I.P.

"Hey, Bo, dig me out another beer."

◆ ◆ ◆

Back at the dock we waited some more. Finally, when a mullet fisherman cast off, we followed him out through the now invisible markers and we were followed in turn by a procession of other sport fishing boats. Lanier and Bo are in one boat captioned by Brian Horsley. Wayne and I are in another boat captained by Sarah Gardiner.

We are not the only ones at Harker's on the trail of the false albacore. There are people here from as far away as Tacoma, Washington; Roseburg, Oregon; Belmont, California; Syracuse, New York; Pittsburgh, Pennsylvania. Some of these men and women have driven all the way, trailering their own boats behind them.

And this is quite an array of boats: Parker's and Jones's. And the motors—massive outboards—Hondas, Suszukis, Yamahas, Evinrudes, Mercurys. 90s mounted side-by-side, single 215s, and 150s. Later you'll see why these boats sport such powerful motors.

On board Sarah's boat we are bundled up in bright yellow full-dress rain suits—hooded jackets over matching coveralls—like fishermen in a Winslow Homer painting. We are heading past Shell Point, the extreme southeastern end of Harker's, toward the Lighthouse Channel about a mile-and-a-half away.

I notice that Sarah's fly reels have her name engraved on tiny brass nameplates screwed down on the side of the reels with tiny golden screws. The reels are Tibor, Pate, Islander. The rods, Thomas & Thomas, Winston. Loomis, and Sage. They are ten-weight fly rods equipped sinking lines—clear ones (slime line), brown tipped ones, intermediate and fast sinking. The flies are neon Clousers, and crease flies.

The crease fly is made by cutting a sixteenth-of-an-inch-thick piece of flexible compressed Styrofoam into a butterflied minnow shape and then folding it and epoxying it over the shank of a straight-eye # 6 hook. Once folded and secured to the hook, the body has a dome-shaped cavity at the mouth end like the scooped-out front of a popper. It is then painted with layers of colorful fluorescent and iridescent paint to resemble a bait fish with a big, yellow rimmed black eye. The end product looks like a bait fish in a Hawaiian shirt. These flies are not easy to cast. They are wind-resistant and tend to flutter and gyrate.

Wayne, a short, powerful man with a well-trimmed white moustache has little trouble punching a crease fly out there fifty or sixty feet, or more. In other words, he can put it in the pudding. This takes powerful, well-timed double hauls, which he executes to perfection. Obviously such an expert caster can cover more water and reach fish well out of the novice's range.

Also, as usual with two men fly fishing in a relatively small boat, the angler in the bow must cast backwards—this means casting conventionally facing front but making the release backwards. This is to avoid casting down the center of the boat. What's more there's an arsenal of fly rods sticking upright like antennas against the side of the pilot house. Before I mastered, rather managed, the proper protocol, I snagged my line several times in the upright rods. Not a good thing because I was using one of Sarah's Thomas & Thomas rods, and the others stacked up there represented an investment of, let's say, something like $3,600. That makes you very careful.

Wayne, being by far the much better caster, is able to manage his line better in the wind and get it up over any obstacles in the boat—including me. So, Wayne, positioned in the stern, is catching 4 or 5 albies on the crease fly, to my one. These fish are big ones. Up to 16 or 17 pounds. But few—none of Wayne's—are able to snap the 25 lb tippets and on our first day out, only two are lost on the way to the boat.

These albies have incredibly tough mouths and hook themselves with their violent, high-speed attacks on the lure. Yes, the strikes are savage, the struggles long, 20 minutes or more to bring most fish to the net. One fish bent my hook into a grotesque shape from the strength and duration of his struggle. I still have that hook in my table of fame.

It was Wayne who caught one of the largest, a 17-pounder. He was making a magnificent cast into the center of a riot of gulls and pelicans feeding on the bait fish chased up to the surface by the marauding albies. I saw his line go over the back of a pelican in the water and when the fish struck, the line went taut and sank the pelican. He bobbed up to the surface ten seconds later.

One day Wayne actually hooked a pelican casting into the maelstrom. The bird flew off with the fly in its beak and Wayne played it masterfully back to the boat where Sarah netted it and put a towel over its head before prying the hook out. After the operation, the bird was released and flew off apparently unharmed.

We stay on the water from dawn till dusk. One angler continues to cast while the other eats lunch. We putter to and fro off the Outer Banks, off the islands of Cape Lookout National Seashore—Cockle Marsh Island, Cedar Hammock, Sheep Island Slue, to name a few of the many.

Here's the way the action takes place.

All the powerful boats, maybe a dozen of them, are puttering around on the water watching the birds circle high overhead. What we are waiting for is that frenzied moment then the gulls and pelicans converge over a spot where a school of albacore has attacked a school of bait fish (it's called a bait ball) and driven them in a panic up to the surface. The birds signal this event by rushing in and diving down to scoop them up. Sometimes they even land momentarily on the backs of the albacore. The surface of the water is now a boiling stew of bait, birds and albacore.

All this happens—and ends—as quickly as I tell it.

When it happens, the captain must, first, spot the boil, and, second, rev up his motors to get his anglers within casting range before it stops. In other words, he must get his anglers close enough to cast a fly into the melee of birds, bait and albacore.

In between such spectacular events, you simply cruise around covering a lot of water. You cruise along the beach, between the off-shore wetlands along places like Barden Inlet east of the Lighthouse Channel, then around what they call the "gun mounts." Once in a while you see solitary fishermen standing knee-deep in the shallow water off the banks, casting under a luffing canopy of circling birds.

You are looking for the birds to gather over a particular spot—that's when you and all the other boats converge on that spot. It resembles the start of a Bassmasters' Tournament, except in this case the boats roar into range from different directions, from all the compass points, heading for that one spot. A spot that may be not more than forty yards or less in diameter. Now you understand why these boats have such powerful motors. Because the swiftest win this race.

Again, it doesn't last long because as soon as the bait fish form a ball, they scatter under the attack of birds, boats, and the ferocious onslaught of the schools of albacore. And, again, the prize is won by the fastest boats and the best fly casters.

When the bait fish move out of the shallow waters along the banks, the schools of albacore follow. And the shallow-water action slows. That's when the captain takes you out to deeper water. Once there, we change tactics and do a bit of chumming.

Sarah has a big, white plastic bucket filled to the brim with tiny bait fish, no more than two inches long and a quarter-inch wide. She reaches in, grabs a handful and tosses them into the water. The bait is dead and drifts slowly back on the current, sinking behind the now anchored boat. Once the water is well chummed, Wayne and I cast out neon Clousers and let them sink and drift suspended in the current amid the chum behind the boat.

Suddenly, we see fins poking out of the water. They are crisscrossing behind the boat slashing into the bait. When this is happening, you can sometimes hook an albie by just dangling your Clouser off the gunwale. Even at this close range, their take is never gentle.

Catching them in the chum is not, however, as easy as it sounds. The color of the sinking line matters—whether it is brown or clear—as does the rate of sink. How you move or dead-drift the fly matters also. You have to use trial and error until you find the right combination. But when you do, the action comes fast and furious. At the height of the action, the fish will break the surface to strike odd pieces of floating chum. That's when you switch to the crease fly.

Remember the chum is dead, not moving, just suspended in the water. So you either have to imitate that lazy motion or try to attract a more aggressive fish by twitching your Clouser, or stripping it slowly through the chum. Or you can get some exercise and try to tease the albies up to the surface by fast-stripping and bouncing a crease fly over them.

As any fisherman will understand, on some days, during some hours, the switch is off. The action is slow or no. For example, on our last day on the water, the switch seemed to be "off." The number of boats had increased, too. The birds had spread out. It seemed the fish were choosier, somewhat less enthusiastic than the day before; the bait seemed less inclined to ball up, and, although, as usual, the albies from time to time did break the surface in showy displays of gluttony, and, although even some of the less accomplished casters did manage, in the light winds on smooth seas, to get their flies into the occasional boils, I only saw one fish caught.

It is absolutely impossible to describe the dogged fight these fish put up. They strike with surprising speed and heart-stopping savagery. When they take your fly, the coils of line lying in the boat rip out through the guides like a lightening strike and the line on the reel melts in a microsecond into the backing.

I remember one fish, which followed my darting, skipping, surface-skimming crease fly all the way to within a few of the boat. There he struck the fly and dived under the boat, and when he did, the handle on the Islander reel caught in the sleeve of my slicker. This checked the fish's run with a force that slammed my forearm down onto the gunwale like a hammer stroke, so hard it filled my eyes with tears. It was as if I had poised my arm on a table in the hand-wrestling position, tied a string around my wrist, placed a board in the middle of the table, put a 17 pound lead weight on the other end of the string and dropped it off the table.

I untangled the reel from my sleeve, launching the fish like a shot arrow. This time the handle spun so fast that, as I reached out to palm the rim of the reel, the handle cracked my fingers like a stick run down a picket fence. Later my index finger would look as if it had been slammed in a car door. What's more, the reel was turning so fast that when I did press my palm on the rim to slow it, I could feel the burn. Later I noticed a blister on my palm.

All of Sarah's rods are set up for right-hand reeling. (I am accustomed to left-handed reeling.) The reason she has them set up that way is because, if you are a right-hander, you could never sustain the speed and strength you need to recover line with your weaker left hand.

You fight these fish with both hands on the cork, no reaching up to grab just below the ferrule with your left hand as I have seen guides do while fighting tarpon. Once, with a fish on, when I raised the rod and pressed the butt extension into the palm of my left hand, Sarah cautioned me, "That's a good way to break a rod." Another time while fighting a fish, I put the rod handle into my belly and leaned back. Again Sarah cautioned me, "That's a good way to break a rod."

So you fight them with both hands on the cork with the rod tip down, held to the left or right and parallel to the water. Although Sarah had set the drag on her reels just slightly off the leader's breaking point, you still have to palm the reel to check an albie's runs.

We released every fish caught with a few exceptions caused by deep takes and consequent bleeding. The one or two we kept we cut up to supplement our chum. That's when I noticed that the albie's flesh is crimson. Blood red. So saturated with blood that you could squeeze it like a sponge and watch the blood ooze out between your fingers.

I later learned that tuna have an intricate network of blood vessels beneath their skin, which acts as a temperature-regulating mechanism utilized during long-term, slow swimming. This unusual vascular system, unique among fish, enables tunas to maintain the temperature of their bodies above that of the ambient water, sometimes by as much as 14° C (20° F). Perhaps this is what accounts for the bloody appearance of their flesh. This is also the reason that, as far as I know, false albacore, unlike tuna, are not known for their table quality.

And that's the truth about false albacore. There is no more.

17

GETTING THERE

Once I had a pretty wife who is now, sad to say, somewhere far beyond this life. And once, when I asked her if she would like to join me fishing, she pointed out that the only outdoor activity she was interested in was sipping a Martini on the patio.

Married fishermen will immediately understand my dilemma. They will know that when their partner does not share their love of the outdoors, they will incur a debt of sorts whenever they take off on a fishing trip, a debt that must be paid back rather promptly if marital bliss is to be maintained.

Of course, the payback will have to involve some *non-outdoors* something. A walk in the woods will not do. A trip to inspect the water level at a nearby stream will not do. Big debts—to make up for that trip to Alaska—well, that could involve, let's say, a newly remodeled kitchen.

One solution is, however, to barter the payback with a nice family vacation … and stealthily to combine that vacation with just a wee bit of fishing.

So, here's the approach I used.

"Hey, darling, I have an idea. Let's go to London, stay there awhile and then drive up to Scotland. How does that sound, sweetheart? Plenty of good food, plenty of shopping, plenty of sightseeing. You know, dear, we'll stay for a few days in an elegant London hotel, and then rent a car and drive leisurely up to Scotland, stopping along the way at charming little inns. And up there in Scotland, we'll stay in a little storybook cottage. What fun that will be!"

All the while you're thinking she could never, not in a million years, object to your taking a few days, just one or two, to go salmon fishing.

Well, it worked. And this is the story of my "family vacation," an epicurean jaunt up the North Road to the Scottish highlands with my wife in tow. What a brilliant—albeit expensive—way to earn a few days of fishing, don't you think?

So come along with me on my (*shush!*) Scottish salmon fishing adventure.

Take-off.

We did the limo to the airport thing. No sweat. And once on board the plane, my wife said, "Oh, dear. How very exciting! Look at all the colorful costumes!" I did notice that many of our fellow passengers were Indians. In fact, it sort of resembled what I imagined a ferry chugging down the Hooghly from Calcutta to the Bay of Bengal might look like. And, here we were, like two croutons thrown into a *matter pannier* from which arose the fragrance of hot chilies, turmeric, curry, saffron and chutney.

Our fellow passengers were struggling with canvas totes, knapsacks, pasteboard boxes tied up in jute—trying, with signs of mild desperation on their faces, to stuff them in the overheads, and under and between the seats. We wheedled our way down the fuselage to our seats in the back of the plane. It was worth the struggle because these seats tilted back farther than the others and had the additional virtue of being near the toilets and the galley.

We settled in and soon fell into a groggy slumber. I remember little of our hop across the Atlantic until we arrived over London's sprawling suburbs. The sight from the plane's window reminded me of over-flying Los Angeles—miles and miles of twinkling yellow lights spread out below as if they were on a gigantic fallen Christmas tree.

Landing.

We landed at 6:55 A.M. London time (5 hours ahead of EST.) Heathrow airport, like the plane, was jammed with men, women, and, of course, my favorite thing, children, even a gallimaufry of adorable little wiggling babies. Turbans and saris were everywhere. It took us an hour to navigate the queue for passport checking and customs.

After that we careened through the airport balancing our bags and my four fishing rods on a three-wheeled tipsy cart—I had duct-taped the rod cases together and they stuck out from the cart like a Gatlin gun. This is in the era before the popularity of 4-piece "travel rods," which fit neatly and unobtrusively into a cylinder not more than twenty-four inches long. My rods, of course, were the old-fashioned two-piece rods, one of them, a Powell 10-footer was in an aluminum cylinder 5 feet long. It turned out, however, to be a formidable offensive and defensive weapon as we navigated our way through the crowds at Heathrow.

Taxi to London.

After waiting in another queue, we boarded one of those traditional black London taxis, which someone told me weigh two tons. These commodious vehicles, by the way, offer plenty of room for one's luggage, including my Gatlin gun.

It is morning rush hour and we are cheek-to-jowl with Jaguars, Vauxhalls, Land Rovers, Rolls Royces, BMWs plus motorcycles and scooters darting like angry bees between the lanes. The ride takes an hour and twenty minutes and costs an astounding sum. The driver, amused or annoyed by my comments on the cost, noted that the cab is very old but the meter very new. His wife, he says, polishes and oils it every day. In the evening he turns over all his fares to her and she gives him a guinea back. "So it's a guinea a day I work for," he says. He then pats the fishing rods beside him and says, "You'll be paying far more than a guinea a day to fish in Scotland for your salmon. Right pricey it is, I hear."

The Cumberland Hotel at Marble Arch.

Making a U turn in heavy traffic, we pull up at the Cumberland. The cabbie unloads us into the hands of Robert, the bell boy, saying, "Ay, Robert, got a Yankee angler for ya. Not a wormer mind ya, nor a carper like ya be, but a genuine salmon fly fisherman." "A salmon fisher, heh," says Robert. "Gud, dye ta ya, sur."

At the registration desk, a young lady with a far eastern accent, a flawless almond complexion and anthracite hair tells us that we must wait until 2 P.M. to get into our room. "But check back in an hour or so." So we go across the lobby and have breakfast.

An hour later we're on the lift going up to our room. Robert will bring our bags up later.

The next day, after a room service breakfast, we set out to visit London's shops. A list for her, a list for me. May as well join in the fun.

Shopping & Pubbing.

For the cigar aficionado, of whom I am one, a major reward of foreign travel—given today's embargo—is the availability of Cuban cigars. Not surprisingly, therefore, on my list of shops to visit, was Dunhill's. During the 1941 Blitz, Alfred Dunhill's shop on Duke Street was virtually destroyed. At 2 A.M. once the smoke had cleared, Mr. Dunhill himself telephoned Mr. Churchill to say, "Your cigars are safe, sir."

At Dunhill's I bought some Cohibas Robustos. Expensive? Yes. Beyond belief. In those days, the price of merely "good" Havanas was £12.50 each. A box of Cohiba Esplendidos was £376.00.

At the top of Dunhill's "Cigar List" it proclaims, "*Havana Cigars, undoubtedly the finest cigars in the world. Our present selection includes many rolled with tobacco grown in the famous Vuelta Abajo region in the province of Pinar del Rio in Cuba. All our cigars are fully matured and ready for smoking.*" Below are listed a number of the names cigar lovers know and lust after—Bolivar, Partagas, Punch, Rey del Mundo, Romeo y Julieta, Hoyo de Monterrey, H. Upmann, La Flor de Cano—a choice, don't you think, to warm the heart and empty the wallet of cigar aficionados anywhere.

Next we went to a "her list" shop: Liberty of London, a redoubtable retail fortress where the fabric department, for one example, is of unbelievably vast proportions. It sprawls colorfully behind an elaborately ornate walnut balustrade above an atrium. And the fabrics! Silks, Egyptian cottons, British suiting woolens selling, again in those days, for £136.00 a yard. And fabulously patterned wool challis with the handle of the finest, sheerest cotton.

Then we were off to Fortnum & Mason where the food department consists of delicatessens within delicatessens, a wine shop, a sweets shop, a caviar bar, a cheese counter, a bakery shop. Everywhere we looked our eyes fell upon small jars of exotic comestibles. Young Boar Pate, Quail Eggs, Country Pork Pate with Calvados, and Patum Peperium, "The Gentleman's Relish" with a label that cautioned, " … to appreciate the proper flavour of The Gentleman's Relish, it should be used VERY SPARINGLY [sic]." A tiny black bowl of this delicacy was near the cost of caviar. It is, I learned, an anchovy fish paste more pungent than one could possibly want to imagine. I bought two bowls. What sold me were the words "Gentlemen's Relish." It didn't say pungent, brown, foul-smelling fish paste. I ended up depositing the contents of one bowl down the sink at our cottage in Strathtay. The contents of the other found its way down the sewer pipes back home in Gwynedd Valley, Pa. The empty bowls serve today as paperclip holders on my desk.[1]

Our shopping was punctuated with pub visits where we tasted such colorfully named brews as Strongbow and Woodpecker Cider and Merrydown Original Extra Strong Dry Vintage Cider ("matured slowly in oak vats to enhance its extra strength with extra body") and Poacher's Bitters, Younger's Tartan Special, Theakston's Ale, Flower's Best Bitters, Murphy's Irish Stout, Whitbread Feggles Imperial, Baddington's Bitter and that premium lager, Stella Artor's. All served by the pint at room temperature beneath a sign proclaiming that according to the Licensing Act of 1964, "Drinking up time" is 20 minutes after "permitted hours." A violation brings the promise of a £400 fine.

Dinner in the Grill Room

The highlight of our stay in London was a sumptuous dinner in the Grill Room at the Connaught Hotel on Carlos Place. It was my second visit to the elegantly small and refined Connaught.

In the early 70s I was working in New York as an editor at Macmillan Publishing Company, a job that required me to travel to England to acquire American rights to British books. On one of those trips, a British friend of mine recommended that I stay at the Connaught Hotel. I accepted his recommendation and he very kindly made all the necessary arrangements. He even instructed me to bring pajamas, slippers and a bath robe. After all, one does not sleep at the Connaught in one's skivvies.

---

1. In 2007, at the age of 68, Sir Robin Knox-Johnson, attempted his second solo sail around the globe. "Almost all of the food [aboard] is freeze-dried, the main exception being several bottles of Gentleman's Relish…., which he spreads on crackers when he decides he has done something worthy of celebrating." He also took along "a supply of scotch and several two-liter cartons of wine."

At that time, I had no idea how special a place was the Connaught. Nor, indeed, how expensive. What's more, I had absolutely no idea of the towering international reputation enjoyed by the hotel's dining room, the imperious Grill Room where reservations must be made months in advance.

So before leaving on the trip that is the subject of this recollection, I wrote to the general manager, Mr. P. Zago, told him how much I had enjoyed my previous visit, and asked about the possibility of making dinner reservations in The Grill Room. His reply read as follows: "I am delighted that you will be coming here for Dinner during your visit to London. We have made a reservation, for two, in the Grill Room on Tuesday the 13th, and, unless we hear from you regarding an alternative time preference, Mr. Donato, our Grill Room Manager, will look forward to welcoming you at around 7.30/8.00 P.M."

I cannot resist sharing with you some highlights from the Grill Room's à la carte menu. First the specialties "to order in advance": Oeuf en Surprise Connaught, Zephyrs de Sole Tout Paris, Mousse Homard Neptune, Noisettes D'Agneau Edward VII, Mignon de Veau Prince Orloff, Filet D'Angus Farci en Croutte Strasbourgeoise. (Do you notice the French accent?)

Now for a selection of what you might call the *fare ordinaire*: such entrees as Turbot Poché, Grillé ou Rôti au Four Berre Nantais, Pintadeau en Croutte Grand Mère ou en Salmi aux Morilles et Champignons à la Crème … and among the "savouries," Scotch Woodcock and Canapé Baron … and among the "legumes," Chartreuse de Lègumes Saisonniers ("to be ordered in advance.")

Unfortunately I cannot remember what we chose from this astoundingly rich and diverse bill of fare. But I do remember the blindingly bright table cloths, the tall vases of yellow flowers, the sparkly crystal, the translucence of the Limoges China, the subdued air of relaxed elegance, the splendid company of fellow diners, the bubbles in the Dom Perignon, the incredible invisible service … not to mention that bottle of 1935 brandy of a most exquisite character.

Off to the north.

The next morning, trailing clouds of glory, we picked up our little Seat automobile, and with the Eurocar clerk's directions in hand, "dove" into the turbulent stream of London traffic heading for the M6 North. We immediately got lost.

We must have circled Victoria Circle five times before we found signs pointing the way to the M6 and managed to position ourselves in the correct lane to follow them. The traffic was unusually aggressive and bumper-to-bumper for three or four miles. That's when we saw a sign—*Expressway ends 1 m*. How could it end; we were not aware that we had even got on it. But we were in the wrong lane and the inescapable exit ramp dumped us into Kensington, an incredibly congested area of incredibly tiny streets, big trucks and large crowds of pedestrians.

Finally, I found a pull-off and sat in the car sulking over the map. A small, frail man with an Einsteinian head of hair accompanied by a large, robust woman poked his head in the car window and asked if he might have my parking space when I left. Yes, he could, I said on the condition that he gives me directions for getting back on the expressway north. He agreed.

He took a notepad and pen from his pocket and, leaning on the hood of my car, began to draw a map. As he drew, he said, "Go up to the end of the road, turn left; go to the light, turn left, go to the next light. There's a round-about, stay on the inside like this, I've shown it here, and bear left, then turn left, go past the butcher shop, you'll see the sign, then turn left again at the petrol station—what you're doing is going in a circle, because, see there," he looked up and pointed down the street toward the bakery, "there's the road you seek but you cannot get there straightaway from here, but you *can* get there by following my directions and going round the other way until you see a sign for the M6." (Tell me this was not the stuff of bad dreams.)

By some miracle, however, with his map, and oral directions, we did find the entrance to M6 North. After that we had little trouble following the road because it was marked repeatedly with big, reassuring signs with big, reassuring red-and-white arrows pointing to THE NORTH.

The Shakespeare Hotel, Chapel Street, Stratford-upon-Avon.

When we finally pulled up to the Shakespeare, (a mere 58 miles from the infamous Victoria Circle in London), we were wrecks. At the registration desk there was a silver tray and a crystal decanter of sherry surrounded by a circle of small crystal glasses. I picked up two of the glasses, filled them to the brim and carried them out to Betty in the car at the curb. I returned to the desk and poured myself two Sherries.

That evening we dined at the hotel. The dining room was stiffly formal with the usual crystal, china and silver sitting on starched brilliantly white table cloths. The other guests were dressed, as we are, in coats and ties and elegant dresses. Except for two elderly Japanese couples, the guests were middle-aged Brits.

I ordered Guinea Fowl and when the waitress placed it in front of me, she said, "There now, sur. I hope it eats well." At the next table I overheard a gentleman ask a lady "Are you Australian?" To which she replied, "Not yet."

And I remember our wine that evening was a Rèmole 1992 Chianti Rúfina Frescobaldi. Unfortunately the previously drained glasses of sherry and double whiskies dulled my appreciation.

Some of the original sections of The Shakespeare Hotel date back to the 17th century, and have dark ceiling timbers, and white plastered walls just as you'd expect to find in an historic English inn. The huge fireplace in the low-ceilinged lobby has large and had black iron pots hanging from it. There are brass sconces lined up along the walls with lit candles in each. The sweet smell of wood smoke was wafting among the oak-topped tables, overstuffed chairs and sofas.

After dinner we sat in the lobby and when a young man asked if he could serve us, we ordered two whiskies. He dutifully wrote down our order and disappeared. When he reappeared a few minutes later, he was accompanied by a middle-aged, matronly woman. She carried a large, iron padlock key. Together they marched past us and through a door in the darkened corner to the rear of the room. They returned momentarily. She cradled the key ceremoniously in her hands and he held a tray with two glasses on it, each with an amber splash of whiskey in the bottom.

Unbeknownst to us, the pub is closed at this hour and the bar cabinet is, therefore, locked. Hotel guests, however, sitting in the lobby, may order drinks anyway. Because we so much enjoyed the procession of the waiter and the matronly custodian of the key, we ordered seconds.

The next day, in a heavy mist and light rain, we walked to Holy Trinity Church situated on the banks of the languid river Avon. William Shakespeare was baptized here in 1564 and buried here in the Chancel in 1616. The church now has a gift shop in front. A sign nearby warned that no cameras were to be used inside.

Curious, I thought, but I guessed the camera restriction was out of respect for the dead. A rosy-cheeked woman sat behind a card table at the entrance. She was selling tickets to permit one to walk inside to view Shakespeare's catafalque. We decided to simply look at it from afar.

I paused to look longingly at the river Avon. There were no rises that I could see.

The Swan Hotel, Grasser, Amble side, Cambria.

On the following day, after our usual leisurely breakfast, we returned to the road north. Our next stop was to be the Swan Hotel, a small, white-plastered two-storey building in Grasser, the center of the famous Lake District.

In The Swan's dining room that evening, we launched our repast with appetizers of potted salmon, a ham and pepper-onion salad followed by an entrée of Turkey Breast with Bacon, creamed mushrooms, onion soup and roast leg of lamb. Our wine was a Chateau Haut Prier, a 1992 vintage Boudreaux, which clung sweetly to the sides of our tongues. For dessert we had a spectacular Brandy Basket of Berries with a Tulip Trifle. The Basket of Berries had a mound of large, robust, unblemished raspberries on top, two or three other kinds of local and in-season berries encircling them below and all were dusted with confectioners' sugar sprinkled onto a crimson raspberry sauce. This ensemble was served in a small, crisp golden pastry boat which was adrift in a dish in a shallow pool of amber brandy.

In the Buttery after dinner, I lit a Hoyo de Monterrey Churchill accompanied by a snifter of Grand Marnier.

An elderly man sat beside us in a Harris Tweed coat, matching wool pants and a tightly snugged-up black tie. He ordered, "Another whiskey, please, on top of that one, please," and he pointed to the center of his glass with the stem of his Meerschaum pipe. We had noticed him here in the bar sitting alone before dinner uttering his mantra, "another whiskey, please," and in the dining room during dinner we had seen him drinking "another whiskey." He was still there in the Buttery when we called it a night. As we left, I heard him say, "Another whiskey, please, on top of that one, please," again pointing into the center of his glass with his pipe stem.

In the Buttery the next evening after dinner, we met a heating and air conditioning mechanic from Manchester. He was not a tourist but was there to fix the hotel's heating system. "Like a holiday for me, it is. Truly is," he said, "Up here in the lakes, the air, why, you know you can catch it in the palm of your hand. Aye, so pure and cool and good. You can, on a foggy mornin', and all mornin's ear about are foggy, you can scoop up a handful, cup it oop to your mouth, and, will ya believe me? Swallow it."

Strathay Cottage by Pitlochry.

That Saturday we left the Lake Country and ventured north again. After several hours, we arrived at the village of Strathay and the stone and iron gates of Dun-an-Choille, the mini-castle behind which sat the cottage that we had rented beforehand. Dun-an-Choille means "fort in the woods," and, indeed, the main house is tucked away in a thick grove of giant, ancient evergreens.

The cottage is damp and chilly. The front door—four tongue-and-groove boards—misses the jamb by a half inch all around. But to warm the living room, there's a wee wood stove, and in the kitchen a little electric blower heater, and in the bath room upstairs there's an overhead electric heating unit.

That night we ate in, dining on our stash from Fortnum & Mason: Young Wild Boar Pâté and Rabbit Pâté and other small, exotic victuals. We spread the pâté on toast points made from bread bought at John Taylor's grocery above the war memorial in Strathtay. The overture to out pâté ensemble was, naturally, a splash of Scotch. For the accompaniment we sipped an assertive Amarone, that extra-robust valpolicella.

We awoke at 9 A.M. and had lean bacon, poached eggs, warm toast, strong tea and sweet marmalade. Afterwards I talked about fishing with Colin McCoshim, the owner's son. He showed an interest in my gear so I spread it out on a table set up in the driveway beside the cottage. This was a simple table made by mounting two wide oak boards on top of two ornate iron legs salvaged from an old Singer Sewing machine. Colin said that many of the flies they used were made from the feathers of heron wings and he promised to give me some heron feathers before we left. He forgot. But I'll write to remind him, sending a bundle of wood duck feathers to sweeten the deal.

Although it was Sunday, McCoshim said that Mitchell's, the anglers' shop in Pitlochry, was open and Nick, the proprietor, would be there. He'd be expecting me to stop by to confirm my fishing arrangements. So we drove the seven miles into

Pitlochry to meet Nick, who confirmed my fishing arrangements. While Nick and I talked about the fishing, his wife Bess, a pin-up pretty woman with loosely curled blonde hair, pastel pink lips and a sprinkling of cinnamon freckles on her alabaster cheeks, talked with Betty, recommending that while in town we should have lunch at the Westlands Hotel just down the road.

Pitlochry is a bustling tourist center that straddles the Great North Road. Its main street is lined with hotels, guesthouses, restaurants, cafes, and a sprinkling of tweed, Highland Craft and woolen shops. So, after lunch, we poked around the shops and got back to the cottage in time for an afternoon nap. I awoke around 5:30 P.M. and since there was still plenty of light, I decide to follow up on Bob McCoslim's suggestion that I fish the waters at the foot of his gardens.

What McCoshim calls a "garden" is really a vast lawn as green and smooth and lush as a putting green sloping steeply down for 150 yards to the river's edge. The upper section of the lawn is terraced to a point where it is bisected—about 50 yards below the house—by a stately stone wall. In the center of the wall there is a wide set of stone steps and at either end of the wall there is a granite bust. I never thought to ask of whom. Looking closely, I failed to recognize the person depicted. Probably a McCoshim kin. The bottom section of the lawn, twice as long as the upper section, ends at the banks of the River Tay itself, reputed to be one of Scotland's longest and one of Europe's most productive salmon rivers. The record British salmon, a monster of 64 pounds, was caught on the river Tay in 1922.

First fishing.

When I arrive at the water's edge—I didn't wear my waders—I saw some dainty slapping-type rises in the smooth runs on the far side. They look to me like dace or minnows, but Colin later assured me that they were indeed trout. The river here is about 50 yards wide with heavy rapids to the left and smooth, braided water up to the right. There is a deep, placid pool tucked under some giant trees just to my right. The bank is strewn with gray-black, smooth rocks of assorted sizes. It drops off quickly and sharply to a depth of four or five feet. To the left and right of where the lawn meets the river there are incredibly big trees growing right down to the water's edge. Because of the trees, from where I stand, it is almost impossible to make a proper cast. Even roll casts were difficult. Of course, the few fish I see dimpling on the far side—as noted—are well beyond the reach of even my best roll cast.

The large pool to my right, the one tucked under those big trees, looks promising but it is so well bunkered by overhanging limbs that getting a fly in there seems nearly impossible. Beyond this, about 40 yards upriver, I see a narrow, green iron bridge. It starts just in front of the antique shop on the other side of the river and ends just below the "war monument" that marks the boundary of the village of Strathtay, which itself is just below the gated entrance to Dun-an-Choille.

The river above the bridge is filled with a boiling expanse of white water. It is staked out there and below the bridge with what look like the slender red-and-white poles used to define a slalom run. I later learn that the poles actually define a kayak run through the rapids.

I fished for an hour or so as best I could but with no success. That was no surprise because there is always that first get-acquainted encounter with a new river. It is like chatting up a woman at a bar. Hello, how are you, where are you from, where are you going? So I sat down on one of the larger rocks to begin the chatting-up ritual.

While gazing at the water, I spied something small, round and white lolling in the water between two softball-sized rocks near shore. Turned out it was a golf ball, a Titleist 4. Seems there's a golf course not far upstream, no surprise, this is, after all, Scotland and according to McCoshim, he harvests, oh, "at least a dozen balls" along the river's edge every year.

I put the ball in my pocket and today it perches proudly on a block of highly polished walnut on my mantelpiece, a tiny brass plaque affixed thereto proclaims, "Taken on the River Tay, Scotland, September 1994."

Around 7 P.M. a kayaker appeared on the river in the twilight, and, back paddling, he positioned himself in a broad, flat tongue of water below the upper rapids, then released and shot through the rapids below winding his way between the slalom poles. A hawk flew a lazy semicircle overhead. As I was re-climbing the lawn to the cottage, a doe and her two fawns minced along the wall above the river and disappeared into the stand of evergreens.

Betty had masterfully started a fire in the stove. She had found a classical music station on the radio and had positioned a bottle of Scotch on the kitchen table beside a glass and a tall bottle of sparkling spring water, namely, "Britannia Elderflower Sparkling Spring Water." Since there was no Scotsman around to give me a reproachful glance, I fetched a couple of ice cubes from the fridge, dropped them into the glass and poured thereupon a generous helping of Scotch. I finished it off—tell not a Scotsman!—with a splash of the spring water. I went in to join Betty on the couch, sat down and sipped the Scotch. It tasted sickeningly sweet. Vile, in fact. Then, in a stroke of brilliant surmise, I realized that "Elderflower" was the *flavor* and not, as I had thought when I bought it, the *brand.* Thus my Elderflower enhanced Scotch ended up in the sink instead of the stomach.

I leaned back on the couch with another Scotch sans Elderflower water and thought, aha, now, at last, after eating and drinking our way up the spine of the United Kingdom, at last, at last, my days of salmon fishing had came.

Fishing days.

I had written ahead to Bob McCoshim to ask about the fishing thereabouts. Here's his reply: "September is rather past the best of the trout but is about the peak for the end of the summer salmon run. You can fish for trout at the foot of our garden, and I am told there are plenty of fish in the river, the constant trouble appears, however, to be to get one of them on your hook."

As I have said, our cottage was only seven miles from Pitlochry, which lies in the Tummel Valley in the northeastern corner of Perthshire, a district dominated by the River Tay, which runs a 120 mile course to the sea. Along the way it is fed by a number of lochs (lakes), namely Rannoch, Tummel, Ericht, Isla, Lyon, Braan and Almond.

Most of these are artificial lakes formed when a vast hydroelectric power system was built in the Highlands. All of these lochs are stocked with trout.

The main attraction near Pitlochary is the Hydroelectric Power Station with its salmon ladder, an arrangement of ascending pools, which enable the salmon between April and October to move upstream to their spawning grounds. The ladder consists of 34 pools, three of which are resting pools. They rise in succession to the level of the impoundment, Loch Faskally, which was formed when the Tummel valley was dammed. It is the last of the dams to be built in the hydro scheme and a major power station lies at its base. There is a fish observation room with windows looking into the ladder itself. This gives visitors an up-close aquarium view of the ascending salmon. It is said that around 5,400 salmon ascend this ladder each year.

The impoundment, Loch Faskally, is approximately two miles long, and about 800 yards wide at its narrowest point. Its shores consist of steep cliffs and heavily wooded hills which make shore fishing difficult or at best impossible.

According to the guide books, Faskally holds a plentiful population of brown trout and the native fish are supplemented by annual stockings of one- to five-pounders. McCoshim says 7-pounders are caught every year. Records show that in 2001, 54 salmon were caught in the lake. The best being a fish of 14.5 pounds. However, salmon up to 28 pounds have also been caught in other years. On the lake, trolling is the most common method and the best lures are a Copper Tom or a Black-and-Gold Toby.

The morning of my rendezvous at Mitchell's, I woke early, drank a cup of coffee and Betty drove me to Pitlochry where I was to meet my ghillie, Andy Gray.

We pulled up in front of Mitchell's behind an ancient faded green Land Rover with a tan canvas top. In it sat, Andy Gray, his legs hanging out of the front door. Gray was a rotund chap of I'd say 36 or so. He had dark, thick curly hair poking out beneath a tweed cap pulled down to his ears. His full, black beard was neatly trimmed. He wore a buttoned-up Harris Tweed coat belted in the back, a white shirt, black tie, woolen knickers, high argyle socks and brown, Vibram-soled brogans.

"Well, ya ready ta meet the river, Mr. Quigley?" he said.

"Ready," said I.

"Well then let's put your gear in me truck and be on our way."

We stopped down the road for petrol and because the tank is under the front seat, I had to get out while Andy filled it. Good thing because having gotten out of the truck, it was easier for me to reach for my wallet. You see, Andy indicated that it was the custom for the client to pay for the petrol. He must have drained the tank the night before and driven into Pitlochry on fumes because toppin' up the tank took quite awhile.

We pulled out to the petrol station and rattled out of Pitlochry, climbing into the highlands and down again toward Kirkmichael in the vicinity of the River Shee. The Shee Water, the head waters of the river Ericht and a tributary of the Tay, according to the guide book, *"provides exciting, salmon fishing, where sport can be expected to come thick and fast. the fishing begins in June improving as the grilse arrive through the season."*

Our destination was the Shee, which I believe is locally known as the Black Water. On the way we encountered an old woman with a shepherd's staff who waved and blocked the road. Andy slowed and pulled up beside her, leaned out and said, "Hello." She smiled and said, "Careful now, lads. Got me lamb's in th' road oop ahead." "Just a minute now." At that, over the crown in the road came a man with a border collie and a dozen sheep. The dog was zigzagging behind the sheep, his shoulders hunched, his head down, ears up, eyes alert. He formed them into single-file and guided them around Andy's truck. Then with a wave the woman sent us on our way north to the Black Water near a place called the Spittal of Glenshee.

The day was hot and bright, unusual to say the least for this country and this time of year." Hasn't rained in weeks," said Andy. "But the Black Water appears to me to be running well, wet and happy, deep and dark as ever."

We pulled up to a wooden gate in front of a farm house. Andy got out and came around to my side of the truck. "I'll be needin' £20 to pay the rent."

"Pay the rent?"

"Gotta pay the Campbell's rent for treading on their land and fishin' the water runs through it."

I dug out a £20 note and Andy went through the gate to turn it over to Mrs. Campbell.

Then Andy pulled the truck off the main road and drove it down a bumpy path toward the water. Although the morning was rushing toward afternoon, it was still a bit chilly when we stopped near the river. Andy swung out from behind the wheel and went to the back of the truck, pulled open the hatch, and dug out what he called "a flask," really a conventional one-quart thermos bottle filled with well-creamed coffee. He poured some into the thermos cap, rubbed his hands and took a sip.

For the occasion, I had brought along a real sterling silver flask (Scottish made by Grant's of Dalvey). I had filled it with Jack Daniels. It seemed a wise thing to do considering the morning chill.

"Andy," I said, "would you like a tot of this in your coffee, or beside it?"

"Don't mind if I do. What's that ya got inner?" he said.

"American whiskey. Tennessee whiskey. One of the best, Jack Daniels," and I handed him the flask.

He pursed his lips stroked his beard and poured a generous amount directly into his creamed coffee. And took a swig.

"Ah," he said, smacking his lips, "she stands oop well to me caffee. And that's what it's good for, American whiskey, good for nothin' but fur pourin' inta hoot caffee with plenny a cream, but ah, ah got ta tell ya th' truth, wuldna wanna drink it neat."

Thus I learned that here in this ancient land famous for its Scotch, poor Jack from Tennessee is a nothing but a pauper. Good only for spiking well-creamed coffee.

I had, the night before, picked up four bottles of Sweatheart Stout from among the dazzling array displayed in the floor-to-ceiling refrigerator at the Westlands. Being completely unfamiliar with the myriad brands, I had made my choice by the attractiveness of the label, and the one that caught my eye was emblazoned with a beautiful and bosomy smiling blonde, not unlike the St. Pauli Girl label.

That afternoon, when we stopped to dig into our lunch bags, I revealed my stash of stout and offered one to Andy. He smiled patronizingly, reached for the bottle and held it up to the sun. "Ah, good choice ... that is, if me grandmother were here with us. Yes, sur, Sweetheart Stout. We always keeps a bottle or two in the cupboard for the grandmothers to drink at our family gatherings." He gently set the bottle down. "No thanks, got me own."

A second rebuff. But that's when I discovered, all deference to Andy, how sweet the Sweetheart really was. Phew! Virtually undrinkable. Thus, after an introductory sip, I poured the rest of the bottle out on the ground.

"Now, now, I don't mind ya passin' that stuff through ya gut and pissin' it out on th' ground, but I do mind ya pourin' it on the ground outta th' bottle so near ta th' water. God, I hope it don't get inta the Black Water and kill th' fish."

Perhaps the Sweetheart did leak into the river and put the fish off their feed. Because I caught nothing all morning—or what was left of the morning by the time we started fishing.

After lunch we returned to the riverr for another try.

Standing on the grassy bank, I made a roll cast with my ten-foot Powell Legacy Light and landed the fly slightly downstream four inches from the bank on the other side. Not much of a casting feat because the stream was not much wider than a two-lane road.

"Ah, Mr. Quigley, ya gotta keep your cast not beyond th' center o' th' stream. Can't fish that t'other side."

"What? The center?"

"It's true. We paid the Campbells to fish this side only. It's the rules ya know."

"£20 pounds for half the river?"

"It's the rules."

After what seemed like hundreds of half-stream casts, I felt a tap and caught a parr (a young salmon of about 4 inches long).

"Well lock a' that," said Andy standing at my shoulder. "Lemma have a look a' that." He held it in his palm and looked down on it wistfully. "Ah, they look like broaches, they do. Like ya can pin 'me on your collar." He threw the brooch unceremoniously back into the water.

Just then, below us, a great, bright salmon leaped completely out of the water—a 15-pounder. My heart stopped.

"Andy! Andy! Did you see that?"

"I did."

"And he's in the center of the stream, right?"

"Right, you are."

I immediately lengthened my cast and put my Garry Dog, one of the flies recommended and sold to me by Nick, just upstream of where the fish leaped. I did that, I'd say, forty or fifty times, drifting it down and swinging it across the exact spot where the salmon broke water. Nothing happened except that at regular intervals the salmon—or perhaps others like him—would leap clear of the water, stopping my heart each time. But he—or the others, if there were others—never took the fly.

Andy went back to the truck and got a crab about as big as his hand and dyed as red as a cooked lobster. "Gimme your fly," he said. He embedded the hook of the Garry Dog deeply into the belly of the crab and handed it back to me. "Flip 'er out there and let 'er drift well below the fish, just flip 'er out en drift 'er down. Let out the line. When I tell ya, pull it back through the pool fast as ya cin. Overhand."

"But, Andy, is this legal?"

"Legal? Just do as I say if ya wanna catch that salmon."

In general, "fly only" is the rule in "sea trout only" waters. But once permission is obtained, the average water is virtually without restriction. Even worm fishing is tolerated and practiced in many places. So I'm told.

I flipped the red crab out and across the stream and drifted it way down into the broken water below the pool. Way down. When Andy whispered "Now!" I placed the rod under my right arm, and using both hands, I ripped the line back overhand through the guides and right up through the fish's lie. In between my drifts and frantic retrieves the salmon continued periodically to leap out of the water, obviously undisturbed by the passage of the jet-propelled crab.

Andy went back again to the truck and dug out what looked like one of the wooden plugs we use to fish for muskellunge in New York's Thousand Islands area. It was a yellow and green tiger-striped, torpedo-shaped six-inch-long hunk of wood jointed in the middle with treble hooks dangling fore and aft. "Gimme your fly." He removed the Garry Dog from the belly of the crimson crab and tied on the musky plug. "Now do the same. Flip 'er out, drift er down, way down, and bring er back fast as ya cin, overhand."

I did as he instructed, again and again, with the same result. Again and again at regular intervals that salmon leaped clear of the water, but never so much as looked at the plug.

"Ah, now I know, now I know what ay forgot," he said. "Nick put that bloody can of worms by the back door and I forgot to pick 'em oop."

"Worms?"

"Sometimes in desperate situations ya moost, even a gentleman moost, what dew ya say, 'improvise.' Too bad I forgot that bloody can 'o worms."

At twilight, still fishless, we drove back to the cottage. "See ya early in the mornin', early now. Seven. On the button. G'night."

I checked in with Betty, dropped my gear in the doorway and walked down to John Taylor's grocery.

"John," I said, "I've been fishing today and will be fishing tomorrow with Andy Gray as my ghillie. Now I'd like to take along a bottle of whiskey. Something that Andy would enjoy. Something he'd appreciate being a Scotsman and all. He didn't take kindly today to my Jack Daniels. So what would you suggest?"

"Ah, he wuldna like American whiskey. What ya need is a bottle o' The Macallan. And if you've a mind to splurge, take the eighteen-year-old. A sip o' that and I'm sure as the sun does rise in the mornin' Mr. Gray'll git ya a right big salmon."

Back at the cottage, I drained the Jack Daniels from the flask back into its bottle and after rinsing out the flask, I carefully filled it with the 18-year-old Macallan—the price of which was so obscene that I dare not quote it.

The next morning was a repeat of the first. Early and chilly.

But this time we headed for the river Tay, to the Junction Pool where the Lyon meets the Tay below Taymouth Castle and The Point, a stretch of river controlled by the Kenmore Hotel, established in 1542.

We had to check in at the desk and pay the required rent for our assigned beat. I noticed as we entered the hotel that they had a logbook on a tall pedestal by the front door. In it was a list of *every salmon caught*—date, angler, fly, length and weight—on the Kenmore water going back—hold onto your hat!—to the 1500s. If anything, the Scots are as serious about their salmon as they are about their Scotch.

When we pulled up beside the water, Mr. Gray again pulled out his thermos and I repeated yesterday's offer: "Want a tot of this beside or in your coffee?" To which he replied, as he had the morning before, "Don't mind if I do."

As before Mr. Gray poured a generous portion from the lips of the flask into his well-creamed coffee.

"Well here's to ya, Mr. Quigley, and may we have better luck today. " He raised the thermos cap to his lips and took a gulp. But he didn't swallow. Instead he ballooned his cheeks like great round plums, like Louis Armstrong trumpeting a high note, and rolled the liquid once around … then, with a great flushing sound, spit it out onto the dirt behind his truck.

"My god, man, why in the world wuld ya do a trick like that? Why would ya make me—trick me ya did—inta pourin' a precious draught of, ah, 18-year-old Macallan, inta me coffee?" He rubbed his lips vigorously with the back of his hand, poured out the remainder of the coffee in the thermos cap and wiped it clean with his handkerchief.

Now, I am here to tell you, if there ever was, if ever there was living, breathing proof that Scotsmen know their whiskey, this was surely it. Unless, of course, that weasel John Taylor told him—but if he had, Andy would have taken the drink beside his coffee, neat, not *in* it. I had, just like yesterday, given him the choice. No, the only way he knew—the brand and age, by God, of that whiskey diluted in the sweet depths of his well-creamed and sugared coffee—the only way, by God, he knew was by taste.

"Andy, I'd offer you a cigar, a Cuban, of course, purchased at Dunhill's in retribution for my 'trick', but after that display of educated taste, I fear you'd reject even the best handmade Cuban if it weren't the size, age, and brand that matched your finicky fancy."

"Ah, well, ya might try me. The Cohibas I do prefer, Robustos. I'd compromise, you know. But, first, if ya'd give me a splash o' that precious liquid in your flask—ta refresh me palate, you know, then all will be forgotten and forgiven."

The particular Kenmore beat, which we'd rented for the day, gave us access to a wide section of the river with deep pools on the far side and a smooth dogleg of water below that swirled and slowed into a large, deep pool just below the ninth green.

We had parked Andy's Land Rover beside a sign that read: "ACCESS FOR GOLFERS AND SALMON FISHERMEN ONLY" with an arrow pointing left. Below that sign was another: RESTAURANT AND BAR. Its arrow pointed to the right.

When I was on the Kenmore beat, the water was low due to the lack of rain. But it was nonetheless swift, thigh-deep, and relatively easy to wade. Andy had brought his fifteen-foot two-handed spey rod for me to try.

Now spey casting involves what I think is a rather intricate motion wherein the line is raised into the air with a vigorous forward roll cast and then swung to the right and back around to the left, then wrapped forward forming a figure eight with the line in the air. This motion loads the long rod, and, if one's timing is right, shoots out a stupendous amount of line on the forward cast. Remember the rod is fifteen-feet long to begin with. It is, therefore, a distance-casting maneuver that, in my view, takes a considerable amount of practice to master. I recall that I managed to get it to work about one out of three tries.

Andy had recommended a sinking tip line and I was using hair wing flies tied for me especially for this trip by the late Paul Morrissey of Bridgeport, Connecticut. The patterns were the traditional ones such as Thunder & Lightening, Munro Killer and Blue Charm—tied low-water-style on smaller-sized black double hooks. With Andy's two-handed spey rod and the spey casting technique, I was able to cast the flies far across the stream and drift them through the water on the edge of the pools on the far side. Those casts were three times as far as my best one-handed casts—even with my 10 foot Powell.

After working the water for awhile, we walked up a knoll, stood on the fringe of the ninth green, and looked down into the large pool at the end of our beat. The pool was about twenty five yards across and twenty yards long. It was like a bowl and was deepest, say ten feet, in its middle. The sun was straight overhead. As we looked down we could see twelve long, dark forms suspended near the bottom of the pool. Each was as big as a big man's leg. Andy said they were twelve- to fifteen-pound salmon.

They were resting in that pool waiting for a spate, a rain storm to raise the water so they could more easily ascent the rapids above the pool.

I fished the pool with the spey rod and had no trouble getting the flies over the salmon when I got the cast right. But not a one of them moved to the fly. None responded to either Morrissey's artfully tied hair wings, or the sinister provocations of the heron-winged Undertaker, which Andy had given me to try. Presumably, in these particularly refined surroundings, it would not be proper to try the tomato-colored crab. Or musky plug. Or worms. Or hand grenades. None of the above was listed beside the entry of a caught salmon in the Kenmore's venerable logbook.

That night, our last, Andy invited me to join him for a drink at the Westland's. I said I would but on one condition. Without ceremony I handed him a pasteboard box. It contained my condition. He was to wear the contents of the box that night to our rendezvous at the Westland's.

He took the box warily and opened it. Inside, wrapped in tissue paper, was a brand-new Lands' End turtle neck with alternating horizontal stripes of chartreuse, white and canary yellow. His reaction to my gift was much the same as had been his reaction to the Macallan in his coffee.

He drew back and looked at me with bewilderment, "Ah, no, now. Ya don' mean it? I culdna wear a thin' like that to th' bar. Why me friends would laugh me oot the door."

"Do you mean you are not man enough to wear this, this heartfelt gift?"

"Ah you are a man of tricks you are Mr. Quigley. But since you'll be buying the drinks, I'll make an exception and play the game."

That night, beneath my hounds-tooth-checked Burberry sport coat, I wore the identical twin to his new turtleneck. He arrived wearing his under his brown Harris Tweed jacket with all the front buttons buttoned up tightly all the way to his neck. Only a circlet of the green, white and yellow showed under the folds of his chin like a priest's Roman collar. His cap was pulled down onto his forehead. (Later in the evening, with beads of perspiration glistening on his face, and dripping off the tip of his nose, he was forced to take off his jacket. Standing there in that turtleneck, he looked like a man-sized replica of that yellow- and green-striped musky plug we were playing with on the Black Water. The patrons pretended that they could not tell us apart.

On the way into the bar I had noticed three lads sitting on a bench at the entrance. Hair combed, clean white shirts, pressed pants and polished shoes. They looked to me like caddies, sixteen years' old.

In the bar I asked Andy, "Those 'caddies.' What's that all about? What are they doing out there?"

"Why you're in Scotland, Mr. Quigley. Those boys are there to carry home those among the patrons of the bar who might drink too much ta walk ta home without stumblin' inta a ditch. Ya might say they are insurance. And, ya might say, it's a highland tradition."

To start off the night and as I remember throughout the night, I splurged on "dooble" 18-year-old Macallan's. One for Mr. Gray and one for me. Then another round, the same. We were smoking Dunhill's cabinet select Chruchills.

I cannot seem to recall whether or not I employed the services of one of those barroom caddies to escort me home. Fact is, I cannot remember how or when I got back to McCoshim's cottage.

Journey home.

I had come all that way to fish the River Tay. Now, quick as the fishing began, or so it seemed, it was over. Now it was time to track back to London. More penance for the indulgence of a few days fishing. But this time we decided, instead of driving all the way to Edinburgh (74 miles), to turn the rental car in at Perth (a town about 24 miles away) and catch the train from there back to London, So we bought our one-way Edinburgh-to-London tickets at the train station in Pitlochry and headed for Perth.

With a map and directions courtesy of Bob McCoshim, we took the M6 bypass and arrived in plenty of time for the 9:55 A.M. train. We arrived there (not much traffic on Saturday) before the Eurocar establishment opened. To kill time we went to the Station Hotel for breakfast. The hotel was a fading beauty but the breakfast was a banquet of streaky bacon, eggs, croissants, fruit, orange juice and pungent coffee.

After breakfast, we went back to the Eurocar office and sat there for fifteen minutes until it opened and then checked the car in with no trouble and no waiting. The Eurocar lady drove us back to the station (it was only about three minutes away.)

We mistakenly thought the train would have a dining car and be rather elegant. Not so. Nice train but it had only an Amtrak-like snack bar with a long queue—actually stretching the whole length of the car. While waiting in the queue to purchase some cider, and a sandwich, the train, the Highland Chieftain, unexpectedly lurched forward. The woman standing ahead of me was thrown head first into a cardboard box stowed beside the aisle. As another woman helped her out of the box, she said, "Oh, would you know this here's like being on a runaway train." "Oh," says the other woman, "you've got to live dangerously." "Maybe true," replied the box lady, "but do ah have ta die dangerously?"

The man across the aisle, a Cornwall man in a Panama hat, obviously knew that there were no dining facilities on the train, so like many of the other passengers, he had packed his own lunch rolled up in a newspaper. He had two cans of McEwen's and sympathizing with my state of unpreparedness, offered me one. I accepted.

His name was William Lovelady, a classical guitarist who had just finished a gig at Atholl Blair Castle. The affair was held on the castle lawn where they danced in kilts and drank copious amounts of Scotch. Presiding over the affair, he told us, was a fiftyish incredibly wealthy Scots banker by the name of Sir Ian Moncreiffe of that Ilk. Yes, " of that Ilk." Moncreiffe was a captain in the Atholl Highlanders, the last remaining private army in Europe. According to Lovelady, he has named each of his sons after birds of prey—there is Peregrine, Merlin, Hawk and Falcon. He has his suits made, Lovelady revealed, on Southhampton Street in London and he had his shirt maker add customized frayed cuffs to convince his American friends and business associates of his Scottish frugality.

We arrived in London on time and overnighted at Heathrow's Excelsior Hotel. The next morning boarded the Hooghly Express in reverse to Philadelphia.

Since you have taken this trip with me, and I know were mainly interested in the fishing, you will have noticed that, yes, it *is* true, I was *skunked* in Scotland.

All I have to show for this long epicurean journey and my piscatorial efforts in the Scottish Highlands is that Titleist golf ball, the one that, as I said, is mounted on a walnut pedestal sitting on my mantelpiece. Well, no, not "all." The getting there part, that arduous journey of a thousand meals, not only increased the size of my waist, not to mention my liver, but, most importantly, deposited quite a bit of capital into my payback account, which in the future, would be used to barter for other, hopefully more productive, and much less expensive, fishing expeditions.

18

From The Kettle Creek Chronicles:

GOD'S COUNTRY

Let me begin by introducing you to what some have called "one of the most scenic valleys in all of Pennsylvania" and one of the rivers that runs through it: Kettle Creek.

Named after Black Kettle, an Indian who once lived on its upper reaches, Kettle Creek begins its fifty mile journey south from high on the slopes of Cedar Mountain (alt. 2,500 feet) just to the west of the famous Pine Creek Gorge in Tioga County to a rendezvous with the West Branch of the Susquehanna River near Westport. Its journey takes it through Pennsylvania's North Woods, "a wild, dark land populated by more animals than humans; home to the whitetail deer, black bear, wild turkey, ruffed grouse and mysterious raven, The Forbidden Land,[1] as it was known to the Indian tribes, or the Black Forest as it was called by the Germans who settled there after the Indians were gone." [2]

Up until the 1920s, some say well into the '50s, Kettle Creek was counted among the best Brook trout streams in the United States. President Grant, not to mention other rich and famous sportsmen, fished here. Today browns and rainbows make up most of the creek's aquatic population. Wild brookies still swim in its tributaries.

---

1. This book is now out-of-print. Amazon.com lists the following: **Forbidden land, 1614-1895 (His Strange Events in the Black Forest** (Unknown Binding) 1971, by Robert Ray Lyman.
2. Mike Sajna, **Pennsylvania Trout & Salmon Fishing Guide**, Frank Amato Publications, Portland, OR, 1988.

Although it's not like it was in the past, there's still plenty of good trout fishing hereabouts. For example, there's a long stretch of fly-fishing-only water on Cross Fork Creek, a Kettle tributary. And a 3-mile-catch-and-release section just south of Ole Bull State Park—plus some nice water in the park itself.

Kettle runs through the middle of the vast Susquehannock State Forest, where, on the graphic of the topo map in my Garmin GPS, I see nothing but hollows and trails. Listen to their names: Coon Hollow, Lick Hollow, Rhinehimmer Hollow, Dead Horse Hollow, Turtle Hollow, Poplar Hollow, Blacksmith Hollow, Big Darn Hollow, Calamity, Stout, Tin Can, Bobsled, Pine Stump, Elk, Bank Shanty, Manning, Merriman, Black Stump. Butternut, Railroad.

And the trails: Leib Run Trail, Pfoutz Valley Trail, Darling Run Trail, Gravel Lick Trail, Brooks Trail, Klondike Ridge Trail, Donut Hole Trail, Rattlesnake Trail, Black Forest Trail, Big Darn Hollow Trail.

Whew! Seems to me the Forbidden Land was well-trekked and remains every bit as bumpy as the road to hell itself.

Yes, sir, we're talking about being up here in Potter County, Pennsylvania, in October. Up here amid all the crayola-colored leaves you'd ever want to see in what's called "God's Country." My buddy and I drive up from just outside Philly, heading due north until we pick up route 144, go through Lock Haven (home of Lock Haven State College), through South Renovo (area equals two-tenths of a mile, population 557, foreign-born 0, population growth - 14 percent), then through Renovo itself (population 1,255; famous for its railroad repair shops—hence the name "re-new"), and Tamarack (famous for its swamp) and Cross Fork (population 111), on up to and through, up and up some more to a little spot on the map called Germania just below a little bigger spot called Galeton. We're not far from the New York State border. We'll stay up here the whole weekend. We call it "the whole weekend" because we make it last from Friday noon 'til Tuesday morn. Driving time, four hours or so, included.

We were lucky this time. Ran into a couple of back-to-back Indian summer days. That's rare up here in the mountains this time of year. Mostly, in our experience, you'd expect to find gray, chilly, rainy days and long, cold nights.

From The Kettle Creek Chronicles: GOD'S COUNTRY 165

One year we spent a whole week on our bellies in tents up there near Germania. It was also the month of October. We had come up to bow hunt deer and fly fish for trout. Especially those tasty frying-pan sized brookies swimming in Little Kettle, which runs just below our usual campsite. The creek was too high to fish and the rain too hard to go bow hunt, so, as I said, we spent most of the time belly-down in our tents. Oh, except when we made a beer run into Cross Fork, a cluster of dilapidated buildings huddled just across from the bridge where Cross Fork Creek flows into Kettle Creek—a two-pump Gulf station with a tiny restaurant attached, a bait and tackle shop, a 4-unit motel, and a beer joint with a big horseshoe bar, four pool tables and a Juke box.

Again, except for a couple of these excursions into Cross Fork, and when we left the tent to answer nature's call, we just lay on our bellies and listened to the gurgling of the creek and the unceasing patter of the rain. We did all of our cooking on a Coleman stove in one of the tent's vestibules.

But over the years, I have wised up, or grown soft, definitely older. Probably all three. So, this particular year, I told my buddy that he could rough it all he wanted to. I wasn't going all the way up to our usual campsite near Germania. I was going to stay down here, by God, indoors at one of those Bed and Breakfast places. I was going to be warm, and dry and comfortable throughout those frosty nights and especially during that bitter hour, that coldest hour of the day, just before dawn. Hate that.

So, my buddy dropped me off at Ted and Sally's B & B, and went back down the road to set himself up at Ole Bull State Park[3].

---

3. The words "ole" (even with the accent missing) and "bull" conjure images of bull fighting. Bull fighting? Here in the middle of Susquehannock State Forest, not likely. But almost as unlikely, this park is named for Ole Bornemann Bull, a Norwegian child prodigy who began playing the violin at age five. By 1828 he was conductor of Norway's Musical Lyceum and for the rest of his life toured Europe and America, earning praise from such famous contemporary musicians as Liszt, Schumann, and Mendelssohn, and from writers such as George Sand, William Thackeray, Mark Twain and Henrik Ibsen. The Potter County connection? Curiously enough in 1852 he chose Oleana, Pennsylvania, for the site of a Norwegian immigrant colony. Ole!

Curiously, I was the only guest in this rambling, white-sided farm house. $37.00/night American. It was run by Sally Otis and her husband, Ted, whose most striking characteristic was his beard. (I'll get back to Sally later.)

Now this was a beard of geologic age and prodigious proportions—meaning that he looks like he has just tried to swallow, head-first, a world-record octogenarian tailless raccoon. It stuck half in and half out of what you can only imagine to be his mouth, where ever the hell it might be …'cause you sure could not tell from looking. Of course, you had to assume that he had a mouth—it's true, teeth seem to disappear in these parts, but not mouths. Fact is, although there was no beyond-a-shadow-of-a-doubt visual evidence of his having a mouth, he could and did talk. Very seldom though.

When he did talk, no surprise, the words came out like words spoken by a man with a gag in his mouth. Turns out a person didn't need to talk much around Sally. She did most of the talking.

My buddy, Steve Alexander, drives up from Florida twice a year for our Potter County mountain-man rendezvous. Once in May and again in October. Now as I said, he likes to "rough it." But being a man of considerable means, not to mention years of outdoor experience, rough isn't what it used to be. He's got all the very latest cushy camping gear. Dual-fuel stoves, 'lectric lanterns, folding chairs and tables and a big sky-blue geodesic tent with a folding floor—you can actually stand up in it!—a heater stove, a spacious vestibule. Spread up over it all, he's got this arched nylon roof that makes his campsite look like an architect's model of the Denver airport. A far cry from the days we camped in the woods up there on Little Kettle.

But, after setting up all his portable-comfort camping gear in that $12-a-night space in Ole Bull State Park, he has second thoughts. He pulls up his state-of-the-art graphite tent pegs and drives his trucks back up to join me at Ted & Sally's. He's getting as old and as soft as I am.

That's when we discovered that Ted & Sally's was some sort of Christian retreat, as in Baptist, no smoking, no drinking, A capital E "evangelical" B & B. In other words, a smoke-free, alcohol-free, drug-free and cuss-free B & B.

To make matters worse, you must take your shoes off at the back door. There's a sign there. It says so. That's because, my best guess, besides the usual mud, they have three dogs who poop all over the yard and that stuff gets squeegeed up in those Vibram soles that all sports like us wear these days. Naturally she didn't want us tracking mud and dog poop all through the house.

Right inside the back door was a "Rules of The House" sign printed on two sheets of legal-sized paper taped side by side. Twelve-point type outlined and bullet-pointed. Inside were more computer-generated signs with dingbat borders. Three in the hallway alone. Like Tibetan prayer flags, all were not there to promulgate the rules of the house. Many contained Bible quotations. Like a Church-basement Sunday school.

In my bedroom was a sign reminding guests of the strict prohibition against the use of alcohol <u>of any kind, any amount, for any reason</u>. Even specifically mentioned the ban on "non-alcoholic beer, " pointing out that such beverages contained at least one-percent alcohol.(Being the soft-spoken, accommodating fellow that I am, before my buddy got back, I poured my Listerine and Bay Rum aftershave into the little creek beside the driveway.)

One bullet point in the Rules referred to the use of prescription medications. They could not be used unless first inspected and approved by Sally herself. But I ignored that one and smuggled in my supply of can't-be-without-it Prevacid.

Now take note of that "breakfast" part of "Bed & Breakfast." It means what it says, *breakfast* only. No supper. No snacks. And in spite of the fact that we were the only two guests, no matter how we tried to butter up Sally ("What's a sweet little lady like you doing up here in the woods?") and Ted ("Damn, Ted, I always wanted a beard like that! How long did it take you to grow it? Bet you can't go out back during small game season, heh, heh.") Yes, no matter how much of our city-boy charm we sprayed around, hell, we even offered extra under-the-table money and said that we'd cook ourselves and clean up afterwards and share leftovers with them. Said we had some really thick New York strip steaks in the truck. Plenty for four, with enough left over for the dogs. Well, the answer was still NO.("Don't nobody but me set foot, much less cook, in my kitchen, and that's that boys.")

Sally always stood akimbo when making such pronouncements. She was a reasonably pretty woman, about 50 with a shapely full figure enhanced by tight jeans and revealed by a blouse with straining buttons. Saturday morning for breakfast—served in the dining room—she cooked a batch of bacon, sunny-side-up eggs, sausage links, home fries, buttered toast with homemade rhubarb and strawberry jam, orange juice and all the coffee we could drink.

That night, although we had plenty of high-end grub in the truck, we drove down to Cross Fork to have supper at the beer joint. (A Maalox moment.)

Now that was always interesting. This Saturday night they were having a dance and the characters that came looked like the extras in that bar scene from the original *Star Wars* movie. In particular I remember these two girls showed up holding hands. They danced with each other all night, slow dance, fast dance. Hell, on second thought, maybe they were guys.

Sunday and Monday night we went back to the camp grounds to cook our dinner in the early, frosty evening. ("Naw, you cain't use my grill, listen how the dogs would bark—'sides ain't got no charcoal. Naw, you cain't build a fire neither, land a Goshen' no way. I don't want nobody, I mean nobody, setting up a grill and cooking dinner on one of them propane stoves in my driveway!")

That's right, to cook dinner, and smoke Marlboros and Montecristos and to sip our booze, we had to trundle down to the campgrounds. Then after swallowing a handful of Certs, we'd wobble back up to Sally's, take off our shoes and shuffle into the den to watch satellite TV. From the den we could see Sally and Ted propped up in their twin Lazyboy recliners like a couple of mannequins intently, but expressionlessly, watching Smackdown wrestling shows on another TV in their private nook just off the kitchen. On such occasions Sally would dress more casually in a Smackdown T-shirt, Nike warm-ups and pink-rabbit slippers. They ate hot, buttered popcorn and drank orange Kool-Aid.

Sally said it was a "wonderment." Why is it right now, during the bow hunting season and with trout on their spawning beds in Kettle Creek, yes, indeed, it was a wonderment, she said, that they "ain't got" no guests. 'Cept us, of course.

"By golly ding," said Sally, "mystery to me. We got bigger rooms, cleaner by a long sight, too, and a living room, dining room, and a big TV in the den, and, by golly, even got a game room with ping-pong table and all—why, *why* would you imagine them hunters and fishermen, why would they want to stay down Cross Fork ways at that motel, crost from that noisy bar, Lord only knows." Yeah, right Sally. The Lord and the Women's Christian Temperance Union, the Evangelical Society of North America, the Baptist Convention and the industrious little sign maker. They know.

Monday night Sally wandered into the guest's den to see if we were getting along alright. Didn't offer us any popcorn or Kool-Aid. Just sat down in a straight-back chair and next thing you know, in a moment of unguarded camaraderie, she launched into a nostalgic autobiography. Said she had not been as close to Christ and redemption as she is today. "No sirree, boys, you not gonna believe this but once upon a time I was the worst kinda sinner. My fist husband, a genuine skunk he was, beat me like a rug. Well, I divorced that no-good critter and spite I had four kids, well, I went wild. Acted just like a slut. I mean S-L-U-T. Spent 15 years like that 'fore I met Ted in there, 15 years carousin', why, twern't a night I wasn't drinkin.' I mean straight vodka right outta the bottle, straight, I mean that. And I was huggin' up to every guy I met. Got so bad, well, I hadda go to rehab, signed up for Weight Watchers, too. I did. Got myself straightened out, I did, and now I got faith. I've accepted the Lord God Jesus Christ into my heart. Never once-d, never once-d, have I looked back. Never once-d."

After she finished her spontaneous confession, she wiped her palms on the front of her dark blue Nike warm-ups, tugged at her sweat shirt and calmly went back into the kitchen to stir the rhubarb and strawberry jam bubbling on the stove.

Poor woman. Good woman. Now a saved woman. A mother. Grandmother. And, apparently, after those years of suckling a vodka bottle, a happily married woman. Got to respect that. And Ted, good old Ted, with that beard, he'll always have a way to amuse himself.

That's how it was at Ted and Sally's Bed and Breakfast. Didn't cramp our style though one bit. As I said we just bundled up, laced up our shoes at supper time and went down the road to the State campgrounds, built a fire, seared some thick steaks in hot butter or fried up some sirloin burgers, laid them out on burger buns, covered them with a slice of the best imported Swiss and smothered them with sautéed onions and ate them under that serene Indian summer sky strewn with welcoming stars.

Of course, we washed the victuals down with measured portions of a rather wide assortment of liquor—Dalwhinnie Scotch (me), Captain Morgan's rum and Coke Classic (Steve's drink), Budweiser (both), and a feisty little Italian red from the Francis Ford Coppola vineyards. Variety is the spice of life. After dinner we'd sit there smoking (me a Montecristo, and Steve a Marlboro) and watch the fire wane while sipping a vintage Taylor Fladgate Port and crunching on saltines spread with ripe Stilton.

By the way, since Steve had "checked out" of the State-run campgrounds, we were now, technically speaking, trespassers—camp site crashers. This meant we had to keep a sharp lookout for the park ranger. Steve said they always make the rounds at least once a night in a Jeep—looking for bears mostly, I'd suppose.

That introduced a scary thought because if the ranger had stopped by for a check and a chat, our goose would have been cooked. He would have discovered that we were (a) trespassing, (b) lighting a fire without a permit, (c) drinking (Good God almighty!) *alcoholic* beverages. Why there's not one soul in all of Christendom unaware of the prohibition on alcoholic beverages in state parks. (At least—last time I looked—they still do allow smoking in state parks.)

Tough law. But it exists in spite of the fact that the outdoors' experience, I'd say throughout all of North America, takes for granted the need for sportsmen to have a little booze nearby. Hell, I'm not sure it would be safe to go camping or fishing, let alone both, without each man having a fully loaded six pack of Budweiser at his elbow.

Had we been ranger-caught, let's see, the fine would have been, oh, I'd guess, something like—although seriously I have no experience whatsoever with this sort of thing—what would you say, something like $1,500 in lieu of spending the night in jail. Can they confiscate one's vehicle? Who knows? That would be a tragedy because Steve's got this brand-spanking-new cobalt-blue custom Dodge 3-door hemi stretch-cab pickup.

Oh, the fishing? Forgot to mention that. Well, we caught a couple of nice rainbows and some browns on Woolly Buggers and a few on dry flies. Pale Evening Duns and Blue Winged Olives as I recall. Steve fishes nothing but dry flies. Yeah, we caught enough trout to keep our interest up.

Know what, that old Kettle Creek is worth the trip. Sure is. Nothing special though. The fishing can be tough. But with all those autumn leaves falling and floating by, it sure is pretty up there.

Next year, however, I do intend to make one slight change. I'm going to scout up, let's say, a Methodist-run bed and breakfast—at least there, unlike in those run by the good-hearted Baptists, I might be able to cadge a dance with the inn keeper's daughter. Yeah, right ... with my luck she'll turn out to be the gal who brought the other gal to the Saturday night dance in Cross Fork.

"Hey, Steve, mind if I sleep on the drive back to Philly?"

19

THE LAST PLACE ON EARTH

Most of the fly fisher's experience with Brook trout has to do with catching small, frisky seven- and eight-inchers in small streams. The rap on brookies is that they are rather stupid, meaning easy to catch. Drop a fly on the water and if one is around, he'll take it.

Whether they are that easy to catch is debatable, but what's not debatable is the fact that brookies *are* much easier to catch than the more sagacious yellow-bellied browns. Or wary rainbows. But no one has said that they are not exuberant, and enthusiastic quarry. No one has ever said that they are not gorgeous. They look as if they were fashioned by Picasso's daughter for Tiffany's in cloisonné and onyx. Each one is a jewel.

Yes, beautiful but generally small. Hell, anything over twelve inches where I come from, Pennsylvania, is a trophy.

Case in point: Under the arch of a stone bridge at the mouth of an unpronounceable stream flowing into the Delaware below Lambertville, on a yellow caddis nymph, I once caught a fifteen-incher. Fifteen inches! Hell, I had it mounted.

That's because a fifteen-inch Brook trout caught in near northeastern waters is a trophy for sure. Fact is, in the past in the northeast, if you wanted to catch big, fat brookies, *real* trophies, you had to go all the way up to Maine, to the Rangeley Lakes region, and there you'd catch, maybe, a three- or four-pounder on a trolled Parmachene Belle.

Alas, those days are gone, perhaps, forever.

But there is a place, and they say it is the last place on earth, way up north in Atlantic Canada, north of Nova Scotia, north of the big island, Newfoundland, where, in the waters that first gave birth to the brookie and its relative the Arctic char, nearly every Brook trout caught is trophy-sized. That's right, they *average* five pounds.

Way up there, even today, this pristine breed of native brookie still swims—five, six, seven and eight—sometimes even ten—pound specimens. And these big boys take floating flies.

This place is sub-arctic Labrador, and it is, yes, truly the last place on earth where you can still catch giant Brook trout. I know. I have been there many times. To Jack Cooper's Minipi Camps.

Jack has exclusive fly-in rights to a vast uninhabited area on the famed Minipi watershed where, deep in that impenetrable black-spruce forest, he's built two log cabins, one on the shores of Anne Marie Lake, the other on the shores of Minonipi; and a third, a large prow-fronted Lindal cedar lodge on the shores of thirty-five-mile-long Minipi Lake.

Now "lake" is perhaps the wrong word because these waters are, technically speaking, rather shallow "river-lakes." Wide sand-bottomed rivers that have spread out above and below necks and narrows, outlets and inlets.

We fly to this land of river lakes from Philadelphia via Toronto and Halifax to Goose Bay, Labrador. From there we board a floatplane for the 45-minute flight into the wilderness lodge. An hour later we are stalking giant brookies in a bright red canoe looking for the telltale sign of rises. I should mention that landlocked Arctic char up to twelve pounds, and great northern pike up to twenty-five pounds also prowl these waters.

These giant brookies, unlike their northeastern cousins, are not so easily fooled. When it comes to hooking trophy-sized Labradorean brookies, it takes the right fly and often post-graduate distance casting skill plus well-honed marksmanship. These fish are cruising. So, when you see a rise, you have to be able to shoot *ahead* of the rise. Quickly. There's not a lot of time for air casting.

Besides that, unlike their down-east relatives, these big trout are not stupid. On the slicks, they can be extremely leader-shy. When feeding on the hatch *du jour*, they will refuse a sloppy presentation or a faulty imitation.

This, however, is not the case in the quick waters of the Minipi's outlets and inlets. Here you can blind cast out and across and catch what they call pan-sized specimens (and sometimes a three-pounder or two) on nearly every cast of a Muddler Minnow, an Elk Hair Caddis or a Deer-hair Mouse. There's a place like this below Minipi Lodge called "The Gorge" just below the outlet falls. But the fact is, Minipi guides do not "book" (that is, record your catch in the logbook) unless it weighs over three pounds. Smaller brookies simply do not count.

To catch the really big ones, you have to sight-fish the rises out on the lake. You have to stalk your Minipi trophies with skill, persistence and patience. It's not like rainbow fishing in Alaska. You will not catch Labrador's big boys until your elbow twinges, unless, of course, you are lucky enough to hit the peak of the Green and Brown Drake hatch in late June to middle-to-late July.

That's when, one year, Clint Kellog, a 93-year-old retired Boston lawyer, staggered into Anne Marie lodge. He was balanced and ballasted with a half gallon of hundred-proof vodka in one hand and a big plastic bag in the other.

He introduced himself: "You can call me Clint, as in Eastwood. And Kellogg as in cereal."

"Say Clint, what have you got in that bag?"

"Well, in this bag I have a week's supply of Metamucil. The very best you can buy. And in this hand I have a week's supply of vodka. The very best. Now, the former, that's to keep me regular. The latter, that's to keep me regularly drunk."

That evening after dinner—the best time to stalk the really big brookies—Ray Best, Anne Marie's chief guide, took one of the dining room chairs, and with the help of another guide, duct-taped a bed pillow to it. They carried the pillowed chair down to the dock and secured it in the prow of a boat with more duct tape. Then they helped Clint down to the boat, lifted him up onto the pillow and ran duct tape around his waist and legs to secure him to the chair. Then Ray took him solo to fish down river.

As luck would have it, that was where the Green Drakes were hatching.

In two hours of angling, amid one of the Minipi's legendary and incredibly prolific Green Drake hatches, Clint, who, from his sticky perch, could manage a cast of no more than twenty-five feet at best, caught 5 logbook brookies.

That night at dark when Clint wobbled through the cabin door, I asked him what luck he'd had.

Not pausing to sit down he said, "Got five. One, a male, five-and-a-quarter; a female, six-and-a-half; two more males right at five each; and a bright and beautiful seven-pounder. All on Green Drakes."

I've been going up to fish the Minipi for more than ten years now. My first year, raw and untutored, I caught dozens of smallies in the rapids at the outlet, a couple of three-and-a-half-pounders, some nice fours; a couple of feisty Arctic char, six to seven pounds, and a few of those crocodilian pike. But truth be told, I only got one brookie that qualified for the "book." A five-and-a-half-pounder. Having never seen a Brook trout that big and thinking this might be my only one, I kept it and had the critter mounted. Think about it. Down home you could fish a life time as long as Clint's and never catch a 5-pound brookie.

Once I really got the hang of it, on later trips, I'd catch three or four remarkable "book" fish a day. Last year I caught my biggest ever, an eight-and-one-quarter pounder, a battle scarred veteran—on a big, Deer-hair Mouse. I released him to enjoy some more of his old age.

I don't keep my own log but if recollection serves, I'd say I catch 24 or 25 "book" fish a week up there. But, bear this in mind, I am not a fanatic. I stop to smell the roses, to sip a brewsky now and then, puff on fat cigars, run my mouth something awful. In other words, I give in to distractions. Too often I'll take my eyes off the floating fly to tell a story or two.

By contrast, there's—among others—this retired dentist from Michigan. He's tall, athletic and trim as a rake handle. He distains cigars and beer (and keeps his distance from those like me who drink and puff). I never heard him tell a joke, or take the time to listen to one. He's a fanatic. A truly expert fly-tier and a world-class caster. A persistent fellow who catches twice my catch and scores with uncanny consistency on chubby char (ten-pounders no less!) with that special double-streamer tandem rig of his. Then there's that guy from out West named Duncan Lewis. I just don't want to talk about him.

The dentist was up there last year with his twin brother. The brother is much better looking. To protect the fish, we thought of using that roll of duct tape to tie both of them to the bedpost. I even suggested we could then force-feed them a cocktail of Clint's Metamucil and vodka. You know, as an act of eco-terrorism designed to protect the precious Minipi brookies.

What's great about Cooper's place is that you fish *all* day. None of that knocking off at 3 P.M. business. Here you come in around 5 P.M. for an early supper. Then go out again at 7 P.M. and don't come back 'til dark. And since this is "sub-arctic Canada," that means ten or eleven o'clock.

After talking about those "real" fishermen from Michigan and out West, I must confess that I generally take along an after-dinner cigar and, perhaps, a brewsky. If it's cold, maybe a tot of brandy. Of course, I am not a teetotaler at dinner either and this may explain why the dentist and his brother always book higher scores. One can't help one's handicaps.

As I said, the evening is when we stalk the truly big fish, looking for those toilet-flush takes in the twilight. That's when we cast the big dries—6s, 8s and 10s, humongous dry flies—Green Drakes, White and Black Wulffs, Orange Stimulators and Bombers. And, of course, Deer-hair mice.

Now that's just a wee taste of what it's like to fish for the big, beautiful brookies of you'll only find in Labrador. And although this is not a travelogue, I must say that if you want to experience real wilderness, and enjoy an interesting fly-fishing challenge; come on up to Cooper's on the Minipi.

We'll all be there. Now I can't speak for Clint, because I know he never shares his vodka or his high-end Metamucil, but the rest of us, we'll share the jewels of the Minipi and in case you run out, and are a partaking person, we'll cheerfully share our cigars and a brewsky or brandy or two.

Oh, speaking of my friend, Clint. Come to think about it, I suppose he's too busy to join us this time. He's regularly fishing up there well beyond the wild blue yonder unencumbered with duct tape, not to mention his need for vodka and Metamucil. May God bless him.

20

THE KEYS TO THE KINGDOM

First, let me introduce you to the king, the tarpon, a fish that is better known in Latin speaking circles as *Magelops atlantica*.

Zane Grey, who was among the first to pursue this titanic fish with rod and reel, called him "The Silver King." And, he is, indeed, a king among sport fish. Especially fly fishing. In fact, to compare fly fishing for tarpon in the salt to any of our freshwater fly-fishing pursuits would be like comparing rabbit hunting to lion stalking.

First of all, these are really big fish. Hundred-pounders are not uncommon. They are incredibly strong. So strong, in fact, that some anglers, in the early days, thought they were too strong to catch on a rod and reel. According to Charles Hallock's *Camp Life in Florida (1876)* quoted in McClane's *Game Fish of North America,* "No man is strong enough to hold a large tarpum [sic] unless he is provided with a drag or buoy in the shape of an empty keg attached on the line...." So, if one were to follow Mr. Hallock's recommendation, his gear would include a bobber fashioned from an empty beer keg.

Why a keg for a bobber? Because tarpon, as I said, are really big. A tarpon measuring six feet from lip to tail, not a particularly uncommon specimen, would weigh one hundred pounds. McClane ticks off several more-than-two-hundred-pound catches. For example, on March 19, 1956, in Lake Maracaibo, Venezuela, M. Salazar boated a 283-pounder. On April 16, 1991, Yvon Victor Sebag topped that catch by only four ounces off Shebro Island, Sierra Leone. As of 1996 these were the two all-tackle IGFA records. The heaviest one mentioned by McClane is a 350-pounder "netted by commercial fishermen at Hillsboro Inlet, Florida, on August 6, 1912."

Among the fly-rod-line-weight records are fish weighing 127, 177 and 188, all from places in Florida like the Sebastian River, Marathon, Flamingo and Homosassa.

Jim Holland, Jr. took one of 202 pounds out of a "secret" place known as Hampton Hole, a record for 20-pound line. A man named Billy Pate has held the 16-pound line class record since May 13, 1982. He caught his monster out of Homosassa, Florida.

Tarpon get big because they get old, I mean 60 years old, if they can avoid the bull and tiger sharks which relish them.

In addition to their size, they present a rather malevolent appearance—imagine a stainless steel Hummer. Up close they appear as if they were crafted by a sculptor who had welded thousands of polished silver dollars into the shape of a fish. Add a silver-plated, bucket-sized mouth and yellow-rimmed black-irised, unblinking eyes, again, the size of silver dollars. That mouth, by the way, is so metallically tempered that it takes a special hook sharpened to a double-edged angle to penetrate it. And, even when the honing is deftly done, the hook can only *sometimes* (let's say one out of eight times) secure itself in the tarpon's armor-plated mandibles.

These metallic monsters move with surprising grace like underwater smoke beneath the vast, shallow sapphire flats off the Florida Keys, seen only—and only then by the keen-eyed angler—when they come in from the deep, pass over the turtle grass and then over the bright, barren patches of sun-illuminated sand. When the sun winks behind a cloud, they are invisible even over the patches.

We had driven about seventy-five miles south of Miami, through Key Largo, to a place called Tavernier just above Islamorada—for an appointment to fish for tarpon out of the Matecumbie Marina with a square shouldered 200-plus-pound guy named Captain Ben Taylor. It was the month of May.

Taylor, about 35, had a coppery, wind-polished face, long, sun-bleached hair mashed under a baseball cap pulled down tight to his eyebrows. His big hands were attached to line-backer arms. He wore pale blue belt-less shorts, a loose-fitting white XXL T-shirt and a pair of well-worn Sebago deck shoes.

Taylor told us that he had worked for a time at a bank up in the Colorado mountains, and then he joined up and went to Viet Nam. One day, nearly six years ago, he cashed everything in, sold his house, packed up a trailer and left "for warmer climes." "All I did was fish," he said. "Fished every day in a little tin boat until my money ran out. That's when I started tying flies. Then I did some guiding. Yeah, that was a crime. I didn't know squat."

Today Taylor's "little tin boat" is a 16-foot Hewes Bonefisher. It weighs about 800 pounds and has black Mercury 95 mounted on the stern. There are no seats. The only compromise to comfort is a piece of faded green indoor/outdoor carpeting glued on the top of his cooler. The whole surface of his boat is smooth, covered with a lightly textured vinyl, no screw heads showing anywhere.

Ben is meticulous about keeping his boat clean. Although he chain-smokes unfiltered Camels, he tells us that we can't smoke cigars, or drink beer on the boat. Other than that, he doesn't talk very much. He's too busy being serious and stern.

On the incoming tide, we've motored out onto the flats. Ben kills the engine. He pulls out a fifteen-foot pole and steps up on the poling platform in the stern. He stands there silently scanning the water left and right. Puffing on his Camel. It's warm. 85° F. There is a steady 15 to 20 knot breeze blowing at a right angle across the boat, which is bobbing up and down like the proverbial cork.

Taylor has positioned the Hewes Bonefisher on the edge of a large bed of dark green turtle grass. Now he uses the pole to keep the bow pointed into the wind. Slightly off to the left there is a peninsula of sand showing white beneath the water. Were it not for Polaroid's, you could see very little of the bottom's geography.

David is first. He steps up onto the small gunwale-level platform in the bow. It is not much wider than necessary to accommodate a man's feet positioned at parade rest. He's holding his rod in his right hand and once settled on the platform, he uses his left hand to strip fly line off his reel until six or seven ten-inch-diameter coils lie loosely stacked at his feet, some on the casting platform, some dribbling down onto the bottom of the boat. Between his thumb and index finger, he's holding the tarpon fly, a Roach, with its splayed furnace hackle wings and hot-orange squirrel-tail skirt at the rear. He's got it pinched at the curve of the hook just above the sharpened barbless point. He's set.

At 11:15 A.M., Taylor says, matter-of-factly, "Here they come. At 12 o'clock. 85 yards."

"11 o'clock. 70 yards."

"10 o'clock. 60 yards. Get set."

David shuffles, resets his feet, spreads them wider apart, stares intently at the water—and although he has Polaroid's, he sees nothing but sapphire and diamond sparkles. He sneaks a furtive glance at his wrist watch to verify the direction. 10 o'clock. He looks quickly over his shoulder at Taylor—looks at his eyes—as another check on the location of the in-coming fish.

Without warning, Taylor yells and points, "Now! Now! *Now!*"

David releases the fly from his left hand and with his right swings the rod back throwing the line and the fly up into the air behind his right shoulder. Then, keeping the line in the air, he false casts, once, twice, three times, four times, feeding more line out each time from the coils at his feet.

He has never really seen the fish but when he thinks he has enough line in the air to reach the unseen fish, he double hauls with his left hand, speeds the rod forward and releases the cast. That shoots the remaining loops through the rod's guides. But he's standing on one of the loops and snubs the cast. The fly like a shot duck catapults into the water six feet off the bow.

"Holy shit. Can you believe that? Too late, too fuckin' late," says Taylor slapping his big hand into his hip. "Stroke and shoot. Forget that fuckin' false casting shit."

Those first fish had come in a pod of five. One out front, two more just slightly to the left and right of the lead fish's tail, and one behind, swimming next to each other about two feet apart in a Blue Angel's formation. They passed not more than twenty or thirty feet—maybe less—to the left of the boat. Their speed, in retrospect, appears to be rather leisurely. In other words they do not appear to be moving at a particularly high rate of speed. In third gear. Just cruising. And they look like torpedoes released from *Das Boot*.

This routine is repeated three more times as pods of fish, threes and fives, cruise in over the bare sandy peninsula to the left of the boat's bow. But the fifth time, David sees the fish coming and he manages to get off a cast of thirty feet in spite of the wind, the bobbing bow and other complications. This time, that's enough.

"Let it sink. Easy now, "whispers Taylor. Then he yells, "Strip, strip, strip! Strip, for Christ's sake, *strip*."

David is not an adept stripper. He moves the rod tip left to right every time he pulls line with his left hand. This negates the stripping action and the fly, instead of darting through the water as it is supposed to do, just sits there, slowly sinking.

But David is lucky. What happens next seems to happen in my memory like an extra-slow-mo scene from a *Kung Fu* movie. The fly is suspended in the water, two or three feet below the surface. David can see it. And he sees the lead fish cruise under it. He sees the fish open his great upturned mouth and swallow the fly like a peanut caught in a bucket.

David had insisted, against Taylor's advice, on using his own tackle. I don't remember exactly what kind of tackle he had. Probably an old Shakespeare nine-footer, probably fiberglass, maybe a number 9, and, let's say, a vintage Medalist reel. With Taylor's help the reel has been rigged with 200 yards of backing and a 12 pound, 12-ft leader, a 100-pound shock tippet with a 50-pound butt section.

"Stick him! Stick him! Stick him!" yells Taylor.

David, with both hands grasping the rod handle, heaves back and up mightily.

"Again. Again."

Again, and again, David heaves back.

At the first bite of the hook, the tarpon leaped and somersaulted in the air three feet over the water, then flipped, twisted, turned and with incredible speed, he headed back toward deeper water.

He was into the backing almost instantly, ripping off one hundred yards, then one hundred twenty five yards in a hiccup. He paused halfway to the horizon and jumped again. A silver speck. Then again and again he leaped. David's reel, with the drag set tight squealed like the wheels of a car in a panic stop. Halfway through the tarpon's super-charged run to the horizon, the reel began to smoke, *literally to smoke,* like an over-heated electric motor. Neon blue smoke. Then it began to chatter and wobble. Then it blew a screw; *ping!*, then another *ping!*

In another instant, all the line and backing were gone, and when it reached the knot on the reel's axel, there was this little snap and at that moment, the reel disintegrated. And at that moment, David's rod shattered simultaneously in three places—just above the handle, at the ferrule and eight inches back from the tip top.

Empty-handed now, David shrugged his shoulders, bowed his head and plopped his butt down on the cooler. "What th' hell was that all about?" he said dejectedly.

"That was all about fuckin' up," said Taylor.

It is just downright impossible to convey in simple language or simile the speed of a tarpon's first run, his acrobatic leaps, the overwhelming strength he displays during the fight. Perhaps the way to imagine it is to imagine what it would be like to have a hundred-pound Atlantic salmon on the end of your line. But such an encounter with the Silver King cannot really be imagined. Only those who have hooked a tarpon on a fly rod will ever truly know what it is like to stand at the pinnacle of the fly fishing experience. You will have to ask David.

Now it was my turn. I was using Taylor's gear. He had two rods in the boat, a Sage and a Powell, both nine-footers, an eleven- and a twelve-weight. The eleven-weight had a Billy Pate reel on it. The twelve a Fin Nor. He had floating line on one and Slime Line (a sinking fly line resembling thick, greasy monofilament) on the other.

I had learned from David's encounter that the proper technique is to lead the fish with the fly by about four feet; let the fly sink and then suspend beneath the surface momentarily; let the current work the fly, and then as the fish approaches, you strip in short, fast-as-possible 12-inch bursts to imitate the action of a panicked shrimp. That draws the tarpon's attention. But to make all this happen, you have to place the fly right on a line with the tarpon's nose. Not an easy maneuver when you are balancing on that narrow, bobbing platform on a small boat in a 15-to-20-knot wind.

Taylor has now repositioned the boat, lining it up again at a new bare spot in the turtle grass. Taylor never says much but when he did speak he reminded me of my high school basketball coach, a latter-day Bobby Knight, simmering with half-repressed anger, unfulfilled expectation, downright disgust at the ineptitude of his players.

When another formation of tarpon swam into sight, at least I knew what I was up against. What's more, I had Taylor's 11-weight Powell in my hands. All I needed now was a little beginner's luck.

When Taylor yelled, "Twelve o'clock, shoot, shoot!" I managed a clumsy double-haul and got off a one-stroke cast of about forty feet. Like David, I never really saw the fish but somehow I had managed to place my fly about four feet in front of the incoming squadron of tarpon … and the lead fish took it even before I had a chance to strip.

"Stick him!," Taylor yelled. And I struck him. Once, twice, three times. The tarpon exploded like a depth charge, ran twenty yards and somersaulted into the air.

"Bow when he jumps!" yelled Taylor.

So, I obediently lowered the rod tip each time he leaped. And when he made that first off-to-the-horizon run, I snugged the rod handle into the intersection of my thigh and stomach. When he stopped about a hundred yards out, I pumped the rod. For the first time in my life my knees were knocking. I pumped again and reeled, pumped and reeled until my biceps burned. The rod butt bit painfully into my stomach. Sweat dripped off the tip of my nose and the ends of my elbows.

It took 35 minutes to get the fish back to within 100 feet of the boat. That's about the length of the fly line. To make the fight easier, Taylor had backed the boat down on the fish during the hook-up and now the fish was on a right angle to the right of the bow about 60 feet away, wallowing on the surface and shaking his enormous head. I could see his baleful eye, the hook in his jaw, the blood-red of his flared gills.

"Pull hard. Put the wood to him. Don't let him rest. Turn him. Put that rod tip down and pull to the left parallel with the water. That's it. Down and dirty." Taylor stood behind my left shoulder holding the short, curved gaff.

I did all that and I could now see the fly line hanging over the tarpon's shoulder just behind his gill. When he rolled again, the line tightened and the hook flipped out.

"You got him into the fly line. Not bad. Seventy-five, eighty pounds. Good fish," said Taylor lighting a Camel.

I was covered in sweat. Exhausted. My shoulders ached, my stomach was red and bruised where I had positioned the rod handle. My lips were dry, and my knees were still knocking. I slumped onto the cooler. God, how I could have used a keg of Budweiser and a Montecristo Churchill.

Taylor clipped the fly off the line and handed it to me. The standard trophy, I learned, for one who manages to get a tarpon back into the fly line. I also learned that the ratio of hook-ups to landings is about three in ten. Hey, I guess Taylor's not such a bad sort after all even though he is the Bobby Knight of Florida's tarpon guides.

21

ON THE UPPER DELAWARE

Rivers were the highways of the wilderness. The portals into and out of the vast tracts of forest shouldering their banks. Up and down these rivers flowed the trapper's furs and the logger's logs. Commerce and industry, oh, they dearly love our rivers. The Cincinnati, the Mississippi, the Missouri, the Hudson. That's why, today's highways so often follow river banks and that's why we speak of the "flow" of traffic in a metaphorical bow to the highway's kinship with our rivers.

That's why so often you can hear the sound of traffic while fishing in or sitting beside rivers. That's what I'm doing right now, sitting beside a wide, shallow river, listening to the sound of traffic. It is dusk and I am at a picnic table in front of a small log cabin with a mansard roof of imitation cedar shakes. I've rented the cabin for a couple of nights in the middle of the week. It is situated five miles downstream from Deposit, a little town 166 miles north and west of New York City, via highway 17, which, up here, and maybe down there, too, they call the "Quick Way."

Across the river, through the trees, I see glimpses of cars and trucks on the double-laned highway, cars and trucks heading east toward Interstate 81 and Binghamton, NY, and south toward New York City. I hear their shusss-shuss-shuss. That searing sound like the amplified tearing of a bed sheet, the schwoooooingangish of big tandem rigs, one after another, going up to Binghamton and down to New York. Behind me I hear the chirp of birds and crackle of crickets.

The river, unlike the traffic, flows slow, and silent, rather solemnly. Its dimpled surface, braided here and there, sparkles in the rosy light of twilight. At this point, the river is about one hundred and fifty yards wide. It looks unwadeable, but is, in truth, only a few feet deep bank-to-bank and traveling at only 5.6 miles an hour—which means that if you waded in, it would feel like a big Labrador retriever shouldering gently up against your leg. Its sandy bottom is strewn benignly with small round stones and tangled patches of water weed. Its color is a translucent slate—with touches of green and faded khaki. It looks as if it were a flooded football field. An expanse of smooth water with nervous patches shore to shore.

This river is the fabled Upper Delaware, which, up here, flows along the border between New York and Pennsylvania. You can fish it with a license from either state. South of here it forms the border of Pennsylvania and New Jersey, then doglegs southeast, spreads out into Delaware Bay and loses itself in the Atlantic Ocean north of Virginia's Chincoteague on the eastern shore of the Delmarva Peninsula.

Way up here, it is called "The West Branch," and it is fed by a controlled discharge of chilly water from the bottom of New York's Cannonsville Reservoir. That makes it a "tailwater," a term of excitement and oftentimes frustration among trout fishermen. Excitement because it means near-perfect trout habitat: a good flow of cool water all summer long; warmer water all winter long. Frustration, because, for whatever the reasons, it can mean finicky fish. Big fish in small-fly water.

When most fly fishermen think of tailwaters, they think of the West, of the Bighorn below the Yellowtail diversion dam flowing through the Crow Reservation in Montana; the North Platte's Miracle Mile in Wyoming below the Seminoe Reservoir; Colorado's Black Canyon on the Gunnison below Blue Mesa reservoir; the Green in Utah and Wyoming below Flaming Gorge Dam; the San Juan below the Navajo Reservoir in northwestern New Mexico. And, if he thinks of tailwaters in the East at all, it is perhaps of the Chattahoochee near Atlanta or the White River below Bull Shoals in Arkansas.

The challenge of fishing the tailwaters of the Delaware's West Branch—a river 200 feet wide on average—is no secret to savvy anglers in New York, New Jersey, Pennsylvania and elsewhere. The fish are, indeed, finicky if not down right persnickety. They prefer sparsely tied dries that match the hatches and this river has been called a "bug factory" producing practically all the common northeastern hatches you can name.

It is predominantly brown trout water—rainbow water down below where the West Branch combines with the East Branch—and on this day, measured down stream at Hale Eddy, the controlled release on the West Branch is at 500 cfs (cubic feet per second). The water is 63 ° F. It is the first week in September.

The reservoir, due to a brutal summer-long drought, is at only 36.5 percent capacity. The water being released now is coming from much nearer than usual to the reservoir's murky bottom. It's warmer than usual and filled with slimy green algae and weeds that look like quarter-inch wide strands of green cellophane. It is also reportedly filled with alewives, great fodder for the trout, so they say. According to the Professional Fishing Reports at www.flyshop.com, at a flow of 500 cfs, you can count on "Great wading and floating along the entire river." How great the fishing is, well, that depends.

My cabin, rented from an outfit called West Branch Anglers'[1] is one of ten standing nearly shoulder to shoulder like toy soldiers along the riverbank. Everything around them is as neat and clean as a public park in Ottawa. A gray crushed-stone walk runs in front of the cabins on the river side and there's a gray crushed-stone driveway wide enough for parking in the back. Each cabin has its own raised charcoal grill and a circle of half-inch thick cast iron two feet in diameter to contain a campfire. Bundles of firewood are available at the tackle shop for $2.50 each.

Behind me, on the porch of my cabin, are a couple of green Adirondack chairs. Under the window there's a shelf—great for dumping gear—with a tiny air conditioner jutting out above it. It looks like a normal air conditioner that someone has cut in half lengthwise. It's humming now because I turned it on first thing when I came in today at 2 o'clock and dumped my reels and vest under it on the shelf.

Earlier, while I was on the porch setting up my rod, another fisherman crunched up the walk and said, "Hello." He was a large man, the kind of man who looks like he is made of cinderblocks. He wore a dark brown broad-brimmed felt hat with a braided leather band, stocking-foot no-sweat Orvis chest

---

1. In late June, 2006, torrential rains caused heavy flooding throughout the entire Delaware River Basin, damaging riverside homes and businesses, among them West Branch Anglers'.

waders and a long-sleeve khaki shirt. He carried a delicate Sage four-weight nine-foot with a Hardy reel. His face was broad with high, smooth cheekbones. He looked once-military. Definitely an officer. I fought the impulse to salute.

"Hullo! Been here before?," he said.

"No, first time up here on the West Branch."

"My wife and I, guess it's been 17 times we've been up here this year."

Then, in a generous, accommodating fashion, he outlined all the nearby spots. The hatches and all.

"There's a no-kill section just above here. You passed it on the way in. Probably saw the sign. That's been fishing well. Try Blue Winged Olives, 22s and 24s and ants cast in close to the bank. Small ones. 20s. Cinnamon seems best. Then, above that, above where they've taken the bridge out, opposite the brick building, you'll see it there on the other side, there's some good water. Good slicks and a few riffles. Try that, too."

"I've got my canoe—it's always easier to say "canoe" rather than "Poke Boat"—and the lady at the tackle shop said they'd arrange for someone to take me up stream tomorrow for a float down."

"Oh, got your canoe, do ya, well that'll be great. Just great. Be sure to stop and fish the no-kill section on your way down."

Then he turned with big-man nonchalance and walked down to the river on the nearly invisible path directly in front of my cabin. Did you hear me say, "Directly in front of my cabin"? That's right. He waded into the water, pulled line from his Hardy and began casting. Right in front of *my* cabin. Walked down *my* path. Jeez. I had just got *my* rod set up. So, what the heck, I pulled on my waders, walked in and started casting just below him. It was around 3 in the afternoon and I quit at 6. Fishless. The big guy got skunked, too.

I knew that the cabins came supplied with a little gas stove, an assortment of pots, pans, utensils and dishes, so as I drove through Deposit on my way to the cabin, I had stopped at the liquor store for a pint of Dewars Scotch and a four-pack of Jack Daniel's Blackberry Cooler. (I brought a bottle of 1994 Haut-Medoc with me.) Then I strolled down the street past the hardware store and the Clip & Cut beauty parlor to the Big M Grocery Store for other provisions.

What a shame! They were completely out of tofu, bean sprouts and veggie burgers, so, instead, I bought a package of Ballpark Franks, a half dozen hot dog rolls, four sandwich rolls, a quarter pound of Dutch loaf, the same of pastrami, a half pound of smoke-cured "Gourmet" thick-cut bacon, two steaks (New York strips which had fluorescent green oval stickers on them yelling "THIN" as if half inch steaks were all the rage up here), a half dozen Farm Fresh Eggs, a small bottle of A-1 steak sauce, a wee bottle of Liquid Smoke (original recipe), three anemic "Jersey" tomatoes, an big red onion (I never know what kind of onions to buy, yellow, red, white, Vidalia?), a plastic bag of Romaine lettuce hearts, an itty bitty bottle of Pure Virgin Olive Oil, a bottle of regular V-8 juice, a twelve pack of Miller High Life (In New York they sell beer and wine in the grocery stores, an enlightened convenience not available in Pennsylvania.), a bag of Easy-light charcoal, and a box of Diamond White-Tip Strike Anywhere matches.

As I toted my two bags of provisions back to my Pathfinder, I saw a local fellow giving the Poke Boat on my Thule rack the once over.

As I walked up, he pushed his ball cap back and said, without looking at me, "I do a lotta canoeing. Ain't never tried that tho'. Looks like fun. Yeah, gotta try that some time. Call that a kayak, I suppose."

"It's just like canoeing," I said, "only less tippy."

"That right, ya say," he said and walked off slowly toward the liquor store.

That night I had a splash of Dewars with a splash of soda (brought that from home, too), drank a Blackberry Cooler and ate some pastrami and Dutch loaf while cooking dinner: one of those skinny steaks rubbed with A-1 Steak Sauce, olive oil and Liquid Smoke, done rare on the outside grill accompanied by a sliced tomato and onion salad drizzled with olive oil. I washed it down with a glass of Medoc, sitting shirtless at the picnic table. Later I had an attack of sweet tooth and went out to the car for a roll of wild cherry Life Savers. Ate three that were unlucky enough to stick together when I extracted them from the wrapper. Later still, after watching that depressing film *Philadelphia* on TV, I had a midnight snack—one raw hot dog neat (Love 'em!) and a Miller Lite. Took a Pepcid AC washed down with a slosh of Medoc and sacked out on the lower bunk.

The next morning I woke at about 8:30, brewed some coffee (brought Bucks County Breakfast Blend from home), and fried up three strips of that thick bacon and one egg sunny-side-up. Took my multiple vitamins, which I keep in a Wheatley fly box dedicated to that purpose, and washed them down with V-8 juice mixed with Millers and a dash of Worcestershire Sauce, salt and pepper. That's called a Lumberjack Special. Or a Beer Bloody. There's no accounting for taste.

During the night, condensation from that miniature air conditioner dripped down and soaked the stuff I put on the shelf. Damn. It is not a perfect world.

A man named Frank picked me up at 10 A.M. (this is late-season, and this is *trout* fishing; no need to start early). He drove me about 15 miles up stream for my float down.

Frank has a big old-fashioned Elvis-era hairdo, a male version of the bouffant. Really big hair. Salt and pepper. Lots more salt than pepper. It's cut severely square in the back high on his neck just even with his ear lobes. The big hair makes his eyes look extra small. There are elaborate tattoos on both his arms—fire-breathing dragons, snakes with fangs, that sort of thing. He is wearing a faded melon-colored T-shirt with the Rainbow Anglers logo embroidered on the breast pocket. He is marvelously reticent as he stands there with pocketed hands, evaluating me and my boat. Expressionlessly.

On the way up river, he responds to my questions. Yes, the water is low and running at only about five miles an hour so he estimates my drift down will take about five hours. Counting in the time I'll spend fishing.

"Anything I should know?," I ask. "Any side channels?"

"Just stay to the left, that's all."

Then Frank opened up a bit. "What's that boat called," he said.

"A Poke Boat, cross between a canoe and a kayak. Make 'em in Kentucky. Berea, Kentucky."

"Oh. That so. Had this guy come up here once that rented a McKenzie boat to drift down. We asked him did he know how to handle one. Sure, he said. But he got all fouled up tryin' ta do it with one paddle stead a two. We hadda go git 'em offen the river. I'll tell ya, I seen everything. Not once but twiced. Had a guy my buddy took down, he stuck a hook in his nose, right here. Yeah, not *his* nose, my buddy's nose. John, that's his name, my buddy, he got mad and just ripped it out and said nothin'. Toll me later it hurt like pure-T hell. Just a little hook, too. Swelled up big-time afterwards."

When we got to "the place," a beautiful patch of crew-cut, lusciously green lawn sloping down to the river's edge, he said, "Yeah, just pull'er right onto er."

I hesitated because I had never driven across such a luscious patch of grass and when I did as he ordered, I felt, well, guilty, like a kid who has ridden his bike across the neighbor's newly mown lawn.

Frank lit a filterless Chesterfield and watched as I put on my chest waders, belted them and rolled them down to my waist, set up my three-piece Winston 5 weight with a Bill Ballen reel, grabbed the kayak paddle, a thermos of water, my portable latrine (a doctored Tide detergent bottle), a little cooler pack with two Miller Lites nestled inside, small Orvis chest pack, and dumped all this stuff into the bottom of the boat, adjusted my PFD for a seat cushion and slid the boat into the water. No lunch, mind you. Forgot about that but figured I'd had enough to eat the night before. (Besides I had eaten all my pastrami and Dutch loaf.)

"If ya wanna paddle 'round a bit, try up there," said Frank, pointing up stream. "There's a real good pool ta th' left below that weir up there. See where I mean? Over ta th' left there. 'Nother just there below the bridge," he gestured to the right.

"Yeah, I do." I had paid him twenty-five dollars (that's a five dollar tip) and watched him drive off in my Pathfinder.

Now this is not white-water kayaking. The river is slow and low. According to the International River Rating Scale, I'd call it a Class I—"easy bends, small rapids with low waves. River speed less than hard back-paddling speed." In other words, at most points, if not all, I could paddle upstream. And in most places, like the water in front of the cabin, it is one big gentle gliding riffle. So as soon as I got settled, I closed my eyes and imagined that I am Scott Lindgren, World-class kayaker, all nerve, muscle and lightening-quick reflexes, careening down the mysterious and uncharted Karnali flowing through the mountains of Nepal.

By the way, sitting in a Poke Boat™ is like sitting in a bath tub. It has this low center of gravity and wide-beamed hull design that makes for a stable, dry ride. It also counteracts "weather cocking," the phenomenon of a canoe spinning around in high wind. Reacts quickly to paddle strokes and tracks well. And I use a kayak paddle for better control and a stronger stroke. What's fun is that you can actually see the water rippling beneath your butt through the translucent Fiberglas hull.

My boat is 12 feet long, has a depth (height above the water line) of 9.5 inches in the middle and up to 15 inches at the ends. It weighs 28" pounds (the Kevlar version weighs 22 pounds—sorry I didn't buy it) and is standard outdoor green on the top and yellow-bone white on the bottom not unlike a green shark. It has a 32 inch smooth, keel-less beam, a cockpit much larger than a kayak's. With my little butt in the seat (I weigh 165), the Poke needs only three inches of water, or less, to float.

Kayaks and canoes of comparable size are generally heavier than my Poke Boat. A canoe or kayak of this size would weight 35 to 50 pounds depending upon the material. A kayak, generally, has a narrower beam and sits slightly lower in the water. In fact, kayaks are designed so that water breaks over their bow. That's why, to stay dry, kayakers wear a splash skirt. Because of its hull design, the Poke Boat runs dryer than a kayak so you don't need one. But I have one anyway that fits tightly under the cockpit's coaming and I put it on to keep the rain out when I'm car-topping her. Like a kayak, the Poke's upper hull (what's called the tumblehome in some canoes) levels out almost flat to form the edge of the cockpit. That helps to keep the water out and enhances the bath-tub effect.

Canoes have either flat, round or vee (keeled) bottoms. Kayaks, like my Poke, have a cross between a round and a flat bottom. It's a bottom that slopes up slightly from the center line. Some canoes, called rocker-bottoms, and some kayaks, appear "bent," because they also slope up at the bow and the stern. The Poke sits flat throughout its length making it a little less maneuverable than a kayak but more stable.

Inside the cockpit, there's a black butt bucket with adjustable foot braces up front on either side. I've fitted my Poke with two hard-rubber brackets on the left for stowing the paddle and on the right for stowing the fly rod. So I can paddle along, slap the paddle securely in the left-side brackets, grab the fly rod out of the right side brackets and cast to that rising fish I just spied near shore. And I have pasted in "D" rings at strategic points inside the hull to secure my gear bags.

The Poke Boat looks enough like a kayak that people who see it often say, "Oh, you're a kayaker. Cool!"

My top-of-the-line Werner kayak paddle with its royal blue fiberglass shaft and white elegantly spoon-shaped "computer-designed" fiberglass ends, adds to the illusion. It's a "take-apart" paddle meaning it breaks down into two regular paddles with a T-handle that fits into the end of one. So, when I'm not truckin' down a stream like Stan Lindgren, I can single-paddle slowly, stealthily (and lazily) like a canoeist out bird watching. And when I hit tough water I can rig up the two-ended paddle and navigate with ease.

Now that you know much more about canoes and kayaks then you ever wanted to, you will want to know that it took me five and a half hours to drift back to the cabin. I stopped to fish at about five spots.

The water was discolored and filled with those cellophane-like sprigs of elodea and algae floating just beneath the surface. So it was impossible to get a good drift with the local alewife streamer imitation I bought from the lady at the tackle shop. The knots in my leader, the head of the fly and the hook itself would all pick up algae and weeds on every cast. And you'd have to pick off these little bunches of slime and weed before the next cast. Fact is, it felt like you got a bite on every cast but it was only those weeds snared by the hook. So I snipped off the alewife imitation and tied on a floating ant. No, not a number 20 cinnamon—fishermen take advice to heart—but the redoubtable Chernobyl Ant made by a beautiful blonde woman who lives on the Snake River out in Utah. Now this was serious fishing.

This fly, you see, is a huge—number eight (inch-and-a-quarter long)—imitation of a well-fed carpenter ant. Since I had forgotten my little yellow butterfly anchor, to stop and fish I had to crash-land on shore or on an island and since virtually all of the land along the river is private property and posted (there are only three public put-ins in the upper thirty-five miles of river). I would mostly nose into the islands of tall grass along the way, disembark and cast the giant ant toward shore or into smooth spots between braids of current.

I put my first cast with the ant into a foam-flecked eddy along the edge of a neatly mowed backyard below a cabin with a wrap-around porch. The manicured lawn, a lush green, came right down to the water's edge. The owner must have had one wheel in the water when he mowed the edge.

On that first cast, which landed not 18 inches from the fringe of grass trailing in the water, I got a prodigious, splashy rise. And felt a momentary tug. That was it, so I moved on, after, perversely, switching to a big grasshopper which I repeatedly cast close to shore. Nothing happened.

The ride down the river was smooth and soporific. But every time I've done this, every time I've drifted down a strange river, I've fought the feeling that I have gone around the wrong bend or taken the wrong fork. Is this right? Am I lost? Have I gone down some strange tributary and now had to find my way back? And, so, I drift on wondering where I am and when I can pull into shore and ask a friendly farmer for directions.

"Hey, hi," I'll say, "can you tell me where I am? You see, I am drifting down to Deposit, actually just beyond there, to a place called the West Branch Angler."

And he'll say, "Deposit? Reckon you took the north fork 'stead of the main stem. You're now well nigh right upon Center Creek Rapids. Mighty lotta work ta paddle back up. Yes, sir. Good luck, feller." And he'll start up his John Deere and move on down the furrow. And there I'll be. Stranded on the river.

But, of course, that didn't happen. The West Branch is a wide, smooth river and getting lost is almost impossible. Frank told me to stay to the left and that was easy enough. The river was slow and benign except for a few, three maybe, wake-up rapids. Once I did go to the right and curved around an island losing sight of the main stem. It was a quiet little, dark, narrow place with deep water overhung with oaks and willows. But I opened a Miller Lite, lit a cigar and drifted on, reassured by the little bubble compass mounted on the cowling in the bow.

I ran across only three other anglers. The first was a tall, spidery man in sky-blue dungarees, a checkered shirt, a faded red baseball cap, and a beard as rusty as a shovel left out all winter. His cheeks and the tip of his nose were polished cranberry-apple red. He had just quit fishing and was loading his fly rod into the back of his pickup. So I headed into shore, got out and said, "Howdy!"

"Howdy," he replied, lighting a cigarette.

"Any luck?"

"Naw. Not today. Nothin' much happenin'. How 'bout you?"

"Naw, nothin' much happenin," I said.

"Darn nice day, tho', he said.

"Darn nice day," I replied.

"Where ya driftin' ta?," he said.

"Down to West Branch Anglers' below Deposit," I said.

"Nice day fur it," he said. "Good luck," and he climbed into his pickup.

The next one was an older fellow standing up to his waist 30 or 40 feet from shore. Perched on his head on what looked like a thatched bird's nest was a rumpled khaki hat with the brim turned down all around. He was fishing bamboo. A dark, toasty colored nine-footer. I back paddled to slow down and quartered toward him, approaching from upstream, and when fairly close I cleared my throat loudly so's not to scare him.

Then I said, "Hello."

He turned his head laconically halfway toward me and said, "Hello," then turned back to his fishing.

"Any luck? I asked.

"Nope," he said with his back to me, casting rhythmically and drifting his nymph down stream. I guessed it was a nymph because he had a fluorescent strike indicator on the line.

"Water's low," I said.

"Yep, it is that for sure," he said.

"Well, good luck," I said with a sweep of the paddle.

"Good luck," he said with another rhythmic cast into the current.

The third one was a young guy in his twenties all Orvis-ed up standing with the water flowing around his waist way out in the center of the river. He had a crisp khaki broad-billed fishing cap pulled tightly down on his head, a bright red shirt, a many-pocketed vest with a wood-framed net hanging down in back. He was using a gray graphite rod with a yellow line. I used the same approach but his concentration was so intense that my theatrical throat-clearing startled him.

"Sorry," I said.

"Oh, that's OK," he said, looking embarrassed because he jumped.

"Nice day, huh?, I said.

"Sure is," he said, resuming casting.

"Having any luck? I asked.

"No, not much," he replied.

"Watcha using? I asked.

"Tried an alewife streamer but the weeds were catching on the hook. Trying a Blue Winged Olive now but nothing's rising, " he replied.

"Been here long," I asked.

"No not long," he replied.

"Well, good luck," I said quartering the boat back into the current.

"Same to you," he said, staring intently toward shore at his size twenty-two Blue Winged Olive.

And so it was that I drifted down the West Branch of the Delaware like a debutant lazing in a bathtub. In the estimated five-and-a-half hours, I paddled up in front of my little cabin.

The next morning after breakfast, thick bacon again, and a Lumberjack Special, again, I went up to the tackle shop to settle accounts.

I had had a fishless day on the Delaware. Hey, what could be better?

22
CATCH & RELEASE

A good game fish is too valuable to be caught only once.
Lee Wulff, *Handbook of Freshwater Fishing*, 1938.

I fear that my old pastime has become the blood sport of urbanites and vegetarians, so refined that somebody who actually eats fish is considered to be as spooky and recidivist as a cannibal.
Stephen J. Bodio in "Confessions of a Catfish Heretic."

Catch-and-release angling is becoming a religion. Although in some instances it is essential to the survival of the species sought, in others its major effect is to cloak its more evangelical practitioners in a mantle of righteousness.
Nelson Bryant, *New York Times*

To go a shade further than Bryant, catch and release fishing may be cruelty masquerading as political correctness.
John McPhee, *The Founding Fish*

◆ ◆ ◆

No book dealing with any aspect of sport fishing can, or, perhaps, should avoid some mention of catch-and-release because no fisherman can long avoid wrestling with this conundrum himself.

You have to make a decision. Do you fish for fun, or for a trophy to hang on the wall to brag about and to hand down to your grand kids, or do you sometimes fish (we are whispering here) for a couple of trout to sauté for supper?

Make up your mind because, one way or another, you will have to decide whether you want to kill or cuddle. Oh, yes, and while we're at it, are you going to be a bait fisherman (boo!) or a fly fisherman (rah). A bass fisherman or a trout fisherman. That "boo" "rah" above illustrates that the so-called upper tier of fly fishermen have turned into rather insufferable snobs. Perhaps it has always been so.

What's happened in our day is that fly fishing has risen in the hierarchy of sport fishing to a rather lofty pinnacle primarily on the wings of catch-and-release. However, I think that the motivation goes deeper. Some fly fishers, most especially the newbies, just don't want to get their hands dirty. Why ruin an expensive manicure by cleaning a fish or baiting a hook?

What's more, they don't want that kind of responsibility. It's too grown-up. That's probably why most of them fly-fish in the first place. They abhor those slimy, wiggly worms that bleed red blood. And threading a hook through the tender little lips or bony little spines of struggling minnows, or impaling a blood-sopped hunk of fish flesh on a hook—not on your life. On the other hand, they will stoop—you'll see this on the TV fishing shows—to actually kiss a caught fish before releasing it. Love 'em and leave 'em, they call it. Now, c'mon, that's absolutely disgusting.

Most lodge owners, outfitters and professional guides worship at the altar of catch-and-release for a very obvious economic reason—it makes pleasing their clients easier, their fish stocks more sustainable and their profits higher. Their testimony is, therefore, biased. They are excluded from this discussion.

It will surprise most politically correct sports to learn that even the most finicky dry-fly fishing is a blood sport. Hard to believe, but true nonetheless.

Yes, even the most delicate dry-fly fishing with gossamer tippets and tee-tiny midges on size 24 hooks is still, at root, a blood sport. The death of the prey is its classical denouement. But it is a sport, unlike other blood sports, hunting with a rifle, for example, where the predator can ponder the fate of his prey and entertain the question of whether to kill or not to kill. To make the decision easier for fly fishermen, there are now legislated "No Kill" zones on many of our favorite trout streams. But, aside from the legally designated waters, "no kill" can sometimes be a somewhat difficult choice, especially for youngsters and beginners.

That's because just as a young man can seldom, if ever, ignore the inviting smiles and plunging décolletage exhibited by beautiful girls; so, too, the newly minted fly fisher and the youngster on his first outing will likely find it difficult to release such a hard-won prize. I want Mom to see.

Bragging rights are at stake here. Proof of prowess. On the other hand, it is not so difficult for the seasoned angler, who, over time, has slipped hundreds of trout into his creel and into the pan, to abjure the practice of killing and keeping. One can, I suppose, even grow tired of sex.

Take for example, the reputed father of catch-and-release in America, Lee Wulff. In his early years, I bet he carved a murderous swath through sport fishing before he got tired of having to eviscerate his catches and called a halt. Consider his travels in Labrador, for example. In a 1969 essay, "The Wonderful Brookies of Minipi," he writes that "a couple of 3-pounders was frying over the camp fire." Of a trout he was playing, he says, "He was bigger than the one that now hangs over my mantel. For a brief instant—when I first saw him clearly—I considered taking him down to a taxidermist since I was ready to fly home."

But once converted to catch-and-release, with the fervor of a convert, he decreed that everyone else should call a halt with him. Thus, the seasoned angler, like Wulff, with uncountable notches on the corks of his rod handle, and an ever-lengthening row of holes in his belt, finds it easy to foreswear the killing. He can easily ignore the classical denouement and release his trout with an air of piety born of an angling *Weltschmerz*. I have been there, he says, done that.

Of course, excess *is* excess. And Wulff rightly wags his finger at "one trapper who took 400 pounds of trout out of Minipi for dog food, along with his catch of furs." That, indeed, deserves a finger wag. Hopefully we have all learned the value of moderation.

This catch-and-release thing is, of course, nothing new. It has been practiced by sport fishermen since the time of Dame Juliana Berners. Carp fishermen in the British Isles have raised it to a high art. But, I fear, it has evolved as a robust companion to our more recently awakened respect for the environment. It is part of that feel-good ritual, which prescribes the freeing of one's prey, not so much out of deference to its bestial courage and natural beauty but in deference to its demonstrated scarcity. That sentiment was, after all, Lee Wulff's stated rationale.

Trout are, he opined, too valuable to be caught just once. Then along came hatchery trout and the plant-and-harvest solution to scarcity. But that's another story.

Let's face it, total adherence to catch-and-release bestows a warm and wonderful sense of piety upon its practitioners. However, there are among us still, truth be told, a few who have not yet reached this lofty pinnacle of patrician piety. We still yearn for the more dramatic, natural, classical climax. If the fish is fat and long, we want to kill it and eat it. Or mount it on the wall. That's why a few of us do still keep an occasional trout for the table. Or one for the wall.

Consider what must go through the mind of a like-minded fly fisherman standing knee-deep in a brook casting his tiny invitations into every pocket, pool, glide and riffle only to be refused again, and again and again—until finally there is a take, his line tightens, and, after the struggle, he at last holds the object of his desire—a black-backed, bright and buttery golden-sided trout with neon-blue and vermillion-ringed speckles—in his hand. Or net. If the prize is fat, fat and long, the temptation grows intense. Nearly intolerable. The desire to possess the prize becomes downright primordial. Will this be a trout for the table, or the wall, or will it be someone else's prey on another day?

Sometimes I think we may sacrifice a trout caught at the end of an especially trying day on the water as a sort of revenge of the gods. A quenching of our frustration.

Undeniably this sport, like other field and stream sports, had its origins in man's attempt to provide food for the table. The trout fisherman who nowadays does occasionally keep one or two for the table is only, therefore, acting out an ancient ritual. In this context, to return a captured trout of edible, or trophy size may, therefore, be considered what I call *piscatorus interruptus*, the rather unnatural act of tugging a trout around like a recalcitrant dog on a leash and then releasing him in the hope that he will survive to be tugged and teased another day. Or so that he can later die from the trauma of the struggle out of sight and out of mind. In my experience the high priests of catch and release are not models of probity when it comes to the mortality rate of released fish.(For a more pointed, well, actually pointless example of *piscatorus interruptus*, continue on into the discussion of "hookless" fishing up-coming in this chapter.)

Make no mistake. I do not encourage any angler to keep all his fish. On the other hand, I do not encourage all anglers to adopt the strict doctrine of complete abstinence. Indeed, killing a particularly large fish, let's say a truly record-sized fish, allows the IGFA record book to grow, to be hard-data-verified, and thus to add to our body of specie-specific knowledge through positive proof (certified scales) instead of wishful thinking or speculation.

Killing the occasional big fish is also a way to give little fish a chance to grow bigger. (Fish are cannibals, I am chagrined to say.) But just as the goal of dieting is moderation, not starvation, so, too, the goal of fishing is neither total abstinence nor gluttony. In fact, I subscribe to the commonsense approach of limiting your kill, not killing your limit. Thus, when it comes to the religion of catch-and-release, does this make me an apostate?

Hookless Fishing

This brings us to the latest stalking horse of total abstinence: hookless fishing.

Let me begin by saying that I love the outdoors writer named Nelson Bryant. I have been reading his columns, which have appeared occasionally on the sports page of the Sunday *New York Times* for as long as I can remember. As many sportsmen like him, Mr. Bryant frequently goes fishing and comes home fishless. Goes hunting and comes home duckless and/or deerless. Sometimes when he does creel a fish, nail a duck, or bag a deer; he cooks it and eats it. Usually with the accompaniment of a well-chosen bottle of wine. When he does this, he shares his recipes and the name of that well-chosen wine with his readers.

Last Sunday while looking for Bryant's column in the *Times*, I came across, instead, an article by a Mr. Pete Bodo, a member apparently of the new humane generation of fly fishers. The title of his article is "Hookless Fly Fishing Is a Humane Advance." A more humane advance, indeed, that goes one-step down a slippery slope beyond catch-and-release into the la-la land of *catch-less* fly fishing. This is truly *piscatorus interruptus* redux.

You see, for Mr. Bodo, the mere sight of a rising, taking trout is enough. Hooking and playing the fish to net is too much. Much too much for the humane fisherman.

Now this is a brilliant and wonderfully humane advance, I suppose, in such a mercilessly inhumane sport like fly fishing. What Mr. Bodo has discovered is a way to apply the feminist writer, Naomi Wolf's version of making out to fly fishing. Light petting only. No penetration, please.

I should not be surprised that in Mr. Bodo's world fly fishing should cease to be catching. Much less releasing. Isn't unrequited foreplay enough? No penetration, please.

Don't get me wrong. We should all be concerned about any cruel, unusual or inhumane treatment to animals. But, if concerned we must be, then I would think we should, when it comes to the humane treatment of fish, be more concerned about the practice of luring spawning salmon up a sluiceway that leads to a hatchery where the females are grabbed by the scruff of their necks, slapped onto cold, unyielding stainless-steel tables and squeezed until their eggs pop out their anus. Thus emptied of their progeny, they are tossed into another trough to limp back to the stream. The same method of harvesting eggs is used on lady trout confined to hatcheries.

While on this subject, what about trapping bears in barrels, shooting them with tranquilizer darts, extracting a tooth, a pint of blood, tattooing them with a five-digit number, tagging their ear with a Black & Decker stapling machine, fitting them with a radio-transmitter on a Velcro choker, and, finally spraying a six-inch spot of fluorescent paint on their neck.

Or when white-tailed deer are darted and neutered to save our suburban hollyhocks.

This kind of animal handling in science-for-the-sake-of-science circles must give the creature on the receiving end a heavy dose of post-traumatic stress syndrome.

Yet such animal handling practices never seem to raise the ire of the Mr. Bodos of our world. Instead he and his ilk seem more concerned about penetrating the mouth of a trout with a small hook. What pain and inhumane trauma the prick of a gnat-sized # 24 hook with a barb smaller than a deer tick must cause! Yet, consider this. Fish have no hands or paws with which to grab their food. Only a mouth. A mouth that, by divine design or Darwinian evolution, has been framed with bloodless cartilage, gristle and bone precisely to enable trout to root beneath sharp stones and gravel for such prickly prey as fresh water crabs, crayfish, hellgrammites and bony minnows—without injury. A delicate, pain-prone mouth would not equip a trout to survive in his harsh environment. It's like saying that a pig has a delicate nose.

Surely if a lady salmon can survive such rough treatment as getting slammed around and having her eggs squeezed out of her anal orifice, then their relative, the trout, must surely be designed by some divine or Darwinian imperative to survive that tiny prick and tug of war against a fly rod whose tip is, say, 20 microns in diameter. Surely they can survive being cradled gently in a human hand, admired for a moment and having their image digitized before being released back into the water. Nearly all proponents of catch and release think emphatically they can.

But now Mr. Bodo arrives on the scene to proselytize an even more humane method than catch and release, "catchless fishing." And again I have little doubt that this is a symptom of an excessively prissy bleeding-heart *Zeitgeist* let loose in the land. It is the very bottom of the slippery slope of catch-and-release orthodoxy. Those, like Mr. Bodo, a catchless/hookless proselyte should simply give up fishing altogether and take up knitting, with synthetic yarn, of course. And may I humbly suggest that the sports-page editor of the *New York Times* pass Mr. Bodo's next lacrimonious column along to the editor of the PETA newsletter.

In closing, may I take a moment to mourn the few, proud, gallant fish caught on a day when the anglers, like Nelson Bryant, are hungry for a simple plate of sautéed trout. You could observe that it is the just fulfillment of the trout's bestial destiny. And ours.

23

MINIPI MEMORIES

"For years my plane carried me deeper and deeper into the Labrador wilderness as I sought the last strongholds of giant brook trout. Then I struck the most fabulous area of all. The flow from lake to lake looked perfect. It was deep, with a blue-black sheen of dark peat-stained water, yet occasionally, between the pools, shallow enough for a man to wade from shore to shore. Fast flows tumbled between the shallow lakes, where from the air, the underwater grass beds showed up in wide areas like submerged golden carpets. I pictured the grass as being heavy with nymphs. In June the green drakes would burst their imprisoning underwater cases and rise in clouds to the freedom of the air.

"The secret of Minipi's superb trout lies largely, I believe, in the water, which is organically and chemically rich enough to support great quantities of insect life. The lakes are shallow enough to let sunshine reach their beds and warm them into great productivity. The trout, through thousands of years of undisturbed natural selection, have learned to fit into and use this environment. They grow big and they grow fast."

Lee Wulff, from an essay, "The Wonderful Brookies of Minipi," 1969.

◆　　◆　　◆

The Minipi watershed way up north in eastern Canada's Labrador is to Brook trout what the famous fields of Vuelta Abajo is to Habanos cigars. A breeding ground for the best of the best.

The Minipi River is like Florida's St. Johns River, which the Seminoles called "Walaka" (river of lakes), a river that widens along its course to form a chain of lakes. Minipi Lake is the largest of the Minipi Lakes, flowing 35 miles from a place called Black Fly down river to the rapids at the Outlet within sight of Jack Cooper's Minipi Lake Lodge.

I first went fly fishing at the Coopers' in the early '90s. Probably '92 or '93. I would fly up there and stay one, two, or, when I was younger, sometimes for three weeks. (Your arm gets sore.) Up to this point in my life, I have spent over 27 weeks at Coopers stalking those wide-bodied Labradorean Brook trout.

Now consider this, that's really equivalent to 27 years if you figure that an average angler generally goes on a trip like that only once a year and stays for only one week. That makes me an old-timer, but certainly not an expert. Fact is, fly fishing is one of the only things I can think of that you can do for 30 or 40 years without becoming an expert. Now that's just my point of view because I know plenty of people who think they have become experts in less than one summer.

As I look back, what I remember are the big brookies—and pike and char—the long, accurate casts I made to present dry flies to rising fish; how hot it got, how cold, how those black flies bedevil you, how those mosquitoes bite, how those persistent hornet-like "stouts" attack you out on the lake.

I remember the comfort, the discomfort, and, oh, I almost forgot, I remember some of the people I met. All those incidental characters. The lovable, laughable, and the few, very few, downright intolerable. All those people who become your un-chosen companions for a week of fishing—eating, drinking, smoking, joking and arguing. People, who, for the most part, you will never see again. A very few perhaps you'll never miss. Others you'll miss for a lifetime.

But I cannot remember a single person that in some way, on some level, I didn't find a measure of simpatico with. Whether among the guides or the guests. After all, anybody who loves brookies the way I do and goes all that way to fly fish for them has to be at heart a good and companionable person. So as I tell you about some of them, I want you to know at the start that any of the peevishness, impatience or irascibility you find here lies in my own heart, not theirs. They are and were all good people who had a much harder time, no doubt, putting up with me than I with them.

What follows, therefore, is a remembrance of some of the people I spent time with on the Minipi. I've compressed these three tattle tales into what will appear to be one week. In reality they are plucked from shards of memory stretching over a much longer time span.

My Minipi remembering starts about the time the copper tone, burnished onto my cheeks by the Labradorean sun and wind, begins to fade along with the red mosquito bites, the blue bruises earned while commando fishing with Vermont's illustrious lawyer and adventurer, Jake Wheeler; and when the weeping scarlet lesions left by black flies start to crust up; that's when I think about the characters who had to put up with me for a week. Among them was the late Andy Brown, a true gentleman dressed in his Harris Tweeds and jaunty cap, a true Minipi old-timer. I remember the day he christened me "The Intolerable Quigley." "Mr. Quigley," he would say, "I can smell your foul cigar smoke halfway down the lake."

Now the size of the lake necessitates the use of Crestliner boats and 20-horse-power outboard motors to ferry anglers to and from the forty or so named locations—outlets, inlets, runs and rapids noted on the Minipi map as "hotspots." And also to look for rising fish, especially in the evening. So unless one wants to wade-fish exclusively for smaller trout in the faster waters, one can be stuck for a whole day in the company of an un-chosen, never-met-before boat buddy.

I should note that I usually went to Minipi alone—some say my personality accounts for that—and because the routine called for two fishermen being assigned to one guide on a rotation basis, some poor soul would have to spend time on the water with me. (I have no sympathy for the guides. It's their job.) For the unlucky ones it might be a few days. For those who have come solo, it could mean a whole week, Lord help them!

Some of the better-heeled anglers would pay a premium to fish one-on-one with a guide. Ron Miller from Pittsburgh still does that. Always has. (Some wags say that's because he was unlucky enough to spend his first-ever Minipi week fishing with me.) Others, if they knew in advance that Quigley would be there solo, well, they'd dig deeper into their pockets.

The vignettes that follow concern time spent with Jersey Jim, Bill and Marlene, and finally Jake Wheeler.

Jersey Jim.

We'll start with Jim from New Jersey. He had fished Minipi several times before and was, by the testimony of all those who had previously encountered him, something of a strange fellow.

Take this example: Once when I was with him in the boat, he said spontaneously, no preamble, "They weighed my trout, the one I kept to have it mounted, the one I got three years ago; they weighed it three times."

As he talked he pulled a photograph out of his shirt pocket. It was a shot of an artistically pedestal-mounted, handsomely colored brookie on a table in his richly paneled den. "Three times. Six and a quarter, then seven, and then six and three quarters. Couldn't get it right. But then there's dehydration, the dehydration factor, you know. So, I know it's a seven pound trout. No doubt about it," he says as if I'd asked or cared. "Yeah," I say handing back the well-worn snapshot, "Looks like seven pounds to me for sure."

Late one night we were sitting around the dining table in the lodge munching on chicken wings and popcorn and chosen libations when Jim got up abruptly and went down the hall to his room. We thought he'd gone to bed. But he returned momentarily with a photograph. I thought it was that mounted fish again.

"Take a look at my favorite thing," he said handing me the picture. I expected to see a candid photo of his naked wife or girl friend, some guys are like that, you know. Especially at fishing camps. But it was a picture of his son—"My first born son, " he said. Weight seemed not to be the issue here. The kid, a mere baby, was wrapped up in blankets. You could only see his head.

"Now look at that," I said with genuine admiration, "a trophy-sized kid. "Jim, you can be proud of that. He must go at least seven pounds." I handed the picture around the table.

In the lodge at the same time was a gentle-dispositioned Virginian, a big guy named Bill, a clinical psychologist by profession. He told me that Jim reminded him of some of his patients. That seemed to me a mean-spirited exaggeration. Bill gave me the diagnosis in clinical terms but my Latin was rusty and it went right over my head. Truth is, all that's wrong with Jim is that he is a rather shy, taciturn specimen (glassy eyes and all) of the really serious trophy fisherman who gauges his personal worth by the *size* of the fish he catches.

The joke about Jim is the fact that he would not tell, never had told anyone what he did for a living. He does not seem to purposely revel in the intrigue that that creates; it was just the way he wants it. Occupation? Unknown. But one day out in the boat I asked him point blank

"Hey, Jimmy, whadda ya do back in civilization?"

His reply: "Look, Ed, I'm on vacation here. What I do back home is irrelevant."

Besides, he said, he did not like the idea that in ten minutes everyone is sitting around talking about their occupations and in fifteen minutes everyone knows what everyone else does and they're all talking business.

"Hell, I'm here to relax, not tell everyone my life history."

But the fish weren't rising that afternoon and I had nothing better to do, so, overlooking his comments, I decide to press on with my inquiries.

"Hey, Jimmy," I says, "come on, man, you're among friends here. Knowing what someone does, asking what they do, hey, it's a nice, traditional way to start a conversation. C'mon, really, Jimbo, do we care if you have some, well, strange occupation? Will we think the less of you because of what you do? No way, Jimbo. Besides, hell, I think I know anyway. I guessed the first time I saw you. You've got the look. I know you're an undertaker, an embalmer, or a county coroner, or chief of autopsy at Jersey General. It's the look. I can tell by the way you look. Now watch, watch how knowing that helps the conversation—now that I know you handle dead bodies, I can ask you, just for the sake of polite conversation, all kinds of interesting questions. Like, I've always wanted to know this; do you guys ever comment on, you know, er, the pretty corpses? Do you say things like, 'Hey, Joey c'mere an' look at the body on this body. Huh?' You can tell me, Jimbo. It will be our secret. We're on vacation here. We're alone in the wilderness. C'mon, trust me. We're boat buddies."

Through all of my inane, if not obnoxious chatter, Jim just looks at me with a Mona Lisa smile, a sort of sad stoicism and a "What-the-hell-am-I-doing-here" expression. The guide, David, his expression is blank. He's concentrating on rock-avoidance and looking for rising fish.

Hey, I know, that what I was doing was not funny. It was uncivil. Maybe even stupid. But drinking beers before noon, smoking cigars and sitting around in the middle of a lake when the fish aren't rising, well, that's when stuff like that happens. I give Jimbo a Purple Heart for putting up with my chatter.

That night, after everyone has gone to bed, Jim and I were left alone at the dining room table drinking wine. He's changed into another clean T-shirt. He's got this enormous collection of them. Wears a different one everyday, changing twice a day. Each one with the name and slogan of some exotic place emblazoned on it, like London or Camden. And he says sort of wistfully, "Ed, I noticed your wine. That Bordeaux. Are you a wine connoisseur?" That launches a conversation about wine. Well not really a conversation. He does all the talking and I listen to him and discover he's a serious, well-informed wine collector. He really knows his stuff. I'm wondering how he manages that on an undertaker's salary. They must make good money. Guess I'll never know.

He talks about the five years he spent in London, things like lunching at the Reform Club (Jim says they have the greatest selection of port wine in all of Europe), how he used to eat dinner at the Connaught Hotel's famous Grill Room (says it's one of Europe's best); how he bought a side-by-side at Purdey's Gun Shop, had a suit made on Savile Row. Man, he's a *bon vivant*, I'm thinking. And throughout the "conversation," he retains a cool, strangely detached air. Sort of like he is talking to himself. Maybe the guy is just shy. Hell, maybe he's 007. Anyway turns out to be a nice evening's conversation.

By the way, he never did answer my creepy question about the corpses. I had never asked again.

The next day, while fishing with Jim and David Budgell, our sturdy Labradorean guide, I feel the need to relieve myself off the engine end of the boat. "David, here," hold my rod. Take a couple of casts if you want to while I take a pee and for God's sake watch your back cast."

"Kin a pud on anudder fly, det yeller one ay tied lass neet?"

"Sure. Take your time. I'm not as fast at this as I used to be."

Meanwhile, Jim is blind casting from the seat of honor in the front of the boat. The wind is still. The sun hot. The water calm. On David's first cast, a fish swirls at his yellow maribou-mouse-muddler-bomber creation, follows it and swallows it with a great splash about twenty four inches from the gunwale.

"Whoa! Gud feesh," says David. "Wud I do naw?"

"Ya hold him," says I, "'til I finish here. Then you give me the damn rod."

Jim looks crestfallen but keeps on casting. I finish my boat-end business, hike up my waders and take the rod from David. Now I'm playing the fish to the net. She's a five-pounder.

"That doesn't count, you know. That's not going in the book under your name," counsels Jim in a saintly voice.

"Fuck you," says I affectionately. "Far as I'm concerned, I landed a five-pounder and you saw me do it and you, Jimmy, Jimmy dear, and you, well, you ain't even landed nothin' yet."

"Shit," says Jim. Well he really didn't say that not out loud anyway. He said it with his expression. Fact is, I never heard him curse. Not once. No, he says "shit" with his face, with a sort of paralinguistic scatological ventriloquism. Then he looks up to verify that the sky is still there and still periwinkle blue. And resumes casting.

That night at the lodge, when we're all comparing notes, Bill asks me, "Hey, how'd you do, Ed, catch any big ones today?"

"Well, let's see," I say rubbing my chin. "Oh, yeah, as a matter of fact, out there on the bar, I landed a five-pounder. Nice fight. Took this yellow thing, a sorta mouse-muddler thing. Followed it and took right off the gunwale."

Jim slowly looks over at me and rolls his glassy eyes up toward the high ceiling.

What a difference a day makes!

We're down in the gorge one evening fishing in the foam below the falls. Two boats. David is guiding Bill and his wife Marlene. They're in one boat and I'm in the other with Conway, the guide. Tan caddis flies, size 14s, are skittering all over the water and darting through the air. On the water there are rises everywhere. I'm catching nice 16-, 17-, 18-inch fish on nearly every cast with a tan elk-hair caddis.

Bill and Marlene are catching nothing. David is trying his damnedest to get Marlene a fish. He's sitting next to her. Tying on flies for her. Helping her with the rod. Showing her how to cast. But frustration hangs like a rain cloud over this neighboring boat and the cloud grows darker as I land fish after fish. I'm whooping and hollering. Obnoxious as usual. Perhaps I'll outgrow it.

Conway leans over to me and says, "Next thin' ya know they'll wanna know what fly you're usin'."

Sure enough, Bill yells over, "Ed, what are you using?"

"Elk-hair caddis. Tan with a touch of cinnamon," says I. Then Bill confers with David. who shakes his head. Next thing I know, David ups anchor, putters over and pulls alongside.

"Got an extra one?" asks Bill.

"Sure," and I lean over and carefully place, not one, but three virgin self-tied elk-haired caddis in his outstretched palm.

"Thanks," says Bill.

David looks slightly embarrassed and motors back to their original spot. Marlene catches the first fish. These fish are small by Minipi standards. Only fish over three pounds go into the logbook. But that's what we do down here in the gorge, catch tons of "small" ones—any one of which would be a keeper back home. Bill is also catching fish now on nearly every cast. God is in His heaven. All is well with the world. But Marlene, with trophy blood in her beautiful veins, is still not really the happiest of campers. Bill is loving it.

Marlene, who looks spiffy in her new Orvis outfit, was, at first, like a whiskey sour without the cherry or the sugar. She could find nothing right with the Minipi experience. During the first few days at dinner she let everyone know. The guides, she said, were know-nothings. And why didn't they serve wine with the meals. And this Quigley chap, why, when she told him that she had written a book on eating disorders, he said that he didn't know there would be much interest in a book about food fights. So, for poor little Marlene, the guides were incompetent and surly, the meals substandard and wine-less, the dinner-table repartee crude, smart-ass, uninformed and some of the guests downright ill-mannered.

Bill, on the other hand, seemed to enjoy not only the meals (he said so frequently with his mouth full) but the conversation, too, (he even laughed at my food-fight remark). Maybe that's because he was catching fish and. Marlene wasn't. And, by God, she had taken a genuine Orvis fly fishing course before she came up here.

In the days that followed, as she went fishless, while Bill caught more and more fish, her mood darkened. Her tongue sharpened. The guides, she repeated, were worthless louts. The water barren of fish. To make matters worse, Bill had caught and kept a six-and-a-quarter pounder. His trophy fish. That's right, he kept it to have it mounted. So, if luck didn't change, he'd have a trophy and Marlene would just have to live with that. For the rest of her life.

Then, as the saying goes, the worm turned.

On the third day, having cast a large Royal Wulff upon the placid waters at the narrows, Marlene was lounging in the middle of the boat reading a book. She dozed off in the warm sun. The gentle, almost imperceptible current took her fly sixty feet out from the boat. It is riding high, with a tiny wake trailing behind it. Paulette is their guide. And lo, and behold! A seven pound brookie spies the Royal Wulff and swallows it in a jolting explosion and dives for the depths, hooking itself firmly. Marlene awakes and plays the fish with the kind of oos, aahs, grunts, groans and giggles they say you hear on the sound track of a pornographic film. Paulette is poised with the net.

In the middle of the fight, the fish circles toward the front of the boat where husband Bill is offering advice. "Here," he says to Paulette, reaching out his hand, "give me the net." Quick as a black fly bites, with an expression of "glory be to God" on her face, Paulette complies. Bill nets the fish. Marlene emits an uninhibited and triumphant scream of delight that echoes up and down the Minipi end to end and side to side. She does a little war dance in the bottom of the boat. You can see the pretty shape of her legs through the waders. She then raises her hands and does a bumpa, bumpa with her hips. David, witnessing the affair from our boat nearby, smiles cherubically and says, "Looka dere, look-a dere, she shakes her head likka feesh, and wiggles her bottom likka go-go gal."

Thus it was that both Bill and Marlene acquired his and her trophies to take home. She can live with that. For the rest of her life. They will have them mounted, she confides, side-by-side in a large vitrine. She saw a mount like that in a magazine.

That evening at dinner, Bill is his amiable, old-shoe self. Marlene, she's transformed into a charming woman who thinks that this is the grandest vacation she has ever had. Why, Paulette, like all the guides, is a rare, wonderful jewel; Gladys, why she's the best cook on the continent. On and on she goes sprinkling her kudos with four letter words just like the rest of the guys. Even tells a risqué joke.

At one point, she rolls up her sleeve, stands up, walks over and offers her bare flexed bicep to Quigley. "Feel that," she says. "I lift weights, you know! Feel me!" I reach out slowly and lovingly caressing her bicep with lingering awe and admiration, and say, "Oh, Marlene, how soft your skin, how firm and shapely your bicep. Are all your muscles like this?" She giggles delightfully and asks to feel Quigley's bicep. He obliges, rolling up his sleeve with ceremony. She reaches out with both hand and says, "Oh, Quigley, how hard your bicep is. Are all your muscles like this?"

We raise a toast to Marlene with red wine.

After dinner she goes into the kitchen and thanks Gladys for the "really, really wonderful meal." "The dessert was fabulous. You must give me the recipe."

Soon after Marlene hooked that fish in her sleep, on that same day, Bill hooked one, a good one, too. And David says, "Wonder what they're usin'." "Let's ask," I said, "they owe me one for those elk-hair caddis I gave them in the gorge, don't ya think?" So, I yell over, "What are you using, Billy?"

"Something bright," replies he. "Brown and bright."

"What?"

"Yeah," says he. "Brown and flashy. Something I bought in England."

The next day Bill and I are fishing together within shouting distance of Jim who is fishing solo. We're laughing and joking. I'm getting one strike after another. For some reason I was missing them. Buck fever maybe. Missed three in a row. Maybe the fish are short striking at my luxurious mink Mickey Mouse. On the fourth cast, I finally set the hook. Bill's getting action too. Jim's striking out so just to annoy him, we both pretend not to take the business at hand very seriously. We're laughing, telling jokes, drinking beer, smoking fat Cuban cigars. I start telling the "Zachary disease" joke. A doctor joke that I knew Bill would appreciate. But right in the middle of the telling, Bill hooks a fish. "Bill, you're one damn rude dude. I'm tellin' a joke, a doctor joke no less, and 'stead of waiting 'til I'm finished, right in the middle, you're hookin' a fish. Damned if I'll tell any more jokes."

Bill brings his fish to net. It weighs five and a half pounds. He sits down, lays his rod across his knees, takes a long puff on his cigar and says, "Hey, Ed. I forgot the beginning of that joke. Please start over. Please. I promise, I won't catch another fish till you're finished."

All this cavorting, not to mention all the action, is driving Jim crazy. You can tell. He never says much in the boat anyway. Once in a while, though, he makes an inaudible, sour-sounding remark, probably a put-down aimed at me. Finally he's had enough. "Hey, Ed!", he says in a let's-get-serious tone. "What are you guys using?" "Just something brown and furry." "Brown? Furry? Like what?," he asks. "Brown, you know 'brown' like that something Bill bought in England."

With Jimbo at the Fabled Foam Pool.

One day Mark Pike is guiding Jim and me to the fabled "Foam Pool." You get there after motoring down the lake to the spot where a stream empties in. Then, you leave the boat and portage along a path to a point where another boat is stowed. On the way, there's lots of chatter from Jim—yeah, that's very unusual—about how great this spot is. The great Foam Pool.

Along the portage we have to ford some heavy rapids. Scary. In case I slip, I ask Mark to stand downstream with his hands outstretched. Once across we make our way along the slippery, rock-strewn shore to where that other boat is stowed. Then we take a scenic and leisurely trip up this small river-stream, dragging muddlers behind the boat or casting them into shore whenever we pass likely spots. Here and there we catch small brookies.

At last we arrive below the Foam Pool. There it is, just up ahead. A celestial trumpet sounds, a shaft of light parts the gray clouds and strikes the surface of the pool with a shaft of golden light. Jim quivers with anticipation and trots ahead.

I stop, stand akimbo, and look up at the pool, an eddy spiraling slowly at the edge of the heavy rapids. "You must be kidding, Mark." That's because this fabled pool, snuggled up against those big black rocks on the shore, is little bigger than a dining room table in a boarding house. Not surprisingly it is covered with a thick comforter of foam, a layer of creamy root-beer-colored bubbles four inches thick. Filled with the carcasses of a million bugs. Mark ignores my comment and says, "One of youse fish below an' ta udder fum aboff."

"I'll go above," says Jim speaking over his shoulder because he is already jogging upstream bouncing over the rocks like a mountain goat.

From below, I begin to feed out line, lengthen my false casts each time until I judge that I can drop a muddler on the upper edge of the foam. I'm standing about eight yards below, centered on the pool. I measure out and release a cast hitting the upper edge of the pool and strip the muddler through the foam. Nothing. Then a shadow darkens the foam as if an eagle flew between the sun and the pool. I look up and instead of a majestic eagle soaring overhead, I see Jim. He is standing, spread-eagled like a statue silhouetted against the sky on a high, round rock above the pool. He is poised to cast his fly toward me, toward the tail of the pool. I stop casting to watch. Peeved.

On his first cast his deer-hair mouse lands neatly in the back of the pool at my feet. As he retrieves it, it makes a track through the foam like a part in wet hair. Bang! He has, by God, hooked one of the fabled denizens of the foam, a muscular broad-sided seven-pound Brook trout.

Now, truth be told, I don't think this foam pool, this mere pool table of a pool, is really big enough for two fishermen to flail simultaneously. Unusually, of course, that's not the way it is done. Anglers take turns, flipping a coin to see who goes first.

So, like a spurned lover, I turn, draw my wading staff like a sword from its scabbard and carefully make my way back downstream to fish the large, promising eddy near where we had left the second boat. This pool is also covered with foam.

After digging a three-pounder out of the pool, I go down and dig a Molson's out of the cooler and a cigar out of my pack, sit down on the gunwale and survey the river rushing by. Gladys has slipped a can of smoked oysters in my lunch bag. I open it and spear them one by one with the tooth pick from my Swiss Army knife until they are all gone. I burp a wilderness honoring burp, and enjoy the silence. Then I get up and fish the smooth tongue of water out from where the boat is beached. I'm using a mouse and on nearly every cast a small fish, 14, 15 inchers, jump at up and over the mouse. It's too big to fit in their mouth so I never hook one. This is what I call having a great day at the famed Foam Pool.

Mark comes down and asks to use my other rod, the #6 Winston, to catch a couple of small ones for lunch. He catches four smallies, cleans them on a flat stone at the water's edge, cuts them into hunks, dips them in white flour, adds salt and pepper and fries them in butter in a blackened pan over his Coleman stove. I have another Molson's and eat the crisp hunks of salmon-colored, sizzling golden-crusted trout that Mark offers me on a white paper plate. After lunch, I light another cigar (amazing how many you can smoke in a day on the Minipi) and lean back on a rock, using another rock for an Ottoman. The afternoon wanes. Jim never comes down for lunch. He stays up there flailing away at the foam pool. Mark goes back to the crossing point and motions to Jim, who finally and reluctantly comes down from his perch, joins us and eats some of the now cold pan-fried trout. Time to head back to the lodge.

But before we go, let me say that for all my foaming about the size of the Foam Pool, I should point out that a guest named John and his son Brian, whose turn it was to fish the Foam Pool the next day, each caught a seven pounder there—the father was casting from the spot where I was standing the day before. His son Brian was standing above where Jim was the day before. They had rested the pool after the first fish was caught.

It probably was not so much the size of the pool but the size of Jim's fish which peeved me. And, of course, his lack of stream etiquette, which really means that I was suffering mostly from the bitter taste of sour grapes.

That night I went down to "the guides' shack" and politely ask Conway, the acting head guide, if it is possible for me *not* to fish with Jim the next day. Could I be paired with someone else? I explain that I don't want special treatment, I am not asking to fish alone and I do not want to foul up their schedule of assignments. Whatever is possible is OK with me. Even if that means fishing again with Jim. But Conway says that Bill can fish with me because Marlene's taking the day off. It's settled.

That God-awful Stink of the Stinkin' Slimy Pike.

Later in the week, I'm fishing mice, this time not a deer-hair version but my own delectable, fluffy floating mink-swaddled, Minny Mouse by name. I'm strippin' Minny gaily back to the boat when a Seawolf-class submarine surfaces right behind her, pushing up a big malevolent bow wave. Then there is this terrific splash. The sub dives and in my head I hear the score from the movie *Jaws*. Da da dada dada dada. The fish runs into the backing. Then swirls on the surface and sounds like a harpooned Orka.

"It's a pike," says the guide, yawning. "I can tell by the take."

"Damn, look at that," I yell. The pike swirls again and jumps. My knees are knocking, "I don't care what it is. Look at that." I raise the rod tip high, both hands tight to the cork handle.

My line is as taut as the E string on a Stradivarius. A 36-inch *Esox lucius*, the water wolf, in other words, a Great Northern pike with eye sockets the size of quarters, is on the end of it. But, let me interrupt this fight story to remind you that this is trophy Brook trout water and instead of cheers and attaboys, I hear nothing but the silence of the wilderness, broken only by the thrashing of the pike in the net.

"Hey folks, that's one of the largest freshwater fish I've ever caught. He may stink, be ugly and slimy, he may be a "poik" but he fought like a champ and I want a picture of me holding him." Smile.

Four or five casts later, still using my now bedraggled Minny, I hook another fish. "That's for sure a big trout," says the guide. Of course, he's lying. The fish runs lickety split into the backing. Just like the first one. It leaps, then dives to sulk and shake its head. Then he comes back to the boat at 90 miles an hour, swirls at the sight of the net and runs again. ZZZZZZZzzzzzzzzzzzzzzzzzing.

"That's another pike," Jim says.

"I'm not so sure. Could be the new Minipi record Brook trout. A new IGFA record."

"Took like a trout," says Mark.

Of course, it is just another slimy pike, this time measuring nearly 40 inches lip to tail. Again I insist on a picture and hand my camera to Mark. He hands me the white cotton glove. Smile.

"Well, Ed, that was a good fight." Jim says. "Two in a row. Nice."

Now it's true, most of Minipi's anglers don't come here to catch pike on flies, we come for the giant brookies. That's a given. This ain't Minnesota, Michigan or Manitoba where the Great Northern Pike reigns supreme. It's the Minipi. Here we have the delicious luxury of distaining one great game fish in favor of another. We're trout snobs.

That night the dinner conversation drifted to talk of pike and then shifted to the skill thing. Jim says, "Todd Kennedy here has won fly-casting tournaments, have you, Ed?"

"No, can't say that I have. Could be because I never entered one."

Another guest opines, "Tournament casting aside. Truth is anybody can catch a pike."

"Right," says Jimmy. All heads nod.

Guess they forgot Marlene's sleeper. Truth is at Minipi anybody can catch a trout.

A journey to hell and back.

Having mentioned tournament casting prowess let me now introduce you to Jake Wheeler, the previously mentioned Vermont lawyer. And after that tell you about an Outward Bound journey I once took with him.

It's true. In my book, if you want to talk about skill, concentration and determination, you have to give the devil his due and talk about Jake Wheeler. He is one helluva fisherman. A superb caster and a creative fly-tyer, too. He concentrates like a chess master. I can't remember that he ever missed a strike or failed to put his fly right on the rise, instantly, even in the dark! And I never saw him fail to land a fish he'd hooked. Well, there was one but I bet that one was a stinking pike.

What's more, when he was wading, he would refuse the guide's assistance and beach his own fish in the shallows like Lee Wulff used to do. One day, fishing the other side of a narrows, he caught four fish—all over three pounds—and that was supposedly on the poorer side of the river. (He had conceded the "better" side to me.) He caught his fish over there while I hooked only one on the favored side of the river. And missed three.

One day Jake and I were fishing out of Cooper's cabin on Minonipi Lake with Howard Guptill, that sagacious student of the waters. At Shearpin Rapids, Jake stationed himself at the center-pool position, and began, in his inimitable way to cover the water. There's plenty of water there (unless you go with Jake, the waterhog) and I had gone up stream to fish the dark, swift, narrow tongue of water above.

Once situated, I yelled down to Howard. "Hey, Howard, do they ever catch fish up here." "Nope," he replied languidly.

I saw Jake make a magnificent roll cast, landing his muddler neatly across and down stream. Pow! He's immediately into a fish. Then another. I stop fishing each time he hooks up to watch him fight the fish.

Jake works the water hard and artfully. In a pattern. He works his way down stream landing another fish on the way. He then comes back upstream and starts down again. Up top I'm having no luck.

Shearpin is a deep, fast chute that flows into Minonipi Lake between rows of smooth black boulders on either side. From these rocks, it drops off straight down. It is about ten yards wide at this spot and I'd guess ten feet deep.

On one of my casts, I get a bump and set the hook. It's an eight-incher. That's unusual. Most of the small fish stay further up streams, out of the lake, until they get big enough to venture down here where the big boys play. As this little fish is struggling in the water, hanging suspended by my line and flipping and flopping just on the edge of one of the rocks beside the drop off, a big fish comes up from the depths and slashes at him. He missed. Instantly, he comes again. This time he virtually swallows the little guy. That's right. The little trout virtually disappears into his mouth, which appears as wide as the mouth of a largemouth bass. He's one of the biggest Minipi brookie I have ever seen. That monster swallows the trout in one gulp and breaks me off. Snap. Quicker than I can tell it.

"Howard! Did you see that?

"Big pike, "Howard says laconically.

"No, no. It was a big, really big trout. I saw him. Came at the fish twice. Jeez, I could count his spots. Right here at my feet. Right here. A big trout. I mean a *big* one. Ripped the little trout right off my hook."

"Pike," Howard said.

"No, no, Howard. It was a trout. I swear. A trout. Biggest one I've ever seen."

"Pike," said Howard.

After that I can't concentrate and after about an hour or so, Jake stops casting and says, "Hey, Ed, you should try it down here."

"That's not easy, Jake, at least not while you're there."

"Oh, ah, well, yeah, I'll move up stream. You come on down here. Let's trade places. You got a muddler?"

"Yeah."

"Lemme see it," he says. I show him my #8 muddler.

"Too big. Try this," he hands me a #10 lightly tied mini-muddler. I take off the #8 and tie on his #10. But in spite of Jake's apparent luck with this smaller fly, I have no confidence in it. Fact is, I am still having trouble concentrating after that monster ate my guppy trout. I out my #8 back on the line and cast a couple of times. There's a strong take.

"Whoa, there goes one!"

"Are you using the muddler I gave you," Jake asks.

"No. I put the #8 back on."

"Oh, OK," he says.

I can see him fiddling with his fly. Looks like he's putting on a fresh one. His other one was probably sinking too fast. Took him only a few seconds, then he turns, makes a prodigious double-haul cast from his upstream position and lands his fly downstream in the center of Shearpin. Matter of fact right where I had got my rise.

His fly alights near enough that I can see the splash. It looks like a big muddler, a # 8—just like mine! He moves a step down stream and casts again. This time he gets a hit and hooks a five-pound brookie. He plays it masterfully in the swift water and lets Howard net it. By now I'm drinking a beer in the beached boat, resting my arm, smelling the roses and swatting the flies.

By the way, Jake's fish are never weighed (he doesn't allow it). What he does is declare the weight himself. According to Jake, every fish he's caught today and yesterday and the day before, none are less than five pounds. Yet none are subjected to the scale. None is photographed. Every fish is released quickly with encomiums like, "A beautiful five-pounder." "Nice fish. Five pounds." "A fine six-pounder." "Six-and-a-half." "Big female, seven pounds, fat as a football." Howard always shakes his head in agreement. Every evening, usurping the guide's duty, Jake records his daily catch—poundage, place and fly—in the camp's logbook.

The next day I go back up to Shearpin. This time fishing alone with a guide named Herb. I catch a nice one right there in the center of the run. It tips the scales at six pounds. I miss two others. Jake would have nailed them.

Outward Bound: Expedition to Johnnie Lake.

You know those Outward Bound schools? The ones where executives go to have a wilderness experience and learn self-reliance, survival skills and team work? That's what it can be like to be fishing with Jake when he decides to go in search of virgin waters. Take, for example, our Johnnie Lake expedition with Herb guiding.

To get there we had to lug the big red canoe up a veritable Everest of boulders, with each stage of the ascent growing more arduous than the last. We were dragging that big red canoe straight up a shallow, rumbling boulder-strewn rapids—I mean some of those boulders were the size of VW Beetles.

No surprise, Jake goes first, walking atop the rocks and pulling manfully on the bright green bow line. Herb is up to his waist in the water on the right side of the canoe pushing. I am at the stern pushing. As times I am up to my armpits in the rapids, at other times I am completely out of the water, tip-toeing over the top of a rock. The aluminum canoe sticks to the rocks leaving vivid red marks.

Once, when I sank into a man-swallowing hole, the end of the canoe lurched around like a swung sledge hammer, the force of the blow sheared off my wrist watch (thank God it wasn't a Rolex like Jake's) and slammed me against a rock. The gunwale careened into my ribs just below my little beating heart.

Herb saw it. "You, OK?" he said. "Ah, yeah." I was lying. Fact is, I felt like Mike Tyson had just hit me. I thought I might have cracked a rib or two. But I managed to catch my breath and pushed on.

When we finally reached the end of one of these struggles, I slumped onto a rock, took a deep breath (ouch!) and let out a cautious sigh of relief (ouch!). Although I could not see it, I thought that we had reached the edge of the lake that Jake sought. Whew! Maybe we could now do some fishing. But I couldn't help thinking about the agony to come on the way back. I was, however, wrong on the first count. We had not attained Jake's goal. And I knew I was in deep trouble when I hallucinated and saw, rising from the mists, a sign that said "Welcome to Detroit." At this point I said, "Enough (ouch!). Enough (ouch!) already!"

When I said that, Herb, who had said nothing except, "You Ok," the whole day, and who had worked like an army mule with Jake in the saddle all the way up the rocky streambed, now he showed a glimmer of compassion for my point of view. Up to that moment he had been Jake's uncomplaining portage slave. I was just along for the ride. Jake still wanted to press on but Herb, God bless him, did pause to hear what I had to say. And I said, speaking directly to Jake—"Shit, man, if the world record brook trout, even a ten-pounder, is up there—guaranteed—just around the bend, then let's go for it. But if we're gonna drag this canoe and motor up another mile of streambed and when we get there you're gonna say, aw shucks, water's too low, just another pike hole, let's push on boys, then, then, gentlemen," I turned to look at Herb, " I'll wait here for you. This is getting to be fucking (ouch!) ridiculous."

Jake thinks Johnnie Lake must be just around the bend. My comments mean nothing. They don't even seem to annoy him. He's not even really listening. Herb says it doesn't look so good up ahead and volunteers to scout up there beyond the dogleg in the dwindling stream. This portage looks particularly nasty from where I'm standing. You can see the incline with the naked eye, and the boulders are bigger and closer together with only tiny rivulets of white water running between them.

Herb returns with the report that above the dogleg it looks very tough indeed. There's a big deadfall across the stream. Again, Jake appears not even to listen. He goes up to see for himself. I hang back, shoot some pictures, figuring that whoever finds our bodies will have the film developed and give the pictures to my widow so she can put 'em in the family album as a keepsake for my daughter under the caption, "Your Daddy was a real man."

Jake reconnoiters, comes back and says, "Yeah, you're right," he speaks to Herb, never directly to me, There's deadfall up there. Big tree across the stream."

"Getting late, too," says Herb.

"Alright," says Jake, "let's go back." The triumph of reason over fanaticism.

Now I am here, thank God, to tell you, if getting up there—wherever the hell we were and wherever the hell we were going—was Hell, going back was Purgatory.

What's worse, I'd guess that Jake and I had cast a combined total of, oh, say, six or seven times, on the whole trip so far. Of course, going back, once we cleared the last stretch of the rocky stream and finally got to open water, we did stop and fish a smooth run where I hooked and lost a good fish. (Funny, I've never hooked and lost a bad fish. Unless it was a pike.) Oh, Jake? He landed a six-pounder in that same slick.

Late that night, fortified with Advil, a tumbler of Scotch and a few glasses of wine, I limped down the narrow boardwalk to the guide's shack—humming that old familiar blues tune oo, ah, oo, oo, ah, oo, ah, oo, oo, ah. Once there I prevailed upon Raymond to encircle my chest with duct tape. A day or two later I made Randy, Ray's brother—had to do it at knife point—remove it. He reluctantly put his foot on my butt, grasped the end of the tape and with a mighty pull did the deed. I spun around like a top and toppled onto the ground.

"EEEEeeeeeooooow!"

The hair that I once had on my chest will likely grow back but henceforth I shall be known as ole tit-less Ed. Now that's not true but at the time Randy thought it was.

What the hell, I have bragging rights and an Outward Bound certificate of accomplishment signed by none other than Jake Wheeler. He later said, with a twinge of apology but no remorse, "Gee, Quigley. Had I known you were that old, I wouldn't have put you through that."

It still hurt but only when I breathed, coughed, laughed, swallowed, walked, crawled, hopped, skipped, jumped, burped, sneezed, blew my nose or talked to others about my warm feelings for Jake Wheeler.

The night after our adventure, I longed for a good night's sleep. My roommate at Anne Marie happened to be a lovely little man with a chronic snoring disorder. "Hope this won't bother you," he kindly said.

"No problem. I hope just hope the smell of this Ultra Extra Strength Ben-Gay won't bother *you*." "No problem, none at all," he said.

The next morning at breakfast, Jim Wheeler, Jake's tall, patrician, handsome, scholarly white-haired father (who, by the way refuses to ever fish with his son Jake), asked my roommate if he had slept well.

The lovely little man replied: "Oh, yes. OK, I guess. But I had to tell Ed to turn over a couple of times. His snoring kept me awake all night. And that ointment."

24

WALKER'S CAY

Ashley Nixon pulled up in a shiny Chevy Impala station wagon. She is wearing a fitted buttery-brown leather jacket over a white satin blouse; a pair of tight khaki twills breaking slightly on the insteps of her Bandolino boots. Her driving gloves fit snugly. She is five-nine, a brunette with jade eyes. Not exactly what you'd expect an airport limo driver to look like. Come to think of it, she looked like an actress playing the lead in The Life of Amelia Earhart.

Ashley and I chatted on the way to the Philadelphia airport where I had a rendezvous with US Air flight 1624 bound for West Palm Beach. She told me that she and her mother Marie own a yarn shop in Lansdale. The limo? She drives it on the side to make some extra money. A lady friend owns the company. She helps out when they're a driver short. The extra money will come in handy when she marries George in June.

◆ ◆ ◆

My buddy, the inscrutable Steve, meets me at the West Palm Beach Airport and we spend the rest of the day running errands to provision his boat for the Gulf Stream crossing to Walker's Cay with stops at the liquor store for Southern Comfort and Scotch, to the grocery store for V-8 juice for me and orange juice for him, chocolate chip cookies, thick-cut bacon, farm-fresh eggs, two cases, cans, of Miller's Genuine Draught, Steve's cannot-be-without-them Fig Newtons, and two cartons of Marlboro cigarettes, just to name some of the most vital victuals. Having finished that we stop by the optometrist's to pick up Steve's new pair of prescription Serengeti sunglasses. Special for the trip.

His boat, "The Getaway," is a 29-foot 320 horsepower inboard Luhrs sportfisher "hardtop" with a 12-foot beam and a 300-gallon diesel fuel tank. Remember that fuel capacity because when on a boat like this, you *never* want to say, "Fill 'er up on me, pal." Plus, before I forget, there's a whole complement of electronic navigational gear; all you'd ever need: radar, loran and GPS.

The boat's docked at father-in-law Bill McDonough's home-side slip in Delray Beach. Steve's a free man for a week since his wife Patti and her mother have gone to Greece.

Ship's Log: Friday, October 28th

We cast off in late afternoon and cruise up the ICW (Intercoastal Waterway), stopping along the way to visit Kathy, Steve's sister-in-law and Skip, her husband. They recently bought a 12-year-old sloop, a handsome sailing ship with a gleaming, just-refinished teak deck. Teak parquet floors inside the cabin, too. The detailing is fabulous. There's a hand-painted cobalt blue-and-white Italian sink with gold faucets in the bathroom. Excuse me, "head."

Skip and Kathy are in the final stages of outfitting her for a three-year sail in the Caribbean.

After a tour of their sloop, topped off with tall drinks on the deck, we resume our journey up the waterway. It's now dark and after facing and solving a few of the usual navigational quandaries, we find ourselves at the entrance to Palm Beach Inlet in the vicinity of Peanut Island. On our way, we passed under nine draw bridges. We were heading up through Flagler Memorial and Lake Worth to our night's anchorage within sight of the big ships at anchor in the Port of Palm Beach.

Navigating after dark is accomplished by following buoy-set red and green flashing marker lights. Their position and the periodicity of their flashes have a significance known to the captain. So, when Steve sees one, he notes whether it is flashing red or green and every four seconds as the chart says it should. Thus, we'd sometimes stop within sight of a marker buoy until Steve could locate it on his chart to verify our position. But Steve is an experienced captain in a well-equipped boat and there would be far sterner tests of his seamanship in the days ahead.

Once we were anchored, Steve pulled out the propane grill, which fits into a gimbal cantilevered over the stern on the boat's port side. Not only is Steve a good sailor, but he's an accomplished cook. So, after cocktails, we had a crisp, chilled Caesar's salad with rolled anchovies followed by asparagus and baby carrots, grilled pork sirloin, and warmed rolls. After dinner we sat in deck chairs smoking—me a Monticristo and Steve a Marlboro. We sipped Taylor Fladgate Vintage Port. Before climbing into our bunks at 11:30 P.M., Steve carefully plotted our course to Walker's Cay and entered waypoint coordinates into the ship's GPS.

Because the current at this anchorage flows at about 4 to 5 knots, it makes gurgling sounds throughout the night as it passes underneath the ship's fiberglass hull. It also held the anchor line tight. Very tight it seemed to me, so once I was comfortably ensconced in my bunk, I asked Steve what would happen if the anchor line snapped while we were sleeping. His answer: "Oh, nothing much. We'd just end up down stream somewhere."

I watched the lights go out on the pleasure craft anchored nearby, among them a sleek twin-hulled sail boat named "The Stray Cat," and not far away, I could see the hulking forms of the commercial vessels—a Western Tiger freighter and two container ships with the hot-orange word "TROPICAL" stenciled on their sides. The lights from the Port of Palm Beach stayed on all night putting yellow twinkles on the dark purple water.

Ship's Log: Saturday, October 29th

During the night, our onboard freshwater pump silently expired and we awoke to no running water. That could be fixed at Walker's. (Besides, if we got thirsty, we had those cases of Miller's.) So, unconcerned, we had breakfast: a bagel slathered with Philadelphia cream cheese topped with lox and washed down with strong coffee. I had a side of V-8 juice mixed with a dash of Worcestershire and a splash of Miller's. We upped anchor at 8:45 A.M. and sailed out of Palm Beach inlet into the open ocean.

We set a heading due east for Memory Rock (N 26° 57', W 079° 07'), a small, isolated island about 15 miles north of West End, the extreme western tip of Grand Bahamas Island. It is the ideal place to go safely onto the Bahamas bank, day or night. (It is lit at night, most of the time).

We got to within a mile of the rock, avoiding the sand banks near its western edge, and held our easterly heading for about another 2 miles before turning NNE to pass east of the rocks and west of the sand bank.

By the way, the so-called Sugar Wreck, located near Memory Rock, is considered to be the best shallow water shipwreck in the entire Caribbean because it attracts such a huge variety of brilliantly colored aquatic life.

Our Gulf Stream crossing was rough with 4- to 6-foot seas but we made it to the rock in good time. We made that right turn safely and sighted Walker's around 2:45 P.M. and made our way carefully through the nautical maze of reefs, sand bars and strong currents into Walker's harbor.

Walker's Cay, Abaco, Bahamas, is the northern outermost island in the Abaco chain made famous by Flip Pallot's TV sportfishing series "The Walker's Cay Chronicles." It is a small island, less that one mile long and half a mile wide. It has a 75-slip, full-service marina where the dockage fee includes access to all of the resort's facilities. There's one hotel (62 rooms, three villas), a small airstrip (2,500 feet), a tiny launderette for the more fastidious sailors, a small restaurant, The Lobster Trap, a tiny chapel with colorful stained-glass windows and two shops one of which located in the hotel lobby sells Rum Reggae batik shirts along with other stylish high-end resort wear for gentlemen and ladies. That's about it. (Funny, I don't remember a tackle shop.)

We tidied up the ship and before dinner went to the hotel's club pool for a swim and a couple of Pina Coladas. For dinner at the Lobster Trap—because a wedding party was using the club dining room—we ordered conch salad, conch chowder, cracked conch, grouper and blackened snapper.

Ship's Log: Sunday, October 30th

There's a wedding in the chapel. Pretty people in white, yellow and pink clothes are scattered all about like confetti. There's champagne and laughter. We didn't crash the reception, although the thought was there.

We watched some guys who had speared several dozen "lobsters" by snorkeling over the reefs in 4 to 10 feet of water. They now had their catch spread out in a soldierly line on a picnic table beside their grill. It is against the law to *scuba dive* for lobsters or use spear guns. So snorkeling with a hand-held spear is the approved and widely practiced method. One of the guys was cleaning the lobsters and mistakenly flipped the tail in the water beside the marina. (These "lobsters" are really *all* tail, like a large crayfish.) He got up, put on his flippers, dived in, retrieved it, flopped back onto the pier, shed his flippers and, without comment, kept on cleaning the remaining lobsters already on the table. After all, no one wants to waste a succulent lobster, which these days sell for over $10 a pound.

Counting ours, there are only 12 or 13 boats docked at the marina. Of those, only five show any signs of life. The others await the arrival of their owners—via plane from Ft. Lauderdale. These boats are all expensive. Walker's Cay is, after all, a millionaire sport-fishing paradise. Here the vessels have price tags running from $550,000 up and over $2 million. Steve's Sportfisher is, measured by these standards, a relatively modestly priced toy.

But using Steve's boat as an example, when it comes to boats, the numbers are, at least to my ear, impressive. For example, Steve's radar with a 32 mile range costs around $11,000. The outriggers for fishing add another $4,000. The Penn reels on Steve's big deep-sea rods cost $400; $250 for the reels on the smaller spinning rods. The rods themselves are custom made. About $450 each. Even the anchors cost significant bucks. Take the one on Skip and Kathy's sailboat. They paid $495 for it. That's because they bought it at a garage sale. New it would have cost them $1,000.

Looking at all these expensive boats, I asked Steve, "What's the ideal boat?" His answer: "It should drink six, eat four and sleep two."

Ship's Log: Monday, October 31th Halloween!

We've come here to fish for blue marlin, the fish immortalized in *The Old Man and the Sea*. Blues over 1,000 pounds have been caught here. And there are plenty of freelance guides hanging around the marina willing and supposedly able to take you out beyond the tricky reefs for a crack at them. A day of fishing on a Walker's Cay charter costs $750 per person per day. But we have our own boat and Steve dickers with one of the freelance guides until he gets him to agree to take us out on Steve's boat for $125.

Promptly at 8:45 A.M. our guide, one Curtis Russell, appears. He's a tall, loose-limbed somewhat sleep-deprived individual who seems to be carved from black coral. He's wearing a white long-sleeved shirt, faded powder blue cutoffs and high-topped, black canvas basketball sneakers. An impressive gold chain encircles his neck. On his left wrist is a Casio digital watch, a diver's watch as big as a hockey puck. On his right wrist is a gold bracelet and on his right ring finger is a gold ring with some kind of gem in it as big as and as crimson as a cranberry.

Curtis hops on board, and, with Captain Steve at the wheel, he guides us out of the harbor beyond the reefs to an area 6 miles off Walker's Cay. Once the boat is situated as Curtis directs, we bait the hooks and load up the outriggers with the big rods. We do the same with the small spinning rods and place them in the PVC rod holders. That's when trolling commences. Back and forth, back and forth. The boat is bucking like a bronco. It is too rough to do anything but hold on, watch the rods, and do knee bends to cushion the rise and fall of the deck. Drinking a beer or using the head is impossible.

Curtis tells us, "if you're interested, mon, " later you could go to the Walker's Cay Shark Rodeo. "We famous fur dat."

He's talking about shark watching in scuba gear. Seems there's this 35-foot deep sandy area about the size of two Olympic swimming pools surrounded by coral reefs. In the middle of this aquatic playground the dive masters drop a "chumsicle," a large frozen-solid barrel of chopped-up fish offal—guts, heads, tails. The barrel has holes in it and as the contents melts, the surrounding water clouds up with pieces and particles of drifting chum.

That's when the fun begins. Attracted by the melting chumsicle, sometimes as many as a hundred sharks come to engage in a feeding frenzy: reef sharks, nurse sharks and blacktips, sometimes a tiger or a mako. The scuba divers, positioned on the margins of this frenzy, watch the action up-close and personal.

One of the highlights of this "rodeo"—and it happens nearly every time—according to Curtis, is when Charlie, a giant barracuda, swims into the spotlight. The dive masters have trained Charlie to respond to hand signals like the waving of a hand, which means—"Hey, Charlie, come, boy, come, get this fish head." Curtis says that a young woman from Topeka lost her right hand when she mixed up the signals. "They done do dat no more, nod wid de tourists anyhow," says Curtis.

Curtis regales us with other stories of a similar nature, like the one about the first mate on a charter boat who got his arm entangled in the line while trying to land a client's blue marlin. "That fish was still green and when dat fish roll off the transom, he go down, down way deep, and that mate he go wif 'em. Needer dat fish nor dat mate was ever seen again."

In between Curtis's stories we did, however, have some excitement of our own when a gigantic blue marlin rolled at the back of the boat and nailed the "teaser, " an array of floating plastic lures, actually ours was a dozen miniature yellow ducks strung together and set out from the stern on fifteen to twenty feet of 100-pound test mono. Teasers are meant to attract marlin in close by simulating a pod of panicked, fleeing bait fish. The marlin comes in to attack them but usually shies at the sight of the boat and drops back where the ballyhoo baits are set. Hopefully, stimulated by the teaser, he'll take one of the real baits. But they seldom come in close enough to strike the teasers.

But this time as Steve was looking off the stern, he saw a shadow appear below and behind the teasers. He yelled and Curtis and I turned just in time to see a marlin's giant back disappear in a stupendous swirl … along with all the little rubber duckies.

Because of the rough seas, we decided to come back early and link up with Clark Balsinger, the captain of the charter "Funny Feelin Too" out of Venice, Florida. His clients for the day had cancelled and he was hanging around in hopes of picking up another group. Clark's a big, heavy, middle-aged man with a friendly, relaxed manner and earlier he had invited us to join him to snorkel for lobsters.

That's a good idea because we've only caught one small dolphin, about eight pounds, and we need a food supplement.

When we're piling into Clark's flats boat, Dan Ausley one of the partying college students on the island—six guys and two girls—who have come over from Tallassee in open boats, yells over and asks, "Hey, can I join you guys?"

"Sure," says Clark. "Grab your gear."

Dan runs to his boat and grabs his spear, snorkeling mask and flippers.

Here's the drill: Each man has a cotton net bag hooked to his belt. He swims over the reefs looking for lobsters wedged in the folds of the coral. When he sees one, he pokes the tip of his spear into the hole or bumps it around the edge to coax the lobster out. Then he spears it and deposits it in his net bag and snorkels off looking for his next victim.

In spite of his size and bulk, Clark is at the top of this game. He's a veritable reef vacuum. Fact is, he single-handedly, in not more than an hour and a half, spears twelve lobsters. Dan gets two—one a granddaddy of about five pounds. Steve, who's not in the best of shape, and hasn't done this in a long while, gets only a belly full of water. I watch the action and tend the small the boat.

That night we had a lobster feast on the pier with Steve's famous stuffing, bowls of melted butter, Clark's slow-cooked beans and dolphin steaks as the side dish.

It's Halloween. Whoopee! Steve goes up to check out the Halloween Party being held at the airstrip. He's back at 1 A.M with a warm Budweiser for me, but I missed the Bud and his stories of ladies gone wild. I had gone to bed at 10 P.M.

Ship's Log: Tuesday, November 1st

Steve slept late. I got up early and walked to the pool house for a shower and a shave. When Steve finally got up, he tried his hand at fixing the water pump. For Steve, fixing meant hitting it with a hammer while muttering unprintable words.

The island's chief mechanic was working on the manifold on "Liquid Assets" docked next to us. The owner, Joe, an Allstate executive, and his son Rich had nothing to do so they helped Steve disassemble our water pump. But, once it was spread out on the pier, they couldn't get it back together. So we left it there for the mechanic to look at when he finished with Joe's manifold. The pump, what was left of it, ended up at the "Powerhouse, " the island's repair shed and machine shop.

Futzing around with that water pump kept us off the water until 11:30 A.M., and now at 12:55 with no breakfast, we were again out there trolling in 600 feet of water north of Walker's. As usual we're trolling ballyhoo baits. some lures and a new teaser set up. Steve lamented, "That damn yellow-ducky thing cost me $25 bucks."

We had no knock downs (that is when a fish pulls the line out of the outriggers) and went back to the marina at 4:45 P.M. Steve washed the boat down with fresh water from a metered hose ($0.30 a gallon) on the pier. Fresh water cost for the week for 126 gallons was $37.80. Dockage for the week was $215. We spent about $55 for the ballyhoo bait.

When I go to the pool house to take a shower, I meet a writer named Pat Smith. He's here with Kurt Gowdy (remember the American Sportsman Shows?) and Kurt's son to make a segment on bonefishing for ESPN's "Walker's Cay Chronicles." Smith tells me that they're also doing a retrospective on some of Gowdy's adventures. And Smith is working on another project titled "Voices of Baseball" consisting of live interviews with announcers like Costas, Barber, and Mel Allen. He himself had recently interviewed Ted Williams who's in rather good shape considering he recently suffered a stroke.

That night we had planned to go over to a place called Rosie's for dinner. It's a short boat ride away on Grand Cays, a neighboring island where most of the locals live—but the water "taxi" never showed so we ended up having dinner with Joe and his son Rich and Jim and Lucinda Pynes, a couple on holiday from Switzerland, who call the sail boats "blow boats."

Ship's Log: Wednesday, November 2nd

The next morning we walk up to the hotel for breakfast. The usual: two eggs over light, cracked conch, and a rasher of bacon. You know, the works. Then we hook up again with Curtis who, this time, is taking us bonefishing in his small outboard motor boat, "Top Gun." We putter past Grand Cays, pass by Rosie's and head over to the flats surrounding Sandy Cay. This excursion is costing us $100 each for half a day.

It's nearly 10 A.M. before we leave and we're back at 12:45 P.M. because the wind was kicking our butts. And now it had shifted and, in Curtis's small boat, it was get back now or get stranded.

While we were there, we waded the shallow flats and used Curtis's decrepit spinning rods baited with small hunks of conch to cast to incoming schools of bonefish. You can see them coming in because they make what appear to be rain squalls on the surface of the shallow water. Then you see their dorsal fins sticking out of the water. Sometimes you see their tails when they tip up and nose down to root along the bottom for shrimp. When coming in, they swim like lightening strikes in pods of 25, 30, 50 fish moving like a single organism through sometimes not more than six inches of water.

We throw our hunks of conch ahead of these in-coming schools. Almost every time we get nibbles but few takes ... until we master the technique, which is to cast and then throw the bale off the reel to let the bait sink. Then when you feel the nibble you let the fish pick up the bait without feeling any resistance. If he feels resistance, he drops the bait instantly. Then when the fish swims off with the bait in his mouth and the line has free-spooled for a few seconds, you throw the bale and set the hook. And you do this gently because they have small, soft, circular mouths that resemble the mouths of a freshwater suckers or carp. But the bonefish mouth is more delicate, not as rubbery. When we did it right, we caught some nice three, three-and-a-half pounders. And as soon as you stick them, they turn tail and streak like a scalded cat for the deeper water. They'll run for a hundred yards easily before you can turn them. They never give up until they hit your hand.

When we got back I noticed that there are no more than 18 or 20 people on the island. At night the locals get into their small outboards and go over to Grand Cays. Things in general are laconic, if not soporific on the island. The little gift shop at the hotel has a "Closed" sign hanging on its door knob, in spite of the fact that it is open. Same thing at the grocery store. The sign on the door says "Closed" when it's open and "Open" when it's closed. No one seems to notice, or noticing, to care.

By the way, those college kids from Florida State in Tallahassee had hauled over—I am not exaggerating—40 cases of beer. Remember, they came across the Gulf Stream in open boats. Outboards. Lots of ballast.

Ship's Log: Thursday, November 3rd

Sunshine eggs this morning on an unmade bed of buttered grits and cracked conch. Orange juice and coffee.

Kurt Gowdy, his son and the film crew go out again for bones on the flats. In spite of all their sophisticated high-end gear, they are not having much luck and Kurt, protected from the sun in a Tilley hat, long-sleeved shirt and long pants, looks bored and tired.

Bill, Steve's stepson, arrives with a case of beer on the 3 P.M. plane from Fort Lauderdale, a 150-mile flight. Bill's about 30, tall, blond, fit, handsome. A nice, serious kid. Something would happen on the trip to change his opinion of me, but, no matter what, I still think he's a good kid and was glad to have him come aboard.

Besides Bill's arrival, the excitement today day centered on the arrival of a super yacht, a Starlight brand, a 96-footer, which has been grounded beyond the reefs at the entrance to the harbor. Now on high tide, it has managed to nose its way into the outer-most slip at the very end of the pier.

You should see this thing. It's the shape of a "cigarette" boat with a sleek, low silhouette. It is painted shimmering ebony with touches of intense, iridescent cobalt and gleaming chrome. It is creamy white at the water line. She's the El Devino, "The Divine." And were she mine, I'd name her El Diablo, and in English I'd say that that means, "Satan of The Seas." She flies the Panamanian flag and has four red-white-and-blue seadoos poised for action on her afterdeck.

She is the new toy of the Ramirez brothers, bankers from Mexico City.

According to John Gordon, whose big yacht lies next to ours in the marina, El Devino would cost something like $60,000 a year just for the insurance and probably $250,000 for the crew ($50,000 for the Captain of the ship, $35,000 for the Chef). Plus the four mates, two female and two male. John says that like a lot of these boats, this one was built in Italy and easily cost $5,000,000. This is not to mention the cost to ferry her across the Atlantic on a freighter to Miami. That means the trip from Miami to Walker's Cay was her maiden voyage.

An hour or so after the El Devino arrived, I had the honor of meeting one of the female mates as she's wheeling a hand truck along the pier with two canvas bags balanced on it.

When she's opposite our boat, I say, "Hello, what's with those bags, Captain?"

"Darlin', this here's nothing but plain ole dirty laundry."

Turns out that in spite of her size and splendor, El Devino has only one small washing machine aboard. So this morning the mate has to do seven loads of the Ramirez' family wash at the marina's three-machine launderette.

"Well then, Captain," I said, "you'll surely need some help."

"Sir, I shore do and I warmly accept your most chivalrous offer."

Now this 20-something Texan is as cute as a button. Her blonde hair is twirled up in a stylish chignon and she's dressed in a starched white shirt open at the collar with blue and gold epaulettes on the shoulders. Her just-above-the-knees pleated skirt is dark blue. Her shoes white. Her name's Christie. Her father was a CHIPS (California highway patrolman) who moved to Houston with her and her two brothers from San Diego to open a bar. She says, reference being a mate, that she's "been in the sailing business" all her life. She tells me that El Devino will sail for Treasure Cay in the morning and then on to Nassau from where, after a week or so, the banker brothers and their families will fly back to Mexico City. Christie and the crew will "play" for a few days and then sail the ship back to Miami.

So I help her wheel seven loads of laundry to the launderette. Along the way we talk and kid around with each other. While waiting for the first three loads to finish washing and drying, we sit by the pool drinking gin and tonic. Naturally we get chummier on each trip. And while we're waiting for the last load to go through the dryer, I persuade Christie to help play a joke on Steve and Bill.

Here's the setup:

On our last trip Christie and I would stay up there at the pool longer than usual, killing time consuming more a gin and tonic—and to kill even more time, we'd throw in a tour of the chapel. Before we start back, Christie, as part of the sting, would pull out her shirt tail, unbutton three buttons on her blouse, unpin her hair and smear a smudge of lipstick on me.

Then, hand-in-hand, we'd walk back to where Steve and Bill are lounging on the Getaway drinking afternoon beers. When we get directly opposite them, we'd stop. I'd place a grandfatherly kiss on Christie's cheek and say, in a stage whisper,

"I'll miss you Christie." She'll reply, "Eddie, I won't forget you. That was special. Y'all *will* write to me? Promise?"

After our emotional parting, according to plan, she'd continue down the pier to El Devino. I'd stay there looking longingly after her. Half way to the yacht, she'd turn and wave to me wistfully. Then, just before she boards, she'd turn again, raise her tiny hand to her lips and blow me a kiss.

Well the plan as outlined above worked flawlessly. Even better than expected because the ever playful Christie—whether it was true love or gin-and-tonic-induced infatuation—she responded to my grandfatherly peck with a real hug and a deep and loving kiss.

When our little contrived drama unfolded before the unbelieving eyes of Steve and Bill—they were not more than four feet from the loving couple on the pier—young Bill's face contorted into a mixture of surprise, bewilderment, envy and red-faced, gut-wrenching anger. Steve, he just sat there looking like a deer caught in the headlights.

When the curtain fell, I hopped on board and said, "Hey, Billy Boy, got one of those cold Beck's? I've worked up quite a thirst."

"Why you son-of-a-bitch. Get your own beer."

Steve, always unflappably ready to dispense fatherly wisdom, said, "Bill, there's no reason to get upset with Quigley; you could just have easily offered to help that little lady with her laundry. He who hesitates, son. is lost. Oh, Bill, while you're up, get *me* a beer too."

"Get your own f-ing beer!"

Ships Log: Friday, November 4th

The next morning at 9:00 A.M. sharp the three of us, with Curtis on board, set off to troll again for blue marlin in the still rough seas. Before noon we had two serious takedowns and lost some baits and lures but by the time we headed back at 3 P.M., we had managed to catch only two small black tuna.

That night we had cocktails and munchies onboard John Gordon's yacht, the Ashton Gordon and then joined the Gordon's for dinner at the hotel. The only other people in the dining room that evening were Kurt Gowdy, his son, Smith (the writer) and the ESPN camera and sound crew. That's about ten people counting us.

While waiting for dessert, I went over to talk with Kurt, a most gracious gentleman, and we ended up exchanging cigars. I got the best of the deal. His were Cubans, mine Honduran.

When I came back to our table, there was the inevitable boat talk going on. For me it was a revelation. Let's take, for example, just one more money fact: the very special paint on the hull of John's boat costs $269 a gallon. (I would hope it's barnacle-proof!) This means that it would cost $18,000 to dry haul and paint the five-ton Ashton Gordon, a boat that was "built to spec" for John.

Over after-dinner coffee, John, a tall, amiable, blue-eyed man with snow-white short-cropped hair and a deep tan, starts talking about what it's like to be a *former* CEO and how one becomes habituated to the good life. Take note of "former." Now he's got to cut back a bit, he says, at least for awhile.

That means his boat is up for sale. And just in case you know anyone who wants to buy or charter John's great, big, beautiful motor yacht, here's the complete description verbatim from the brochure he gave me:

Built by Seaway Yachts in 1985, the dimensions of this "Trawler" type yacht are 67' 6" by 20' x 4' 6". It is powered by a Caterpillar 3406 Turbodiesel. The fuel water spec in gallons is 2250/500 plus a watermaker. Cruising speed 11 knots. Berths 10. Heads 4. Electronics: radar, satnav, loran, (2) VHF's, SSB, fathometer, knotlog, autopilot w/interface.

This extraordinary and unique motor yacht was designed by Charles Wittholz and features a one-off fiberglass hull and superstructure construction. Drawing only 4'6", this graceful and sturdy yacht is ideal for cruising the shoal waters of the Bahamas and Caribbean.

The Ashton Gordon sleeps up to 14 in air-conditioned comfort. The galley is larger and better equipped than most yachts twice the size, and includes a range, 17 ft.[3]

refrigerator in 14 ft.³ freezer, microwave, dishwasher, trash compactor, garbage disposal and icemaker. A utility room forward of the galley has a full-sized Maytag washer and dryer.

The Master State Room features a round king-sized bed, and a private bath with marble-topped his-and-her vanities.

A 600gpd Sea Recovery watermaker replenishes the water supply with clean, mineral-free water. The enclosed pilothouse offers air-conditioned comfort in even the most inclement weather, and visibility is enhanced by its 24-foot height above the water.

Diving enthusiasts will be pleased by the yacht's ability to fill scuba tanks even while anchored at remote locations. A Bauer compressor is located in the engine room and air is pumped to the upper deck.

Man I love these boats! John and Patsy had given us a tour of the Ashton Gordon before dinner. I was amazed. You can actually go down four or five steps into the engine compartment and walk, although a bit cramped, around the huge yellow engine. The "Master State Room" is a bedroom suite nearly as elegant as a suite at the Plaza. The captain's chair in the pilothouse looks like a millionnaire's custom-made Lazyboy. It is a real work of art—chrome, creamy leather and polished brass. The control panel is spread out like a fabulous collection of pristine gadgets under glass.

Anyway, John continued his former-CEO lament.

"You know," he went on, "back then, if I saw something I wanted, anything, I just bought it. If I wanted to go somewhere, I just went there. Took four Colorado ski trips every year. London, Madrid, Rome, Singapore. You name it. We went there. Owned homes in Boca Raton and Connecticut. Had an apartment in New York. Owned my own plane. Still do." (He'd leave his boat here so it would be available for charters and his pilot would fly over from Fort Lauderdale to pick him and Patsy up later in the week.)

Ship's Log: Saturday, November 5th

Having tasted the high-tone-teak-and-chrome elegance and social élan of Walker's Cay, I asked Steve where the hoi polloi stayed in these parts. On second thought, was there any common ground at all under these paradisal skies? His answer was, "You can see for yourself. I'll stop at West End on the way back. There's heavy weather coming and we can wait it out over there."

So that morning we set sail for West End, the very western tip of Grand Bahama Island, in six-foot swells and gusting winds, an estimated two-and-a-half hour voyage.

And here I would find my answer. It would be an economical move, too, because at West End's Jack Tar Marina everything is, no surprise, cheaper. Water costs only 20 cents a gallon. Diesel is far cheaper too. Steve took advantage of this by taking on 75 gallons. That's when I first noticed the forsaken character of this place.

Patches of rust ate away at the pump pier itself. And from there I could see stray cats wandering around on shore seemingly everywhere, even a few had found their way out here onto the rusty pier itself. In shore I could see several dilapidated and abandoned buildings surrendering to the invasion of the tropical forest.

Chief among these relics is a forbidding ruin of a once seemingly grand resort hotel, which now stood with its balconies and parapets bowing in decay. What was left of this building stood in tatters like a castaway, the last, long suffering survivor of some horrible calamity. It looks a hundred years old, yet only five years ago, soon after it was abandoned, it was ransacked of all furniture and fixtures, everything worth taking. Now only the chirping birds and meowing cats are here to sing its requiem.

What economic or natural catastrophe caused this collapse, I have no idea. But Steve says he thinks the owner/builder ran out of money fighting the Bahamian bureaucracy.

To my eye, preened by the luxury of Walker's Cay, this whole place had a difficult-to-describe air of neglect. Ours was the only motor boat in sight. All the others appeared to be vintage, wooden-hulled sailboats with names like "Tropic Venture, Philadelphia;" "Banker's Holiday, Hilton Head, S.C.;" and "The Boo Boo," "The Candy Joy," "The Wet Dream." They were all lined up at the slips like neglected houses on a forgotten street in a forgotten town.

Some appeared to have been here for months, some perhaps for years. And I thought that one or two, like us, had just pulled in the night before to wait for smoother seas. In fact, Steve has continually stayed in touch by radio with Rich on "Liquid Assets," which along with several other ships, elected to wait out the weather back at Walker's.

After taking on fuel, we pulled into a slip between two of these decrepit senior citizens of the sea. No sooner had we tied off when a black boy, let's say sixteen-years-old with legs as skinny as a spider, scampered up the dock. He was barefooted and wearing only a pair of white shorts. He had the usual heavy gold chain around his neck.

He offered to drive us in to town. "Git you anythin' ya want. Name it mon, I get it. Fast. Just name it, mom. Wine, women, song. All's ya gouta do is name it."

Steve tells him we will need a ride into town, come back in an hour and a half, which he does. But we're not ready. Steve tells him to come back in an hour.

Steve is below deck fussing around. I'm mopping the deck with fresh water. Bill's leaning on the rail opening a Beck's. That's when I look up and notice two curious guys with cherry-red cheeks leaning shoulder-to-shoulder over the rail of their sail boat the "Hermitage," which is docked alongside us.

Like the I-can-get-you-anything spiderman, they have on nothing but white shorts. Their twiggy legs poke out of them like straws in a vanilla shake. Both are as tan as burned toast. Both have white stubble on their cheeks and chins. Their heads are shaved. Both are in their seventies.

Looking down on us from their perch, the one on the right says, "Zat nice tan you 'ave tere, you two. You dere," he's looking at me, "you look like ze papa, ze Papa Hemingway. What you think, Andre?"

"Ya, tan like a bunny, both. And Papa, ze yellow bandana looks nice against dat salt-und-pepper hair. So, hullo, dere, you two! Vhere you come from? Vhere you going?"

"Hello," I answered. "From Walker's Cay. Going to Delray Beach when the weather clears."

"Say, you vant to 'ave a drink vid us vhen you've tidied up your boat? You and your friends? All tree of ya."

"I don't know what we've got planned."

After one glance up at Hans and Andre, Bill slipped below deck. He's there now grabbing Steve by the arm and saying, "Steve, Steve, did you *see* those guys? We gotta cut the anchor line and get the hell outa here fast. Move to another slip. C'mon, man."

Bill lets go of Steve and starts fumbling around his bunk, grabs a pair of jeans and goes through the pockets.

"Bill, what the hell are you looking for? Steve asks.

"My friggin' Swiss Army knife, what else?"

Steve turns and sticks his head out of the cabin and says, "Hello." There's a big grin on his face as he looks up at Hans and Andre.

"Ve vas vundering if you boys vant to come 'ave a cocktail vith us?"

"Maybe after dinner. Yeah. How about that?" Steve answers.

"Vunderful. Vunderful. Time doesn't madder much here. So you come ven-efer. OK?"

The spiderman doesn't come back a second time, so, while we're at the marina office checking in and paying up, we ask the clerk to call us a taxi to take us into town. In ten minutes, Bruce arrives in a Dodge Dart as speckled with rust as a Dalmatian is with spots.

The road into town, two miles, is hard-packed, charcoal gray sand. The vividly green jungle stands close on both sides like crowded spectators at a St. Patrick's Day parade.

The "town" is nothing more than a quarter block of unpainted, jerry-built wooden structures tottering wearily on either side of the street. Each building, one-storey shacks in truth, has weathered to light gray so that the street looks like one of those long-abandoned mining towns you see out West.

According to Bruce, there's only one place to eat a proper meal, Yvonne's. And there, we are served by Yvonne herself, a 55-gallon drum of a woman in a faded, nothing-underneath-it pink satin shift decorated with splashes of grease. The shift is spaghetti-strapped and scoop-necked. Her breasts are veritable mountains as black as a moonless night. Her seemingly perpetual smile reveals teeth as bright and white as a full moon. In spite of her size, she moves back and forth from kitchen to table with the liquid motions and balance of a ballerina.

We order beers and Cracked Conch Salad. It is as hot as a three-alarm fire. To put the fire out, we take gulps beer and eat fresh baked bananas and take bites of hard-crusted bread. For the entrée, we each have a brimming basket of fried conch.

Bruce waited for us outside, passing the time smoking the Honduran cigar I gave him. After dinner he took us to the liquor shack where we bought 3 cases of clear-bottle Beck's. Much cheaper here than at Walker's so we were stocking up.

Back at the boat, we noticed that "Hermitage" is lit up like a Christmas tree. Hans and Andre are expecting company for after-dinner drinks.

Bill's plumb tuckered out and tanked up on Beck's. No surprise that he demurs—"You gotta be kidding. Not on your life!" He flops onto his bunk.

Steve and I climb the gangplank and board the venerable "Hermitage."

Hans and Andre are all scrubbed up and dressed as if they were twins: Rum Reggae batik shirts and yellow, white and red stripped silk belts knotted around the waist to hold up their long, white linen pants. Both wear thongs. Andre's toe nails are painted a wistful lavender blue.

Their ship's cabin looks like a Victorian sitting room. There are fringed lamp shades and delicately tatted antimacassars on the back and arms of two red-velvet

Queen Anne wing chairs. What appear to be votive candles are flickering here and there sending small scampers of gold light throughout the room.

Hans and Andre insist that we drink Rusty Nails, an after-dinner drink ordinarily consisting of an ounce-and-a-half of Scotch and the same amount of Drambuie poured over two cubes in an old-fashioned glass. But Hans says, "Andre is an expert ad dis mix. You'll see," making me think that he might have in mind some more sinister variation. The only variation, however, from the standard formula is in the glass itself. Andre serves his Rusty Nail in stemmed champagne glasses balanced on a silver tray. How elegant.

Steve and I settle down into the twin velvet chairs to sip our drinks. Hans and Andre pull up two straight-back canvas deck chairs and begin to chatter on the subject of their itinerary since early September.

"Oh, I think," says Hans, "that soon ve'll sail over to Marsh Harbour; ve 'ave friends dere, you know, and den on to da Virgin Islands to celebrate Christmas. Don't you think, Hans, that Christmas in da Virgin Islands vould be special? Ve've never done dat before."

"Well, why not? Why not, indeed? Let's *do* do that. Ah, but, oh, allow me this flight of fancy, Hans. Think how wonderful it might be to spend Christmas, *Christmas* on Christmas Island. But, I know, I know, we must be careful with our resources."

"To hell vith dat. De time for dat is long past. Besides I am told you cannot take it vith you. So vat ve must do, Andre, it to spend it vile ve're here. My motto is, *die broke.*"

Andre laughs a small laugh, "He-he, what I want to do is one better. I want to make out my last check to the undertaker and have it, how you say, *bounce!*" He throws both hands up and they both laugh as if there were no one else in the room.

Steve abruptly makes an excuse to leave—"Oh, Ed, I've got to make that call." He looks at his watch. "You were supposed to remind me. I almost forgot. Patti'll kill me. Ed you stay here. Have another drink."

He turns to Hans and Andre: "Hey, guys. Thanks for the drink. Look, this is Ed's first time in the islands. He needs to absorb the atmosphere. Give him another drink; show him around your boat; regale him with stories of your travels. But, sorry, I gotta go."

So much for friends.

Yeah, I stayed, had another drink to be polite, listened to more prattle, declined the tour, and then wobbled down the Hermitage gangplank and across to our boat. Steve and Bill were snoring contentedly in their bunks.

Later that night, a storm blew in bringing heavy rain and high winds. The Getaway rocked and rolled all night long.

Ship's Log: Sunday, November 6th

At dawn, across the water at the mouth of Walker's Cay harbor, half a dozen boats are lined up with their motors purring, making ready for their dash across the Gulf Stream to various towns along the Florida coast. El Devino, immune to rough weather by virtue of her size and power, had left days ago. Here on West End, we got up at 8 A.M., later than planned, and sailed solo down the channel to the sea.

From the National Weather Service reports, we learned that that was a big blow last night and we are in for a rough sail today. We carefully secure everything, especially the stock of Beck's.

Once we clear West End's harbor channel, Steve's boat starts acting, in his words, "like a big, untrained dog on a leash." He keeps checking in by radio with "Liquid Assets," which got a pre-dawn start from Walker's. She's traveling at 21 knots (we're at about 17), and, given her head start, she will eventually overtake and pass us. Over the radio, Rich, on "Liquid Assets," advises a heading of 5 degrees south. We correct to that heading.

The sky is clear, but the seas are filled with processions of mountainous swells driven by the still high winds. Steve is wrestling with the wheel. After mounting one of the swells, the Getaway's bow tips over and noses deep into the trough, then stabilizes, and tips up to start the climb again—slowing and straining in the ascent. By the time it reaches the top of the wave, our speed has dropped to 4 knots. Then as she slips over the top and plunges down the other side, our speed jumps to 23 knots. The boat is like a kid on a sledding hill, slogging up to the top, then plunging down to the bottom. Again and again. Never having experienced rough-seas travel, this, to me, is beyond imagination. It is worse than the most gut-wrenching roller-coaster ride. All you can do is hold on until your hands go numb.

Under these conditions, it is difficult but critical, to keep a sharp lookout. Steve, Bill and I are standing in the pilot house straining to see through the windshield, which is constantly awash with wind-driven spray as if we were in a carwash. The radar is humming away. We can see "Liquid Asset's" as a blip ahead and to the right. Nothing else.

The seas are strewn with flotsam and jetsam: Styrofoam coolers, boards, garbage, seaweed.

"Good God," I say, "how will those kids from Tallahassee get back?"

Steve answers: "No way. Not today. They're still on the on the island, running out of beer and money."

Suddenly, off to the starboard, I see a big white something wallowing in the waves, riding very low in the troughs and very high on the crests. It is big, square and bright white. It is moving on a line directly toward us propelled by the wind and current. It is closing fast.

"What the hell *is* that? " I yell. "Over there! It's coming right at us!"

Bill sees it—"Oh, shit. It's a f-ing double-door refrigerator, a f-ing refrigerator for God's sake." Steve turns the wheel abruptly. The boat pauses, wallows for a moment, then responds to the rudder.

The big white thing slips by just ten feet off the bow. It is, in fact, a big double-door refrigerator-freezer. It was too low in the water for the radar to pick it up. It is definitely what you would call a hazard to navigation.

"Well, well. Will you look at that? Will—you—look—at—that," says Steve with a John Wayne cadence. "Gentlemen, that is exactly why you would never, not ever, get me, you couldn't pay me enough to make this crossing at night. Even in the calmest seas."

"Hey, hey," says Bill, "that thing, it could be filled with cold beer and steaks. C'mon, guys, what do you say, let's circle back and run her down. What do you say?"

25

AN IRISH COTTAGE

Among the recollections in this book, you will find the tale of how Divine Providence intervened during my fishing trip to the banks of the Culdaff in the north of Ireland. This poem, which pays a tribute to a lovely Irish cottage and recounts a ramble in its environs, lends the back-story to my Culdaff tale. You see, I was staying in this cottage when I set off to find the Culdaff. And it occurred to me that you might like to visit the cottage and join me for that ramble up and down the nearby hills.

Although this poem itself has nothing whatsoever to do with fishing, *per se*, it stands as but one example of the beguiling provenance that so often surrounds fishing adventures. I offer it as yet another proof that there's more to fishing than catching and more to home than a hearth.

◆ ◆ ◆

So, here we are at Carrowhugh
That cottage with ah, oh, so panoramic view
Perched far above, and an ocean away
From the cares that launched us on this holiday.

Now, at Carrowhugh, truth be told, we'd never get up 'til the sun was bright,
The morning mists well out of sight, and the scattered clouds a sparkling white.

That's when we'd commence our morning chores
With many a pause to gaze far below upon Lough Foyle's shores
And count the pa-pa-pa's echoing 'cross the lake from Miggilighan's Camp in the North.

(Ah, how politicians from tranquility do always seem to scrape the sweetest froth!)

Then we'd have a bit of streaky bacon, honey toast and tea
And glance out once again upon the distant, rolling sea.
Then we'd sweater up, pull shut the sturdy door
And set out in our little motor car to explore.

One such day, bright and clear, we headed toward the pier
Down and 'round about the Fort and the Lighthouse we did steer
Till we happed upon a crooked sign. "Inishowen" it read,
Pointing its wooden finger up a tiny path as bumpy as an unmade bed.

Left we turned onto this path with its knobby spine of gorse
And ruts on either side as bony as the ribs of a neglected horse.

Our little motor car, it jolted, jerked and jilted
Waking curious lambs from their beds of heather quilted.
Like wakened jurists, they peered at we two tourists
And bleated in a scornful tone like none-to-friendly choirists,
Reminding us that we were trespassin' through their high domain
Where, but for our intrusion, they would have, undisturbed, all morning lain.

As we crept farther up the rugged path like stealthy, cautious feral cats
The lambs' chorale was now replaced with buzzing bees and busy gnats.
And then it was we came upon a fork—Left? or Right? No signs in sight.
So here we halted in a fright.

Which way to go?

From me pocket, quick, I fetched an Irish pound
And flipped it harp over stag onto the ground.
Thus, to dispel our fear and dread,
I let that coin tell us where to head.
But not far had we rid on the chosen road when a gate we spied
With a rusty latch and a bright blue cord around it tightly tied,
And a ruddy bucket sittin' like a bonnet on its crooked post.
"Lord! This path leads to a farm not down the coast!"

But the gate, we soon surmised, was only there to keep the lambs about
And not so much to keep the tourists out.
So I undid the cord and swung the gate aside
And motored through like a sea bird gliding toward the tide.

Oh, let out a cheer, we did when far below we spied the sandy coast
With a regular road beside it as black and firm as burnt up toast.
And down we goes like bats a wheelin' out of a cavern
And come straight way to Frances McGonagle's Tavern.

Once inside, I orders me a double Irish and me wife a double Russian
And we commenced to tell how up the hills we prayed and done some cussin,'
Told how the path, up there Madra Cruia way, was, oh, so steep and coarse
And how we feared we might end up at night a sleepin' in the gorse.

Fair Frances, she did listen. Every word she was a reapin'
And then she said, with a smile across her lips a creepin',
"Did this high journey take ye very far away from where ye be stayin'?"
"Oh, yes," did I reply, "miles and miles away and 'tis a price we're payin'."
"Where, pray tell, my dears," said Frances, "<u>do</u> ye be stayin'?"
"The cottage Carrowhugh, far from here I fear," I was sayin'.

Sweet Frances tossed her head with Gaelic glee and did exclaim,
"Why Carrowhugh, 'tis down the road just a house or two, the very same."

The wife and me did look aside, and, quick, replied,
"Ah, well, Frances, me dear, now that we're a sittin' here,
Another double Irish, and a Russian tall, you'd best to pour,
Maybe, in time, three or four, or, who knows, maybe more,
'Cause, truth be told, 'tis a long way we come and round about did roam
To find ourselves, at last, where we begun, right here, indeed, at home."

978-0-595-44682-7
0-595-44682-5